MARXISM AND EDUCATION

This series assumes the ongoing relevance of Marx's contributions to critical social analysis and aims to encourage continuation of the development of the legacy of Marxist traditions in and for education. The remit for the substantive focus of scholarship and analysis appearing in the series extends from the global to the local in relation to dynamics of capitalism and encompasses historical and contemporary developments in political economy of education as well as forms of critique and resistances to capitalist social relations. The series announces a new beginning and proceeds in a spirit of openness and dialogue within and between Marxism and education, and between Marxism and its various critics. The essential feature of the work of the series is that Marxism and Marxist frameworks are to be taken seriously, not as formulaic knowledge and unassailable methodology but critically as inspirational resources for renewal of research and understanding, and as support for action in and upon structures and processes of education and their relations to society. The series is dedicated to the realization of positive human potentialities as education and thus, with Marx, to our education as educators.

Series Editor: *Anthony Green*

Renewing Dialogues in Marxism and Education: Openings
Edited by Anthony Green, Glenn Rikowski, and Helen Raduntz

Critical Race Theory and Education: A Marxist Response
Mike Cole

Revolutionizing Pedagogy: Education for Social Justice Within and Beyond Global Neo-Liberalism
Edited by Sheila Macrine, Peter McLaren, and Dave Hill

Marxism and Education beyond Identity: Sexuality and Schooling
Faith Agostinone-Wilson

Blair's Educational Legacy: Thirteen Years of New Labour
Edited by Anthony Green

Racism and Education in the U.K. and the U.S.: Towards a Socialist Alternative
Mike Cole

Marxism and Education: Renewing the Dialogue, Pedagogy, and Culture
Edited by Peter E. Jones

Educating from Marx: Race, Gender, and Learning
Edited by Shahrzad Mojab and Sara Carpenter

Education and the Reproduction of Capital: Neoliberal Knowledge and Counterstrategies
Edited by Ravi Kumar

Social Change and Education in Greece: A Study in Class Struggle Dynamics
Spyros Themelis

Education and Social Change in Latin America
Edited by Sara C. Motta and Mike Cole

Mass Education, Global Capital, and the World: The Theoretical Lenses of István Mészáros and Immanuel Wallerstein
Tom G. Griffiths and Robert Imre

Constructing Twenty-First Century Socialism in Latin America: The Role of Radical Education
Sara C. Motta and Mike Cole

Constructing Twenty-First Century Socialism in Latin America

The Role of Radical Education

Sara C. Motta and Mike Cole

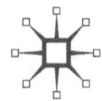

CONSTRUCTING TWENTY-FIRST CENTURY SOCIALISM IN LATIN AMERICA
Copyright © Sara C. Motta and Mike Cole, 2014.
Softcover reprint of the hardcover 1st edition 2014 978-0-230-33823-4
All rights reserved.

First published in 2014 by
PALGRAVE MACMILLAN®
in the United States—a division of St. Martin's Press LLC,
175 Fifth Avenue, New York, NY 10010.

Where this book is distributed in the UK, Europe and the rest of the world, this is by Palgrave Macmillan, a division of Macmillan Publishers Limited, registered in England, company number 785998, of Houndmills, Basingstoke, Hampshire RG21 6XS.

Palgrave Macmillan is the global academic imprint of the above companies and has companies and representatives throughout the world.

Palgrave® and Macmillan® are registered trademarks in the United States, the United Kingdom, Europe and other countries.

ISBN 978-1-349-34124-5   ISBN 978-1-137-08921-2 (eBook)
DOI 10.1057/9781137089212

Library of Congress Cataloging-in-Publication Data

Cole, Mike, 1946–
   Constructing twenty-first century socialism in Latin America : the role of radical education / Mike Cole, Sara C. Motta.
       pages cm
   Includes bibliographical references and index.

   1. Educational sociology—Latin America. 2. Neoliberalism—Latin America. 3. Social movements—Latin America. 4. Education—Philosophy. 5. Radicalism. 6. Latin America—Social conditions—21st century.
   I. Motta, Sara C., 1973– II. Title.

LC191.8.L37C65 2014
306.43—dc23   2013047123

A catalogue record of the book is available from the British Library.

Design by Newgen Knowledge Works (P) Ltd., Chennai, India.

First edition: June 2014

10 9 8 7 6 5 4 3 2 1

We dedicate this book to the memory of Dave Cole (1973–2011) who, while on a visit to Venezuela with me (Mike), saw that another world is possible. We also dedicate the book to the critical and visionary educators in Latin American and beyond who in their everyday lives continue with dedication, endurance, and imagination to construct worlds beyond capitalism and pathways to twenty-first century socialism.

Contents

Series Editor's Preface   ix

Acknowledgments   xxi

Introduction
Pedagogizing the Political and Politicizing Pedagogy   1
Sara C. Motta

Part I Epistemological Hegemonies and Counterhegemonic Epistemologies in, against, and beyond the Capitalist State

Chapter 1
Militarized Neoliberalism in Colombia: Disarticulating Dissent and Articulating Consent to Neoliberal Epistemologies, Pedagogies, and Ways of Life   19
Sara C. Motta

Chapter 2
Brazil and the PT as the Popular Face of Neoliberalism: A Contradictory Terrain for Education and the Politics of Knowledge   43
Sara C. Motta

Chapter 3
The Bolivarian Republic of Venezuela: Education and Twenty-First Century Socialism   65
Mike Cole

Part II Counterhegemonic Epistemologies and Decolonizing Pedagogies from Below

Chapter 4
The Alternative School of Community Organization and Communicational Development, Barrio Pueblo Nuevo, Mérida, Venezuela   97
Mike Cole

Chapter 5
Epistemological Counterhegemonies from Below: Radical Educators in/and the MST and Solidarity Economy Movements   117
Sara C. Motta

Chapter 6
Decolonization in Praxis: Critical Educators, Student Movements, and Feminist Pedagogies in Colombia   143
Sara C. Motta

Part III Constructing Twenty-First Century Socialism in Latin America and Beyond

Chapter 7
Constructing Twenty-First Century Socialism: The Role of Radical Education   175
Sara C. Motta

Annexure 1: MANE Methodology of Programmatic Construction of the Alternative Project of Reform of Higher Education   201

Notes   205

References   209

Index   227

Series Editor's Preface

Sara Motta and Mike Cole's monograph is a welcome companion to their edited collection on radical education and the struggles for socialism in Latin America (Motta and Cole, 2013). Their focus, as with the previous work is *praxis: action, radical critical doing-as-being* working for progressive social changes. As such this is a valuable addition to the Marxism and Education series further consolidating its aim of supporting the continuing dissemination and development of the legacy of Marx and Marxism as, to and for radical educational practices that both inform and learn in action for twenty-first century socialism. To contextualize, laissez-faire–individualized liberalism has now morphed into hegemonic *neoliberalism* while contemporary global capital remains in the throes of attempting to recover from its deepest crisis since the Great Depression of the late 1920s/early 1930s. (Kliman, 2012; Stiglitz, 2010). By the 1970s the period of post-1945 growth in Europe, North America, and beyond in advancing developed economies ended what appears to have been a relatively successful period for poor and working people with rising relative prosperity, a modicum of social mobility consequent on occupational structural changes. These relatively progressive consequences of class struggles began to reverse, especially so during the 1980s where we saw the appearance of "rolling back" the state with its combination of evermore state regulation of the working poor combined with market liberalization. The 1990s and onward have brought consolidating national and global capitalist plutocracy in the developed world spreading globally through expansively applying neoliberal strategies with severe social and economic policies of austerity to the working poor and precarious as the solution to the crisis post-2008; in effect relentless successful class struggle from above. These processes mediate, underpin, and realize structures of domination, both ideologically in myriad cultural forms and in maximizing corporate and private capital accumulation, abstracting, and hoarding value while institutionalizing cultures of monetary profitability as the metric for everything. Nevertheless, capitalism continues in global crisis consequent on its systemic nature recently evident in the financial convulsions of 2008 and since and yet to emerge secure in a new upward spiral of accumulation. In all, as Che Guevara remarked in another context in 1967 but still apt for the present phase: *La lucha continua no terminará fácilmente!* The struggle will continue. It will not be easily concluded![1]

Set against this broad backdrop, the book marks and profiles processes, moments, and structures in humanitarian class struggles in Latin America, specifically focusing on Venezuela, Colombia, and Brazil. The emerging circumstances are consequent on wider interconnecting national and global mechanisms, notably the democratic deficit played out as institutional inefficacy for identifying and expressing the wills of the exploited downsiders, the working classes, the impoverished working, and un- and underemployed who are disempowered in precarities of contemporary political economy despite the abundant global capacity for security in food production and distribution, as well as failures for democratic health and educational arrangements to realize political and cultural well-being for all. Power from below is deflected by market-oriented neoliberal fatalist dogma and "free-market" economistic obfuscation. The potentiality of organized labor for anything approaching relations in production of *industrial democracy* is trammeled in politicized regulation for trades unions, legalized support for structured inequitable relations of capital accumulation; continual redesign of all production, distribution, and exchange represented as "modernization" while enabling intensification of exploitation with managerial forms across the public and private sectors modeled as competitive entrepreneurialism within and between production units; massive failure and evident corruption in finance capital markets; and state financial and monetary policies realizing emergent forms of financial socialism for the corporate and individual rich thereby doing little but encouraging the rates of systemic plutocratic elite consolidation. Each of these structures represents continuing socially illiberal and contrademocratic encroachment on all aspects of the commons, undermining while appropriating the social benefits of the collective and social nature of all human activities that necessarily underpin production of useful goods and assets, whether material or nonmaterial. The political economy continues to be dominated by expropriation and relentless commercialization of all dimensions of human routine normalities as well as creativity in propagating marketable commodities, and capitalized property as acquisitive assets in individual and corporate forms (see Gindin and Panitch, 2013; Harvey, 2005). Especially important in the Latin American focus of this book is the ongoing reach of US global financial and military hegemony. Its domains of power played out in the stock and bond markets under the guidance of the most powerful global institution mediating that influence the US Federal Reserve to realize Pax Americana. It stands in the global center, ably supported by networks of global institutions, not least International Monetary Fund (IMF) and World Trade Organization (WTO).[2] The Federal Reserve and its ever available military alter ego, the US armed forces are the real institutions that are too big to fail, the guarantors of last resort of confidence in global finance capitalism making the bankers and financial sector the main beneficiaries of economic productivity since the 1970s and thereby constituting an evermore deeply entrenched global financial rentier class empowered by its expanding property ownership rather than positive contribution to lubricating productive growth to enhance expansive well-being. These are the gross mechanisms articulating the contemporary *military/industrial* complex (Mills, 1956) as a *military/financial* global class complex that is both mediating and continuing the global crisis, extending neoliberalism and its ever-deepening potential capability for massive instability triggering meltdown, with mayhem and potential for barbarisms in its wake.

There are numerous manifestations of inhumanity as well as glimpses of immanent possibilities and some solid demonstrations of democratic socialism lurking in negation—there to be built through inspirations of the Marxist traditions of analysis, agitation, and humanitarian political movement. It cannot be repeated too often that where there is capitalism and its dedicated rationalists there will always be Marxism, its dialectical foil, interrogator, and specter, haunting and inspiring alternative possibilities for human progress, locally, nationally, regionally, and globally, to redesign social reality while taking up the challenges of shifting from commodity to all manner of possibilities of community as its renewable resource for making history and to socialize capital. The task remains an immense one of rejigging the social forces and relations of production to capitalize on the social as democratic forms: socialism for all. Thus Marxist critical analysis aims to reappropriate the democratic and humanitarian political possibilities in the social structuring of value generation to reengineer it and redirect it for sustainable growth, democratic empowerment with redistribution of resources for multileveling, open-ended creative complexities of global organic solidarity.

These progressive potentialities stand globally full square against exploitation, structural and structuring inequality, either directly in production or indirectly in the massive capitalizing in the powers of financialized forms, appropriated in rentable capacities for production, exploiting control and corporate manipulation of debt and credit *as scarce resources* required in lubricating productive growth (Dienst, 2011; Graeber, 2012). Thus operates huge and complex globalizing power of financial stratagems for appropriating the wealth already established. It's fluidly monetized debt and credit both lubricate the system while leaving huge volumes of such credit possibilities standing idle but available to expand its own volume in corporate acquisitions and mergers. The effect is realizing relatively evermore narrow political contexts of control and undemocratic boundaries of its own expansion. It's dialectical alternative faces are the toxic "assets" and omens of disaster in dissipation of confidence in the viability of more tightly connected, surveilled, and disciplined world of production and structures of intensifying global class plutocratic-elite consolidation. All appears secure so long as the financial system-in-chaos does not shift into reverse, literally undone by its own *incredibility*. The progressive struggle therefore is as much about transforming the democratic mechanisms of the national states as of resisting the globalizing plutocratic state forms. At stake are the articulations and outcomes of class struggles to realize progressive humanitarian political economy highlighted in the United States by the fact that virtually all the rewards of policies taken to tackle the 2008 crash have gone to the wealthiest, particularly the megarich, the pattern repeated across the globe.

Power and representation: In this context the vitality of the politics of representation is never more evident for class-struggle relational forms of language use and progressive imaginaries coming into radical *educative* play as reality, materially effective *language usages as rhetorical forms*. These are representations as instantiations of powers, which encourage movement, identity formation in struggle and critique. Currently, a straw in the wind perhaps, a tiny shimmering moment in the dialectical fortunes of the representation of Marxism itself with its potential for critique of all forms of mystification arises in many apparently unlikely places. Thus was Pope Francis's recent denial of his own harboring Marxist sympathies indicating perhaps that like God, material truths about Marxism emerge in mysterious ways? Among any number of hermeneutic possibilities such pronouncements provide encouragement to Christian socialists of Roman Catholic persuasions, encouragement too for rejuvenating

Liberation Theology activists in Latin America and beyond working in their global entity and its deeply ambiguous mission for the poor!

Noteworthy too for this Preface is its drafting in the wake of the passing of two global figures in class struggle for progressive state formation, Hugo Chávez and Nelson Mandela. Each has been powerfully influenced in complex and distinctive ways by Marxism in his own struggles for and in progressive education and emergent socialist possibilities. Each remains an inspirational and inevitably deeply controversial figure with respect to his historic impact and symbolic legacies, which are now being struggled over in Latin America and Africa, respectively, as well as globally for constructing radical cosmopolitan political narratives and strategies for representing the possibilities of a better twenty-first century world. They have left much to work on and with moving forward. However, while looking in Latin America for inspiration in the afterglow of such distinctive figures *das ist nix so einfach* (it is not so simple) for *educating the educators*. Such are class struggles in pedagogy of critique. And necessarily so for addressing relational forms, not least when considering the complex ramifications of financial and trading partnerships in Latin and South America dominated by the US economy despite or perhaps because of new trading arrangements.[3] What's more, when we consider the express purposes in critical Left hegemony are to identify the burgeoning power of neoliberalism, it is well to keep in mind its inauguration in South America by the Friedman inspired Chicago Boys in the 1970s Chile working on behalf of expansive Monroe Doctrine, as Manifest Destiny (Martínez and Díaz, 1996) Militant Pax Americana is always already overshadowing in its continental and global reaches.

Ongoing themes: Motta and Cole's work raises many time-honored Marxist themes and complexities in analysis for workers and progressive movements where tensions in specificity of political practices arise. Thus, when does positive individuality manifest as distinctly progressive practices compared with relations of possessive individualism? When are state forms liberating and democratic? When is egalitarianism to be cast as neoliberal and when deemed *socialist*? When is socialist egalitarian ambition significant merely as hollow words only, as narrative and ineffective when it comes to outcomes and active means to achieve them in substantive forms? Where lay the significance of sociohistorical aspiration, as hopes and visions that contribute to progressive momentum, even if never to be absolutely realized, as such. Thus there are different ways in dialogue and materials practices of approaching the histories and politics of enhancing social reciprocities involved in generalizing social egalitarianism where there are points of antagonism between social democracy and radical socialist politics. Each moment is an important site of boundaries in critical transactions and struggle, merging with and between Marxism and humanitarian liberal forms and relations of state and civil society. Not least on the unresolved individual, family forms, individual and communal collective property, as well as their takes on meritocracy, claimed in all modernized states as part of its democratic foundations and aspirations.

Inspirations in complexity echoing Ernst Bloch: A vital recurring element in the educational dimensions of class analysis and class struggle is the need to pay attention to renewal of hope in collectivist, nonindividualist forms of what Ernst Bloch referred to as *concrete utopian* thought and practices, and doing so without thereby reproducing debilitating idealist contemplative practices—utopianisms and their products as ends in themselves (Bloch, 1959a; Thompson and Zizek, 2013). The point, of course, is to change the world not just in thought but also in reality, which reality necessarily includes thoughtful experience in cultural forms, too, as living tools in and for mind(s) in action; the ontological imperative critically tempering while working dialectically through the epistemological analytical resources of critical materialist inspiration. Bloch's work and potential for contemporary service is especially pertinent in the context of the Marxism and Education series, given its ongoing commitment to dialogical openness and to the collective self-forming project in complexity of educating the educators and to thus regarding Marxism most vitally as necessarily an *educational* project, itself emergent in the course of struggling across each of the interconnected dimensions of the social.[4]

At many points Motta and Cole identify moments, processes, and structures of such hope across their national cases with regard to alternative sustainable futures. They are indicated by struggle, working critically with, on, and through the possibilities of Venezuelan Chavismo, for instance, in the contemporary *Bolivarian* project and focused program, as well as in complex and delicately and possibly contradictory themes in the cultural politics of democratic socialism for Venezuela, Columbia, and Brazil. Hope and realistic transformative practices operate not only through the politics of the state but such politics are strategized by appreciation of the states of politics, too. Together these are always already complex cultural dynamics, performative and iterative in forms, while critically, the practices of making history must occur in and against potentially oppressive cultural institutional and state forms also, and such forms themselves ever available to be transformed in struggle. In Gramscian terms, this is the context of struggle for hegemony, leadership in models of hope and realistic aspirations for sustainable futures of sustainable progressive change. In Freirian terms, *conscientization* with and through such practices is important as we may note reactionary potential in such traditional forms, too. Nevertheless, there also arises potential and hope in progressive wisdom and the *good senses* of established practices, too. Thus traditions in social organization and production as well as religious forms and cosmological practices may be both strategically ambiguous and ambivalent in real historical contexts of struggles working *both for and against* sustainable progressive movements. The ongoing issue is to distinguish the one from the other. Nevertheless, working through cultural politics is not in contradiction to working on, in, and against the state to transform the state. It is not a matter of these being evidently separable or stark alternatives. Class analysis and struggles are open and complex, and always *both/and*, rarely if ever a simple *either/or*, so far as progressive praxis in hope as against its privatization are concerned. This is so and inevitably the case for the emergence and strategic potential for successful leadership, as ever complex, uncertain, and incomplete for *educating the educators, them/ourselves in struggle*.[5]

Lessons to be learned: Motta and Cole's work demonstrates that crucial lessons can be learned for the cultural forms of progressive socialist politics for the *developed* world from the experiences of the *developing* world, for instance, in rethinking the private/public relation, to challenge and resist the hegemonic privatization of life. Or, on depoliticization in cultures of fatalist possessive individualism where the dominant political cultural forms are fundamentally reinforcing structures of acquiescence. In the popular refrain of irresponsibility among the developed world's middle classes, for instance, *we don't like or believe in neoliberalism in moral and ethical terms but what can we do?* This *TINA* (there is no alternative) of moral and ethical pragmatic futility drains progressive political energy into a sump of cynicism, while simultaneously drawing personal comfort from impotence through personalized nonidentification with dominant powers, frequently wrapped in rhetorical sophistication in all manner of critical fun, too. These modes reinforce the essentially contemplative relation to the ongoing crises of the commons as pleasurable consumption arenas. Thus the public sphere is left to the market and its capacity for action relevant only in individualized contexts of acquisition of immediately local leverage. All of which sits happily with liberal conservative "meritocratic" mantras, articulating middling- and upper-classes hegemonic consumer hypocrisy as "parental responsibility" in education, for instance, and undermining possibilities of democratic and socially comprehensive *systemic* educational possibilities. These are fertile pastures for cultural petty neoliberalism, expressed in all manner of familiar forms from celebrity culture to various types of de- and antimutualization of financial and all other possible "services" whose social rationalities cynically trade on and appropriate the materiality of social capital emergent in the relational nature of all kinds of material and cultural production.

This volume provides many worked critical case examples, problematics, and struggles to be addressed currently occurring across Latin America illustrative of both personal and collective identity themes as unavoidable and vital terrains of struggle that inspire possibilities of alternative socially progressive practices. Their articulation of ideology critique with materialist immanent critique reminds us too, that *belief and fully articulated knowledge* is not required for action to retain power by the already well capitalized. In fact, formation of *self-repressive* social structures of power and opportunity for capitalizing on empowerment in acquiescence are extremely effective modes of liberal self-control with system reinforcing implications. In such contexts what is *not said, not done* are just as important as what is said and done in the emergent structures of (dis)empowerment by the positionally ill-placed themselves. Thus powerful elites of the plutocratic classes, at each level, are daily beneficiaries of such *nonaction* that is so important for practical demoralization of critical energy for educating the educators.

By the same token, much of the *educational* struggle in and for hegemony is not simply against intellectually committed neoliberals, to persuade them away from beguiling market ideology. It is worth reflecting that while fully informed intelligentsia with programmatic perspectives and formulations are most important but they are relatively rare. At least as important are also the "don't knows" and all who glimpse the complexity but look away with irresolvable capacity to confidently envisage *other* feasible possibilities, along with the "not bothered," "can't be bothered," and all those whose actions are fully preoccupied with *more pressing priorities for survival in precarity* that provide structural neoliberal with solace. Alternatively, petty and more substantial philanthropy also works the same magic at all levels of institutionalized acquiescence. Competitive possessive individualism as responsible self management becomes the dominant self-reproducing "realistic" while mistaken response to the commonsense existential projects representative of *that's the way life is*. In Gramscian terms of counterhegemonic organic intellectual practices, the potential for good sense in common collective actions, *cooperation* and *mutuality* are the other side of the coin of individualist practices of all kinds, expressed in all manner of folk wisdoms, and so on. Many direct and indirect indications of these things come though in this volume. So while abstracted individualism operates to regulate, discipline, and control populations, they are also open to and for transgression, ridicule, challenging, and storytelling in *magical* modes for alternative socialist forms of *real* solidarities. All this operates at each level of the community as *social mind*, lived and recognizable right up to critical representations of the "necessity" of the state guaranteeing the market, in neoliberal and classical liberal parlance. These are interconnecting sites of struggles, inevitable contestation within and with which to combat abstracted individualism, for instance, over the meaning of the term "liberal fascism" as it may be applied to and by opponents and adherents of the US Tea Party and/or in relation to US surveillance policies as exposed by Edward Snowden.[6]

Motta and Cole demonstrate complex themes playing out and being resisted in Latin American experiences. What we find are many instances and worked critical exemplifications drawn from struggles for securing democratic-socialist practices running counter to neoliberal defaulting to abstracted individualism. There is much to learn from and with socialist feminist and indigenous peoples' perspectives on the social as collective and in each perspective esteeming the individual in the local histories of identity, of recognizing humane performance of kindness, ecological respect, and uninhibited generosity as social cementing. In Bloch's terms these constitute ongoing, living partial fulfillment of concrete utopian practices as *speculative materialism*.

Dialogical forms in "faith" may also be counterrevolutionary if they settle for *therapeutics*, helpful as necessary balms and support for putting up with the intolerable but *fatalist* if embraced as ends in themselves where the historical materialist, critical realist object is to understand and address causal mechanisms of oppression, both "inner" and "outer," personal, cultural, as well as political and economic with all their attendant ramifications. Dialectical materialism can/should only be manifest in real negation of negations. Most valuably in this context Motta and Cole's interests serve to articulate the personal, the political with and as the economic: the political as the fully articulated dialectical materialism of personal practices, making history, emergent at all levels of its manifestations and makings.[7] Nor can we rule out the downside of potential for social controlling through *repressive tolerance* manifest in co-opting application of liberalism in the social-capital spaces of freedom that *controls*. That is to say where the mission, perhaps inadvertently despite both positive humanitarian intentions, slips into real forms of *combat surgery* mode; patching up and returning the wounded to the futile struggle without effective attention to the objective political, economic, cultural contexts, namely, of addressing the causal mechanisms of conflict. It runs the risk of contributing thereby to moving the context of struggles to *coping with while disempowering, deflecting from consciousness of alternatives and from reality of being alive to the possibilities of generating new living forms for improved conviviality.*

All easier said than done, of course, and never "completed." The historical reality is always of an array of open horizons of possible modes of conviviality and therefore of intensifying sites of demands for and denials of equity in face of recognized inequalities. Perhaps Bloch is of value to conclude this welcoming Preface with some bottom lines:

> The emotion of hope goes out of itself, makes people broad instead of confining them, cannot know nearly enough of what it is that makes them inwardly aimed, of what may be allied to them outwardly. The work of this emotion requires people who throw themselves actively into what is becoming, to which they themselves belong. (Bloch, 1959a)

In such terms, Marxist activist traditions derive continual stimulation from reflection on previous experiences in contexts of the present, realizing that history is alive and continually being written and acted out positively with hope in humanitarian forms to update awareness and knowledge of all the ramifications of the social relations of capitalism, its potential for transformations, and their restless modes of multiform availability. The focus is on class struggles over emergent social wealth built essentially through cooperative human endeavors in face of evident inequitable appropriation and distribution that operates by filtering and funneling its primary credits into plutocratic elite and corporate financialized controls, all of which are presented as systems that are too big for us to be able to tolerate the consequences of their failure. Uncertainty remains, as ever, at its center and with Marx we can appreciate the complexity of finance capital. It is both currency and fluency of social reality as "production," as significant for contemporary neoliberalism was in nascent forms in nineteenth-century market ideology and institutionalized practices for class struggle from above. Today, it continues to be represented in political economy as civilized "responsible" domination. Thus, contemporary neoliberal forms defend its position in part through the very unknowable, complex uncertainties at its center. So too is it at the center of Marx's formulation of finance capital as a *fictitious* capital (Marx, 1863–1883).

More broadly for class struggle in and for reality today, we might reflect again on the nature of artistic practices, sciences, religions, and indeed all humanity as foundation-free practice in face of the *unknowables* concerning what our individual and collective doing does and what our individual and collective knowing (mind) knows. It is now a Left intellectual cliché, but one perhaps worth dwelling on from time to time, to recognize that the French Revolution was many years in the sociocultural making, as indeed was the Russian. Part of the legacy of Marxist traditions in analysis and action is attention to complexities in addressing the problems of capitalism, recognizing that while they are systemic and structurally global, the *solutions* while necessarily systematic too, must be simultaneously *personal* and *political* for socialist development and renewal. Moral and ethical themes are vital, and it is only with democratic transformations that we will be able to address the depths of the system's flows and flaws. In these terms, educating the educators as class struggle is unavoidable and inevitable. Emancipation has to be owned, realized, and made by working people themselves. This volume both keeps the ongoing project alive and kicking while adding contextualized critical descriptions and explanations, contributing in material complexity to practices of hope and expectation for real movements in social transformation. The struggles for twenty-first century socialism continues.

ANTHONY GREEN
December 2013

Acknowledgments

This book was a long journey in its making. Navigating the personal journeys of its authors, it inevitably changed and now in its completion it is, we hope, a relevant, timely, and meaningful contribution to the praxis of constructing pathways to twenty-first century socialism. Written by critical educators in dialogue with critical educators in Brazil, Colombia, and Venezuela, it aims to open horizons of emancipatory possibility in our practices as scholars, teachers, activists, and carers.

For both of us it was a difficult journey. For me personally (Sara), it was a journey of facing and transgressing my fears that I didn't have a right to have a voice and to speak as a political subject. This journey took me to my depths and to walking through the shadows of soul wounds that I have carried and that are the result of the logics of patriarchal colonial capitalism in my life and that of my mother-line. The practice therefore of writing the book was a practice of unlearning some of those parts of my subjectivity that remained alienated and in pain, and of learning to produce myself differently. Its process of production was thus a pedagogical process which pedagogized the political in my everyday life.

There are numerous people that I would like to thank for supporting me in this process; my Brazilian soul family who inspire with their dedication, commitment, and compassion, Sandra Gadelha de Carvalho, Ernandi Mendes, Pedro Vítor Gadelha Mendes, Maíra Gadelha, and Ana Clara Mendes; my beautiful Colombian soul sister Norma Lucía Bermúdez Gómez who creates and nurtures with her poetic politics and emancipatory embrace; my mentor, sister, and friend Katinka Sostens for all that she enabled me to transform and change; my loving soul brothers Jamie Heckert, Andrew Robinson, and Jonathan Mansell for teaching me trust with their tenderness enabling my diving into deeper depths of critical knowing in thought and practice; my soul sister Jennifer Martinez for helping me recognize and heal the wounds; my soul sister Sarah Amsler with her energy, criticality, and caring; my hermana Chilena Maria Loreto Urbina for her sheer determination and loyal commitment; my mother Felicity and auntie Carolyn for all that they taught me and in recognition of all their pain; my two daughters, Sujey and Jaiya Mera-Motta, for teaching me to love; and my beloved Andrew for standing by my side literally and metaphorically through this journey.

For me (Mike) the gestation of the book accompanied a mix of extreme experiences: excessive stress in the form of a difficult divorce; tragedy, with the sudden death of my son; the great joy of getting married again with the added bonus of the pleasure of a lovely stepdaughter; and heart-warming relief in recovering from a life-threatening illness.

We would also both like to thank Sarah Nathan and Mara Berkoff at Palgrave Macmillan, New York, for their patience, understanding, precision, and commitment; and Anthony Green, editor of the Education and Marxism series, for his unwavering support and for the integrity of his scholarship.

Introduction

Pedagogizing the Political and Politicizing Pedagogy

Sara C. Motta

This book is written as a means to rupture the apparent end of history and closure of emancipatory horizons proclaimed by the prophets of neoliberal capitalism. It is written by, and through engagement with, critical educators who are committed to forging worlds beyond capitalism in thought and practice. Patriarchal colonial capitalism has at its heart an epistemological project that is deeply pedagogical. Such an organization of social life and relationships seeks to enact monological closure through producing alienated and instrumental rationalities and technologies of governance that silence all other knowledges and ways of producing our society. Such an epistemological project produces itself through the creation of its underside—the unruly, uneducated, and irrational others whose experiences, wisdoms, knowledges, and ways of life are delegitimized and violently denied.

The epistemological politics that are at the heart of reproducing the hegemony of patriarchal colonial capitalism have explicitly taken center stage in the representations, practices, and prescriptions of neoliberal globalization. From Tony Blair in the United Kingdom declaring that the modernized Labour Party would put "education, education, education" at the heart of their Third Way agenda, through to Álvaro Uribe in Colombia declaring his intent to implement an "educational revolution," education (and by implication epistemology) has become politicized.

This educational project is an increasingly globalized project that reinforces the unequal and uneven relationships between countries, and within countries between communities and ways of life, deepening the lines of exclusions that characterize this stage of capitalist development. At its heart is a continual reproduction and expansion of neoliberal capitalism into every element of social life, along with the deepening of economic inequalities, social and cultural exclusions, and unsustainable ecological practice. As part of this global production of power Latin America is reproduced as the epistemological underside of capitalist coloniality; represented as the passive receiver and consumer of knowledge and research, designed and developed by unelected transnational actors (often of the global North) from international financial institutions, international agencies of development, and representatives of transnational capital.

The neoliberal project fosters practices, policies, and rationalities that seek to deepen a monological and inherently antidemocratic closure of political possibility. As De Angelis and Harvie describe (2009, p. 10),

> We can sum up some of these processes under the terms "quantification," "standardisation" and "surveillance." In all cases, chores are imposed and barriers erected that cut across and interrupt the flows of communicational, affective and creative relationships.

Importantly, however, this does not involve the eradication of the state (even as it involves the definancing of public education) but rather its restructuring into a deeply antipopular and disciplinary state. As Rose (1993, pp. 294–295) argues, "we are dealing with a new form of governmentality" that has two distinct kinds of control. The first being quasimarket mechanisms epitomized as competition, localized entrepreneurial initiatives, delivery of value for money, and competitive tendering; the second being direct state controls in the form of imposed targets, outputs, efficiency gains, and performance criteria. As Coté, Day, and de Peuter argue (2007, p. 319), "These allow populations to be divided and managed, and our daily lives to be more intensely immersed in capitalist exploitation and state-based rational-bureaucratic control."

Thus externally implemented systems of ranking and evaluation are imposed on educators in ways that create disciplinary mechanisms and self-disciplining subjects that devalue local, indigenous traditions of pedagogy, education, and epistemology. Instead the logics of a marketized vision of education, in which education is viewed as a commodity to be accessed by consumer-students, infuses teacher training programs, school curriculum, and university strategic plans. The objective of education, as the rhetoric is reinforced, is to provide the skills necessary to ensure successful entrance into the globalized competitive workforce as laborer and thereby have the income to partake in the market as successful consumer.

In this paradigm the educator, particularly acute in the global South, is deintellectualized, deprofessionalized, and depoliticized, presented as a mere transmitter of skills and neutral knowledge. The resulting mechanisms of evaluation and standardization discipline the teacher-subject in pernicious ways, including devaluation of their teaching and expertise, deterioration of working conditions, and increasing precariousness cumulating as the threat of loss of employment. Indeed in some cases, those educators that are viewed as dissenting to this neoliberal paradigm can suffer death threats and the actual loss of life as teacher-unionists are targeted by militarized neoliberal parastate forces (see chap. 1). Such processes attempt to eradicate the subjective, social, and cultural conditions for the emergence of critical educators and pedagogical-political projects committed to fostering the self-emancipation of oppressed communities.

In the name of modernization, the state has become more deeply embedded in the privatization of education through the defunding of public education and the deregulation of educational markets to enable private investment in educational institutions. This is often justified by attacks against teachers and teacher unions who are presented as privileged interest groups that have "sucked the public purse dry" through their self-interested demands on the educational system. It involves developing a discourse that naturalizes the market as the regulator of social goods as opposed to the state. In the name of democratic access to education, processes are enacted that erode public education, augment social fragmentation, and deepen inequalities.

This educational and epistemological project also seeks to produce certain student subjectivities that ensure the naturalization and reproduction of neoliberal globalization. The ideal neoliberal student is a consumer-student prepared to become indebted (through private finance) to ensure their access to education and by implication success, inclusion, and dignity in the neoliberal economy as producer and consumer. Such a process of subjectification is embedded in instrumental rationalities that produce social and cultural terrains of competition and separation. In this the individual (student, student's family, and/or teacher) is represented as primarily responsible for social and economic success or failure. This acts to mystify the structural nature of such exclusion, particularly the consequences of standardized curriculum that speak over local needs combined with reduced public funding for education and an economic model that produces structural unemployment.

Such a discourse is often internalized into poor student subjectivities fostering a structure of emotions in which happiness, self-worth, and success become focused on access to educational services. Thus failure is often experienced as self-failure and internalized in processes of blaming, shaming, and devaluation. Not only does this link in the oppressed to the parasitic processes of global financialization of capital but it also culturally and subjectively fragments and individualizes poor communities. These people and their families and communities end up carrying the burden of the privatization of education, often accessing poor quality technical courses that lead to precarious unregulated employment or no employment at all. They are left indebted, facing the disciplinary mechanisms of debt-collection agencies. Such logics of disarticulation of political possibility and critical imagination within the subaltern are a pernicious, dehumanizing form of enacting the politics of knowledge of neoliberal globalization. These processes deny the subaltern the cultural, intellectual, and affective knowledges and wisdoms through which to transform the realities of exclusion and oppression.

Yet the processes of privatization and marketization of education, in which access for many subaltern communities remains a myth and when it is possible results in indebtedness and no certainty of decent employment, has created fractures in the epistemological politics of neoliberal globalization. As the promises of inclusion, modernity, choice, and development remain unmet for many people, fault lines have become cracks of political possibility out of which have emerged movements and governments that politicize the pedagogical and pedagogize the political.

Such epistemological and educational alternatives and decolonial practices have most viscerally and forcefully emerged in the Latin American context. Here the neoliberal projects' attempt to disarticulate alternative epistemological and ontological horizons of the political has been resisted. This is manifest in the election to power of various governments falling under the broad rubric of the "pink tide." Examples include those of Luiz Ignácio (Lula) da Silva of the Workers' Party (PT) in Brazil, Hugo Chávez in Venezuela, and Evo Morales in Bolivia. There has also been the development of social movement and community struggles—for example, the recovered-factories movement in Argentina, the movimento dos trabalhadores rurais sem terra (Landless Rural Workers' Movement, MST) in Brazil, the water movements in Uruguay, the indigenous movements in Ecuador and Bolivia, the urban land committees in Venezuela, and feminist nonviolent movements in Colombia. It should be noted, however, and will be detailed in subsequent chapters, that the pink tide is complex and contradictory. For example, the popular hopes generated by the election of Lula in 2002 have been dashed and disappointed by the PT governments' insidious embrace and deepening of neoliberalism and its epistemological logics and politics in educational practices, policies, and representations (see chap. 2).

Arguably within this multiplicity of experiences are the contours and practices of a reinvention of socialism of the twenty-first century. Such emancipatory horizons and practices are deeply democratic, plural, and decentralized. They develop processes in which communities learn to govern themselves. They foreground the multiplicity that is at the heart of this reinvention and the necessity to speak and theorize in the plural. In speaking with, through, and about new forms of popular politics they suggest—sometimes implicitly, sometimes explicitly—that what is being experienced and built in Latin America is not a model that can be transported from one place to another but emerges from concrete places, bodies, traditions, cosmologies, spatialities of power, forms of capital and the state, and histories of struggle. In short, these emancipatory processes are historically, geographically, and politically placed and by necessity plural. There is no overarching model of transformation as is common in twentieth-century conceptualizations of socialism, rather a series of practices, experiences, and struggles that enable the asking of questions and open experimentation with pedagogical practices from which emerge practices of political transformation and social emancipation.

At the heart of this reinvention is an epistemological politics in which the pedagogical takes center stage. "Pedagogical" is used broadly in this book to refer to an articulation of learning aims and processes in social, ethical, spiritual, and affective as well as cognitive relationships. Hence our conceptualization moves the term beyond its hegemonic articulation and representation as a set of methods that ultimately reinforces a practice of education as a practice of domination. Within our conceptualization, pedagogical practices help to constitute the processes of unlearning dominant subjectivities, social relationships, and ways of constituting the world and learning new ones. More concretely, they enable the conditions of emergence of a reinvented emancipatory politics, the immanent development of their emancipatory visions, and can offer fruitful ways to overcome movements' difficulties and contradictions to foster their sustainability and flourishing.

The epistemological politics of this reinvention has particular ethical and political commitments. First, as Ceceña (2012, p. 118) explains, it develops knowledge for and by those excluded either from, or else on the margins, of political power and theory production. Second, it speaks from the placed body and embodied experiences of oppression (Gutiérrez, 2012, p. 61). Third, it fosters the emergence of subjects historically rejected and ignored by capitalist colonial modernity (Mignolo, 2009). In Ceceña's words,

> Speaking about and from these knowledges involves putting them, from the beginning, on a different plane from the practices of power that have condemned popular learning…It is necessary to dislocate the planes, moving from a Euclidean plane to another (or to others) with multiple perspectives that break up and expand the dimensions of understanding, opening them to the penetration of other cosmologies.

Building from radical and subaltern educational traditions and cultural practices such as indigenous cosmologies, liberation theology, and popular education, such a politics of knowledge is produced by multiple subaltern subjects in multiple spatialities and places of alienation and oppression. This politics embraces multiple forms of knowledge, including the affective, embodied, oral, cognitive, and cultural. It experiments with collective and horizontal pedagogies that enable communities to produce themselves, communities, and social relationships differently. These practices are the descendants of Simon Rodriguez's project of epistemological emancipation. Escobar elaborates on this project (cited in Cendales, Mejía, and Muñoz, 2013, p. 7),

> [Rodriguez] wanted all—blacks, indigenous poor, direct descendants of the coloniser—to be equals; he intuited that education could fulfil this task because he had no doubt of the intellectual capacities of anyone, and believed conversely, that the people should be the basis from (which) popular democracy is constructed.

Such subaltern and radical educational heritages, traditions, and practices dethrone the knowing subject of patriarchal capitalist coloniality, which (emphasizes) *his* mastery of others and production of the word as separate from the world. In contrast, emancipatory pedagogy fosters processes of mass intellectuality and creativity thereby enabling communities to reauthor themselves, their practices, and to reweave their worlds anew.

Such a politics of knowledge and politicization of the pedagogical occurs both in formal educational settings, often on the margins of dominant processes of neoliberal restructuring, although in the case of Venezuela at the center of educational reform and reimagining. It also occurs in the messy spaces where subjects, bodies, epistemologies, and spatialities meet through critical educators in schooling, adult education, and university education. This transgresses the borders and boundaries of education separated from life, and learning dissociated from ethical and political commitments, instead, cocreating pedagogical projects with communities in struggle. Within this the school is reimagined as a site for the development of thinking, autonomous, and innovative subjects, able to collectively produce their self-liberation. Teacher training is reconnected to pedagogical-political projects and a conceptualization of the educator as being committed to an emancipatory pedagogical practice embedded in the struggles and needs of oppressed communities. In the higher education (HE) space, Giroux (cited in Coté el al., 2007, p. 319) describes critical educators collectively as those who "discard the careerism, professionalism and isolation" that structure managerialist logics of educational performance. Hence, spaces are opened for the possibility for other relationships, subjectivities, and rationalities via critical pedagogies of the classroom, broader university space, and the community.

These epistemological-political-pedagogical projects, practices, and struggles often confront the mechanisms of monologue of neoliberalism. In the Latin American case, the Left turn in governments has often had the impact of disorientating and debilitating politically such processes of construction. As is demonstrated in the analysis of the PT governments in Brazil (see chap. 2), their political practice has fostered the conditions of governance, as opposed to facilitating the development of the social power and autonomy of popular subjects. Indeed as Alvaro Reyes notes (2012, p. 12), "The arrival of these counter-hegemonic parties and projects in national office has effectively functioned to dissipate the very organizational autonomy and emancipatory impulses that made the rupture with orthodox neoliberalism possible." In other cases such as in Colombia (see chaps. 1 and 6), these projects, practices, and pedagogies are nurtured as practices of exteriority to the reproduction of militarized, populist neoliberal hegemony. Importantly, this context has resulted in some of the most complex and transformatory pedagogical-political projects of decolonization.

The intention of this book is to explore the epistemological politics and the role of the pedagogical in this reinvention of a multiple, immanent, and becoming twenty-first century socialism. We do this in three countries: Colombia, Brazil, and Venezuela and in two methodological steps. The first step involves deconstruction of the mechanisms of (neoliberal) capitalist hegemony as an epistemological project of monologue, closure, and violence against all "others." This enables us to denaturalize, historicize, and expose the contradictory fault lines of the epistemological politics of the contemporary forms of patriarchal capitalist coloniality. The second step involves an affirmative critical practice that speaks with and from traditions, practices, pedagogies, and epistemological politics of counterhegemonic governments in the Venezuelan case, critical educators in formal educational settings in all three countries, social movements in Brazil and Colombia, and the Colombian students' movement. We hope that this contribution to the mapping, analysis, and systematization of epistemological hegemonies and decolonizing counterhegemonies not only contributes to these struggles for alternatives to capitalism in the Latin American context, but also is translatable to other contexts. With the political, cultural, economic, and ecological challenges of the twenty-first century, it is becoming increasingly clear that it is time to pedagogize the political and politicize the pedagogical as a means of unlearning dominant subjectivities and social relationships and embrace possibilities of learning new ones.

In order to theorize and conceptualize the epistemological hegemonies and decolonial counterhegemonies analyzed, we develop a neo-Gramscian–inspired framework that is deepened to include gender and epistemological politics through engagement with black feminism and decolonial thought.

Theorizing the Epistemological Politics and Pedagogies of Hegemony and Counterhegemony

Gramsci sought to understand the varying forms through which capitalism developed, and hence reproduced, in early twentieth-century Europe. He moved away from a structuralist deterministic reading of the relationship between politics and economics. Instead he sought to place an understanding of the class politics in and around the state, which materialized in different paths and forms of capitalism at the heart of any conceptualization of capitalist reproduction. Gramsci thereby brought contingency, conflict, and political struggle to the heart of our understanding of capitalist continuity, historicizing this particular organization of social relations and opening up the immanent possibility of its transformation.

However, Gramsci took his theorization of capitalist reproduction to a deeper level, thereby rendering more complex our understanding of its dynamics. He expanded a conceptualization of the state to include its relationship with society, particularly its role in constructing consent and legitimacy for its rule. The state's form was therefore extended to include civil society. Civil society he argued encompassed the school system, media, religion, and numerous other practices and discourses. Gramsci conceptualized two forms in which this domination is constructed. The first form is labeled passive revolution, and the second hegemony. Gramsci proposed the concept of passive revolution as a means to conceptualize changes in accumulation strategy in response to crises that are characterized by the guidance of the state and based upon the limitation of the role of the popular classes in such processes of change (Buci-Glucksmann, 1979, pp. 208–209).

In such a situation of passive revolution the state absorbs and dominates civil society, unable to construct a refoundational hegemony and thus subject to fragility and potential crises (Gramsci, 1971, p. 244). As Anne Showstack Sassoon argues (1982, pp. 127–148), "passive revolution" is in fact a technique that the bourgeoisie attempts to adopt when its hegemony is weakened. This loss or weakening of hegemony inevitably leads to the introduction of bureaucratic/elitist mechanisms of social reproduction, and to forms of bureaucratic centralism (Gramsci, 1971, p. 189). This is characterized by limitations in democratic mass participation (Gramsci, 1971, pp. 59–60; Showstack Sassoon, 1982, pp. 127–128).

Conversely, for Gramsci, the most stable reproduction of capitalism is hegemonic as it is premised on the construction of consent within the subaltern in which the particular interest of capitalists become represented and internalized as a universal interest. To become hegemonic, a conception of the world reflective of the particular interests of the dominant must become organic, that is, to incorporate itself into everyday life as if it were an expression of it, and to act as an actual and active guiding force, giving direction to how people act and react. Gramsci is therefore unsympathetic with the classical Marxist idea of "false consciousness," because he thinks that ideas always perform a real function of some kind (Fischman and McLaren, 2005, pp. 426–427). Therefore the construction of hegemony is conceived of as an active process that creates particular subjectivities and practices, or common sense that naturalize capitalism in the contours of everyday life. As Gramsci describes,

> Hegemony within the realm of civil society is then grasped when the citizenry come to believe that authority over their lives emanates from the self. Hegemony is therefore articulated through capillary power—akin to an incorporeal government—when it is transmitted organically

through various social institutions, such as schools, street layouts, names, architecture, the family, workplace or church. (Gramsci, 1971, p. 268)

Hegemonic forms of domination can only be upheld if the antagonisms contained in an antagonistic social reality are hidden from view (Femia, 1975, pp. 35, 91). As Birchfield argues (1999, p. 34), "The masking or denial of the deliberately political manoeuvres vital to the maintenance of a market economy is what constitutes the essence of market ideology." The construction of hegemony is inherently pedagogical as it involves the learning and naturalization of ways of being, social relationships, and subjectivities. As Gramsci (1971, p. 350) stated, "Every relationship of hegemony is necessarily a pedagogical relationship." This learning can occur in the formal arena of schooling and education and in the informal spheres of everyday life. It is thus that shift to a marketization of education and the closure of political and epistemological horizons and possibilities that accompanies this is a key site of the construction of consent, and the disarticulation of dissent to neoliberalism.

The linkage between the structural power or capital and the construction of consent in the subaltern is mediated via the construction of a historic bloc, that is, a coalition of social and political actors whose power becomes articulated via the state. They successfully manage to develop a collective will encompassing several social classes or groups, united through the hegemony (not domination) of one group and capable of changing a historical epoch. Gramsci's conceptualization of a historic bloc that mediates the relationship between the state, civil society, and subjectivity in a hegemonic form of capitalism was not, however, closed, in the sense that the former two determine the latter. Rather the subaltern are also historical subjects with past political struggles, cultural practices, and a moral economy in potential conflict with processes of the construction of capitalist "man."

The residues of such histories infuse everyday consciousness and are conceptualized in Gramsci as good sense, which "rough and jagged though they always are, are better than the passing away of the world in its death-throes and the swan-song that it produces" (Gramsci, 1971, p. 343). Therefore everyday consciousness is contradictory and fragmented even when hegemonic, leaving the immanent possibility of the articulation of counterhegemonic moral economy and political practice in the subaltern. As Gramsci (1985, p. 421) explains, "Common sense is not something rigid and stationary, but is in continuous transformation, becoming enriched with scientific notions and philosophical opinions that have entered into common circulation." His conceptualization of good sense therefore is an internally derived critique of common sense: "One might almost say that he [i.e., the worker] has two theoretical consciousnesses" (Gramsci, 1971, p. 333).

For Gramsci, it is the organic intellectual who can play a role in politicizing the tensions between common and good sense. As he argues (1971, p. 10), "The mode of being of the new intellectual can no longer consist in eloquence which is an exterior and momentary mover of feelings and passions, but in active participation in practical life as constructor, organizer, permanent persuader." The bridge that enables the intellectual to become such a permanent persuader is a pedagogical one. This involves the intellectual taking on the role of teacher in which he/she practices constant self-reflexivity to unlearn privilege and open toward learning to learn from below. The intellectual unites theory and practice, and universal and concrete, by being embedded in subaltern struggle (Fischman and McLaren, 2005, p. 435).

However, for Gramsci the organic intellectual is housed in and operates out of the apparatus of a political party; the party is nothing other than "the organic intellectuals of the proletariat that assume the 'directive and organising' role in the revolutionary socialist movement" (Gramsci, 1971, pp. 10, 16). Gramsci thus frames the knowledge of the organic intellectual as conceptual and this intellectual practice as able to guide the masses to revolutionary truth. As he argues (1971, p. 337), "[The intellectual must] understand them and therefore explain and justify them in the particular historical situation and connect them dialectically to the laws of history and to a superior conception of the world, scientifically and coherently elaborated— that is, knowledge." As Coté et al. argue (2007, p. 322),

> Although the organic intellectual is oriented against capitalist hegemony, this figure's ethical commitments, pedagogic methods, and political vision remain governed by a logic that is itself hegemonic; that is, it is a logic that endeavours "to assimilate and to conquer" a "social group," and that seeks "dominance" over an entire social formation.

Arguably Gramsci's conceptualization reinscribes an epistemological and political logic of representation that is out of place in this historical moment of popular reinvention embedded as it is in immanence, multiplicity, practices of mass intellectuality, and processes in which communities learn to govern themselves autonomously. Such limitations necessitate a move beyond Gramsci that will allow ways to conceptualize, analyze, and engage in solidarity with the epistemological reinvention of decolonial counterhegemonic practices that is being enacted by Latin America's subaltern.

Nevertheless, it is possible to draw out a conceptual apparatus that while developed to understand historically concrete forms of capitalism, offers tools of analysis to understand the elements of neoliberal hegemony. This is because hegemony is conceptualized as relational and historicized and therefore premised upon continued and potentially conflictual political and social struggles and subjectivities. Implicit within this conceptualization is an idea of the state, civil society, and the subject as heterogeneous sites of political struggle as opposed to homogenous entities. Thus as Morton (2007, p. 18) argues, "Rather than literally or mechanically applying Gramsci's concepts, questions can then be promoted about hegemony and the complexity of state-civil society relations, in a Gramscian way, about different circumstances from that in which they were formed."

It is also a way in which to conceptualize the political struggle that is at the heart of ensuring reproduction of the everyday as an inherently pedagogical and epistemological struggle. This implies that the subaltern are not merely acted upon but are active political agents, whose agency is either institutionalized and normalized as part of the status quo and/or implicitly and explicitly challenging of this hegemonic consent and legitimization. It thereby helps to frame an analysis that can help to unravel the concrete epistemological and pedagogical mechanisms through which dominant social relationships, subjectivities, and rationalities are reproduced. It can also build elements of a conceptualization of the inherently pedagogical role of producing counterhegemonic subjectivities, social relationships, and ways of life through the figure of the organic intellectual.

However, as indicated previously, there are certain shortcomings in Gramsci's conceptualization of the organic intellectual and of the nature of hegemony and hegemonic subjectivities, particularly in regard to the epistemological and patriarchal politics and logics of capitalism. Despite critiquing the separation of the word from the world, Gramsci's conceptualization of revolutionary knowledge reifies representational logics of knowledge creation and the knower and fails to problematize processes of gendered subjectification that produce embodied and affective alienations and separations (Schugurensky, 2000, p. 501). Therefore, as a means to build on his conceptualization of hegemony, counterhegemony, and the role and nature of organic intellectuals and their pedagogical practice, it is important to combine the works of decolonial thinkers and black/ Chicana feminists.

Decolonial, Chicana, and Black feminists develop deconstructive critiques of the exclusions and violences at the heart of the Enlightenment project. For them, Enlightenment modernity is built upon alienations and separations embedded within a worldview of individualism and materialism. This produces an instrumental and indifferent relationship to nature, denial of other worldviews, and devaluing of the emotional and embodied, manifesting in relationships of dominant patriarchal power (i.e., power-over), hierarchy, and competition in the subjective and social realms (Anzaldúa, 2007; hooks, 2003). Crucially, these alienated subjectivities and social relationships are also gendered. Emotionality is a feminized construct associated with the irrational, the unruly, and the shameful—something to be controlled to avoid disruption to the so-called normal and rational social and physic order (Anzaldúa, 2007, pp. 38–40; Lorde, 2000, pp. 1–4). Alienation thus becomes embedded in our bodies, impoverishing our bodily relationships with each other and ourselves, and distorting our emotions. This results in toxic blockages and repressions (Lorde, 2000).

The epistemological politics of colonial patriarchal capitalism posits "the thinker" as the pinnacle of the knowing subject. This individualized "Europeanized" subject has particular embodied attributes and affective practices. His detached, masculinized "rationality" is able to control the unruly and irrational emotions and bodily desires and the irrationalities of all others named as disorderly and underdeveloped (hooks, 2001, 2003; Lorde, 2000). Modernity is thus produced through a particular way of knowing that which situates "the West," the individual rational subject, theory as conceptual abstraction, and a project of homogenizing universalism as the pinnacle of development and progress. The result is to situate the European epistemological, monological, and individualized subject as the center through which all other contents and forms of epistemological practice would be judged—and ultimately devalued (Agathangelou and Ling, 2004).

Therefore for Decolonial, Chicana, and Black feminists, enlightenment modernity enacts a monological closure and the silencing of all others. Emotional, embodied, oral, popular, and spiritual knowledges are delegitimized, invisibilized, and denied. Such a conceptualization creates relationships of "power-over" between the knower and the known subject. A particular form of knowing, knowledge generation, and knowledge is transformed into the universal epistemology

(Agathangelou and Ling, 2004). The enlightenment knowing subject—the prophet of "truth"—is an alienated subject enacting power-over others. Such a politics of knowledge reproduces a representational praxis of epistemology (and politics) in which there is a division of labor between doers and thinkers, and intellectual and practical labor. A particular representative logic of the political becomes represented as the ontology of the political. Political critique becomes a ritualized performance of the "knower" who seeks to disprove and eradicate his political opponents and convince others of the truth of his arguments and analysis. Thus as useful as Gramscian analysis is up to a point, it too is guilty of this blindness to the "other" and multiple voices.

Black and Decolonial feminist analysis therefore suggests that practices of revolutionary critique must involve not merely changing rationalities or dominant understandings and social practices but also involve decolonizing our subjectivities in their embodied, affective, and spiritual realms, thus overcoming the dualisms between emotional/rational, public/private, and scientific/nonscientific that are constitutive of patriarchal capitalism. This moves the analysis of the hegemonic construction of subjectivities and social relationships, concomitant with the processes of construction of counterhegemonic subjectivities and social relationships, beyond the conceptual and material focus of Gramscian analysis. It suggests including in our analysis the pedagogies of producing and transforming affective and embodied hierarchies, attachments, and practices, the epistemologies of cosmological and cultural formations, and of politicizing pedagogically the realm of the private and gendered subjectivities.

Decolonial scholars suggest that deconstruction of the hegemonic contours of neoliberal capitalism must also involve a critique of the epistemological politics of capitalist coloniality that posits a monological thinking subject able to control their unruly emotions and body who can separate the word from the world as the pinnacle of knowledge and rationality. Arguably, Gramsci partially achieves this through his focus on the cultural realm and contradictory elements of consciousness in common and good sense. However, the conceptualization of organic intellectuality posited predominantly values conceptual and written knowledge as the objectives of revolutionary educational work, therefore reinscribing the logics of othering of other forms of knowledge such as the spiritual, cultural, oral, and embodied. The organic intellectual is also often posited as the individual educator in a way that also reinscribes the logics of separation and representation in epistemological and political construction of strategic and theoretical knowledges for transformation.

Through decolonial and feminist critique we can deconstruct colonial paradigms of knowing, the knower, knowledge, and knowledge construction. Through this, multiple knowledges, multiple and collective forms of knowledge creation, and multiple sites and subjects of knowledge creation can be embraced. Ultimately, what is suggested and conceptualized are pedagogies, knowledges, and ways of creating knowledge that enable the unlearning of dominant rationalities, ways of life, and social relationships and the learning of new ones. We can therefore move beyond an articulation of twentieth-century socialism that reinscribes a political and epistemological politics of monologue and representation and begin to envision and articulate twenty-first-century socialism of multiplicity, dialogue, and immanence.

We develop our analysis of epistemological hegemonies and decolonial epistemological counterhegemonies through a telling of other stories that demonstrate the educational and pedagogical authoritarianism of neoliberalism and the pedagogies of invention, creation, and experimentation of neoliberalism's others.

Conclusion

In summary, this book develops both a deconstruction of the hegemonic epistemological politics of neoliberal capitalism and an affirmative critical practice that maps, systematizes, and engages with the multiple counterhegemonic decolonizing pedagogical-political projects, critical educators, and epistemologies that are being forged across Venezuela, Brazil, and Colombia. It does this as a means of enabling the asking of questions about the relationship between epistemology and pedagogy, and social emancipation, and in the hope of fostering processes of critical educational experimentation in our everyday lives. It offers an invitation to self-reflect, unlearn dominant epistemological practices and subjectivities, and enact in the here and now worlds beyond capitalism.

The decolonizing epistemological and pedagogical practices of Latin America's subaltern are embedded within complex critical readings of the logics and processes of subjectification of patriarchal capitalist coloniality. These critical readings understand that the pedagogical is at the heart of producing capitalist subjectivities, social relationships, and ways of life. They thus also place the pedagogical at the center of creating alternatives to these alienated and destructive logics of social life.

These processes, projects, and practices pedagogize the political and politicize the pedagogical. They thus reimagine the conditions through which we might learn to produce a deeply democratic life embedded in the embrace of the other, weaved together through a politics of care, and practicing of an ethics of love through which to coconstruct dialogical spaces of transformation and healing. They embrace an ethos of experimentation that is oriented toward creating practices of revolutionary transformation immanent to everyday praxis of communities in struggle.

In this prefigurative popular politics there is enacted a decentering of the hegemonic epistemological logics of patriarchal capitalist coloniality through a dethroning of the prophets who produce marketized monologue and closure of political possibility. Instead pedagogical-political projects of emancipation forge processes of mass intellectuality through the creation of prefigurative epistemologies premised upon the collective construction of multiple readings of the world in which we speak in multiple tongues, rethinking and creating what it means to speak, to write, to theorize, and to construct emancipatory change.

Such decolonizing counterhegemonic epistemologies and pedagogies transgress the limits and confines of dominant conceptualizations of twentieth-century socialism. They enact such a transgression because of the exhaustion of this conceptualization of revolutionary transformation that reinscribed political and epistemological logics of representation that mirrored the subjectivities and practices of the imperial knowing subject of patriarchal capitalist coloniality. Through such transgressions they open our political imaginations to the possibility of creating socialism(s) of the twenty-first century, which are intensely embedded and embodied in the experiences of oppression, epistemologically, and ethically committed to speaking from and through the margins and are of necessity multiple, radically open, and thus unfinished and in the process of becoming.

Part I

Epistemological Hegemonies and Counterhegemonic Epistemologies in, against, and beyond the Capitalist State

Chapter 1

Militarized Neoliberalism in Colombia: Disarticulating Dissent and Articulating Consent to Neoliberal Epistemologies, Pedagogies, and Ways of Life

Sara C. Motta

The regime of the Uribe governments (2000–2010) entrenched exclusionary, militarized forms of domination. Notably, the initial passive revolutionary form of neoliberalism was developed into a fragile and highly contradictory neoliberal hegemony during this period. It was articulated in a populist militarized form in which institutional mechanisms, ideological practices, and epistemological logics attempted to articulate the hegemonic educator as a passive, fragmented, and deprofessionalized subject and the student as an individualized, consumer, and depoliticized subject. However, the continued levels of coercion and eradication against all "others" created the conditions for these external others to continue to develop critical, antiauthoritarian pedagogical-political projects throughout Colombian society (to be explored in chap. 6).

This chapter contextualizes and conceptualizes the populist militarized neoliberalism of the governments of Uribe and, now, that of Santos (2010–present). It then analyzes the epistemological logics, pedagogical practices, and institutional mechanisms through which Uribe attempted to disarticulate dissent and articulate consent to imperial monological knowledge subjects, a commodified pedagogy of results and neoliberal way of life.

Colombia has experienced militarized conflict since the 1960s. Globally and regionally it has poverty and inequality rates that rank among the highest. The nexus of conflict and coercion between the internationalized state and Colombian society sits within a broader political economy of exclusionary developmentalism and neoliberalism in which its vast deposits of coal, oil, gold, emeralds, nickel, and fertile agricultural terrain enable the transnationalization of an export producing economy where profits go to transnational economic elites and national political elites (Bermúdez, 2013; Stokes, 2005). The US continual support for the militarized disciplinary state is partially explained by its geopolitic location in which Colombia sits at the crossroads both by land and by sea to a range of crucial transnational communication links. Political violence has been a constant feature of state-civil society relations for decades with the bullet and the bomb as the preferred options for conflict resolution. Here war as politics and politics as war are in continuum.

The historic bloc of both developmentalism and neoliberalism has comprised political and economic elites (who have had privileged access and relationships with state and political representatives in the making of policy) with the support of the United States. They have developed sophisticated mechanisms, systems, and justifications for relationships with the popular classes. These have been premised upon and articulated through the disarticulation of dissent and the systematic elimination of opposition. Paradigmatic of this nexus of coercive power are the paramilitaries that were set up in the 1960s—with military support and US guidance—by large landowners as a means of protection against guerrilla incursion and to suppress demands for land reform. During the 1990s they were well armed and funded and prosecuted leftist insurgents and their alleged social base. They have complex and conflicting relationships with drug cartels, particular local elite interests, and sections of the military. At the time of neoliberal restructuring, which augments inequalities and exclusions, their relationship with the government was strengthened and legitimized in the name of popular self-defense when President Samper legalized setting up of armed self-defense organization known as CONVIVIR (Servicios Especiales de Vigilancia y Seguridad Privada). While these were officially "disbanded" in 1998, they went on to form the illegal AUC (Autodefensas Unidas de Colombia). The government denies continued links but human rights and solidarity organizations have demonstrated clear evidence of their links through either informal military involvement in their activities or active noninterference in their operations (Bermúdez, 2013; Novelli, 2010).

Arguably the form of capitalist reproduction during these periods is one of passive revolution in which a dominant transnational coalition of forces is unable to guarantee hegemonic consent manifested in the emergence and consolidation of armed guerrillas and an overreliance on mechanisms of domination as opposed to consensus. Political violence thus marks the relationships of the hegemonic historic bloc of both developmentalism and its transformation into neoliberalism with the popular classes. When the FARC (Fuerzas Armadas Revolucionarias de Colombia—Ejército del Pueblo) in 1985, for example, attempted to enter electoral politics, over three thousand of its members were murdered within a decade (Stokes, 2005). The conflict in recent decades is fueled by the international drugs trade and by the geopolitic strategies of the United States in the region that have consistently provided training in counterinsurgency, funding, and materials to the Colombian government and its linkages with paramilitary forces. The particular form of passive revolutionary developmentalism in Colombia and its authoritarian and coercive relationship with sectors of the popular classes has been augmented in the 1990s by neoliberal restructuring, which included policies of austerity, deregulation, and privatization. The facts are brutal: there is an estimated three million people internally displaced, political homicides per annum range between three thousand and six thousand, and Colombia has one of the highest per capita murder rates in the world.

The politics of militarization and militarization of politics has impacted upon the everyday forms of state violence that excluded Colombian communities' experience, both in the shantytowns of urban areas and rural areas at the heart of conflict. The violence is also manifested in the way that everyday forms of conflict within the popular classes are mediated and articulated. Thus, it has been described as a parastate that exists beside the formal state, which exercises sustained and targeted levels of repression (Brittain, 2006; Stokes, 2005). Globally, for example, Colombia has the highest rate of trade unionist murders and levels of death threats, displacement, torture, and disappearances (Novelli, 2010; for further details, see http://www.justice forcolombia.org/about-colombia/). Dominant militarized neoliberalism works to disarticulate the formation of alternative subjectivities, social relationships, and frameworks of the world.

Within this context of passive revolutionary transformation of developmentalism into neoliberalism, the role of educators and education is pivotal as a place in which repression and coercion is enacted, and practices of hegemonic construction created. It is also a space of the formation of counterhegemonic subjectivities, social relationships, and emancipatory horizons. The Colombia constitution of 1991 is contradictory in this regard. In a broader context of a political economy shift toward neoliberal accumulation strategy in which critical educators are subject to the coercive force of the formal and parastate education was defined as "a person's right and a public service that has a social function. With education a man would be able to search for access to knowledge, science, technology and the rest of goods and values of the culture" (Colombian Constitution, 2009, cited in Cadavid et al., 2010, p. 191). It was also made compulsory and the responsibility of family, state, and community, for children aged been 5 and 15 to attend school. While public schools were free of cost, in the same constitution, however, the privatization of public services and state activities was institutionalized (Hernandez, 2004, p. 64). And as Novelli demonstrates in his research (2010, p. 279), "Neoliberalism has been the catalyst for intensifying repression against educators both directly and indirectly." This is because as professionals they can reproduce the obedient hegemonic subject yet they have also historically and in the present been at the forefront of liberation movements and the development of pedagogies and epistemologies of insubordination and emancipation.

Militarized, Populist Neoliberalism in the Twenty-First Century

The election to Uribe to power in 2002 marks a moment of the consolidation of an elitist neoliberal historic bloc and their ability, through Uribe, to develop a populist and fragile hegemonic neoliberalism with high levels of support from ordinary Colombians. This nexus between an elitist transnational historic bloc and large sectors of the informal sectors, concomitant with fostering of the deepening of the neoliberal restructuring of society, is common to the continent. Such a conjuncture constituted the possibilities for the articulation of consent to neoliberalism and the intensification of the disarticulation of dissenting voices.

Uribe presented himself as an outsider from the traditional political elite. This was a pivotal political move as the political class had lost much of its legitimacy through political and economic crisis and stagnation. He like many fellow neoliberal populists represented himself as of the people, against the corrupt elites, and sought to institutionalize direct relationships with the populace in the name of democracy on the back of deinstitutionalizing the Colombian state. He ruled by referendum and instituted changes in the institutional structure. He also enacted fiscal austerity to comply with International Monetary Fund (IMF) proposals, for example, repealing of the special pension's provisions and a freezing of state salaries (Cepeda, 2003, p. 2).

He further dedemocratized the state by bypassing institutional channels and checks and balances, creating informal institutional networks of decision making and appointing representatives of the business community such as Jose Roberto Arrango to key advisory positions. A new round of privatization of public services, including contracting out, were carried out under Consejo Superior de Política Economica y Social (CONPES), which was headed by the president with his ministers, the head of the Central Bank, and representatives from the private sector (Hernandez, 2004, p. 64). In the name of democracy he personalized and concentrated political power in the hands of the presidency with unelected representatives of transnational elites, a common form of state institutionality in neoliberalism (Teivanen, 2002).

In continuity with past relationships between the state and society, Uribe deepened the militarization of conflict and denial of "other" voices. This was legitimized through a populist discourse of security, stability, and democracy in his "democratic" security agenda. He appointed himself the "first soldier of Colombia" (Cepeda, 2003, p. 4). In his first week in office he declared a "state of internal commotion," which allowed him to adopt extraordinary measures including the establishment of rehabilitation and consolidation zones covering several provinces; a onetime wealth tax to support strengthening security forces; a discourse articulated around the fight against drugs for its role in fueling conflict; extraditions to the United States; and naming, like the United States, of the FARC as a terrorist group. Such a democratic security agenda was applied throughout his two presidencies to misname and misrepresent opposition as terrorist and the enemies of democratic stability and peace. This discourse of disarticulation of dissent is a common feature of neoliberal hegemony that delegitimizes all ontological, epistemological, and political others, thereby instituting the end of politics and emancipatory horizons outside of those of neoliberal capitalism (Mansell and Motta, 2013; Mendieta, 2008, p. xii; Motta, 2008).

Uribe deepened the elitist historic bloc of neoliberalism through extending the historic influence of the private sector (both national and transnational) in policy making and state relationships with the popular sectors. As Hernandez (2004, p. 57) argues, the business sector and the political class in Colombia "sustain a relationship in which political decisions and public management are permeated by private activity." Thus, the economic policies of the government (continued under President Santos) have supported preferential agreements with transnational companies and foreign governments, including free-trade agreements with the United States and Canada. Many of these agreements contained clauses that invalidated international treaties that Colombia had previously signed to protect its economy and biodiversity, undermined unions and labor rights, and were detrimental to Colombia's economy and ecology. As Ramirez (2005, p. 35) describes, these included

> tariff rebates, preferential agreements—which are not applied reciprocally to products produced in our country—tax exemptions, tax parity between national and foreign industries, facilitations of profit repatriation, compensations for nationalisation, and special guarantees in the case of lawsuits against transnationals. Cases of litigation between the State and private parties are referred to private arbitration tribunals whose decisions always end up favouring the rights of multinationals over the rights of the national, resulting in enormous losses for the public treasury.

An example of private sector and international influence in policy making in the mineral resources sector is Plan Colombia; a US initiative legitimized as contributing to combating drug trafficking and guerrilla forces. It was lobbied at the US congress by Occidental Petroleum and other US companies that helped finance George Bush's campaign. The plan required the placement of Colombian military antinarcotics bases in three strategic resource zones of the country: south of Bolivar, where there had been an ongoing dispute between transnational companies and small-scale miners over one of the richest deposits of gold in the world; the second, Norte de Santander, alongside the Cano Likmon-Covenas, an oil pipeline that belongs to Occidental Petroleum; and the final area near Ataco, in Tolima Department where transnational companies have shown interest in the deposits of gold and other precious materials located there. In these areas violent massacres by paramilitary groups, supported by US multinationals, are common occurrences. This is also witnessed in Putumayo where agencies of the US government, paramilitaries, and the Colombian army have acted to protect Harken Energy investment in developing and exploiting one of Colombia's largest gas reserves. Such policy nexus and legitimization naturalizes consent to intervention and to the neoliberal development strategy, which is represented both as "democratic and progressive." Thus, Colombia's attempt at hegemonic construction weaves a lethal combination of discursive representation, economic expropriation, and political violence to create docile and pacified popular classes. As Cepeda Ulloa (2003, p. 10) describes,

> Despite unpopular measures adopted in terms of taxes, massive staff layoffs, announcements regarding the abolishment of national, provincial and municipal entities, his public image has grown significantly and thus he maintained high levels of popular public support.

In the area of social policy Uribe launched the Social Reactivation Plan, which had eight pillars: educational reform, social security, social management of the rural sector, social management of public services, creation of a country of property owners, cooperatives, enhanced quality of urban life, and macroeconomic stabilization. The logics underlying the reaction plan were those of privatization, removal and weakening of the public sector, weakening the power of labor, and strengthening a neoliberal disciplinary state in the everyday realities of Colombians lives. As Valencia (2013, pp. 31–33) demonstrates in relation to labor conditions and the creation of cooperatives, Law 798 introduced in late 2002 was represented as giving tax breaks to corporations so that they offered more jobs to unemployed Colombian citizens thereby reducing unemployment. The reform did this through extending working hours (from 6 a.m. to 10 p.m.), depriving workers of earning night pay or holiday pay and reducing the amount of termination pay employers must pay in the case of wrongful dismissal; in short, brutal supply-side economics. There was no report from government to verify if the new law did indeed reduce unemployment. Importantly, Central Única dos Trabalhadores (Unified Workers' Central, CUT) with researchers from the National University in Bogota carried out research that demonstrated there was no impact on unemployment; rather the beneficiaries were employers who were saving four trillion Colombian pesos per year by not paying their employees the wages that the 1991 constitution had previously granted them.

Education and/as Epistemological Logics of Neoliberal Capitalist Coloniality

Exploration of educational reform and its underlying epistemological logics in the Uribe and Santos governments demonstrates the continuities and the differences in the Colombian state's relationship with the popular classes in the neoliberal period—both in its coercive and consensus driven aspects. It is clear that educational politics, practices, and institutions play a pivotal role in the consolidation of a neoliberal disciplinary state. However, what also becomes visible is the pivotal role of education practices, struggles, and experiences in the creation of counterhegemonic epistemologies, subjectivities, social relationships, and ways of life. The government's discourse in relation to education reform was couched in the language of modernization, efficiency, and quality as the means to modernize Colombian society through the education of its population into competitive and compliant members of the global workforce and recipients of the "alleged" fruits of globalization. As Light, Manso, and Noguera (2009, p. 5) describe,

> Colombia's leaders believe that education is key to addressing two of the country's biggest challenges: a) the concern for social peace, inclusion and social integration; and b) the need for economic development in an era of competitiveness and globalisation.

Yet this type of education is primarily to create workers to reproduce uncritically neoliberal capitalist logics and satisfy financial and business interests. Education is conceptualized as a commodity that is consumed in order to obtain particular measurable skills and competencies that will ensure successful entrance in the job market. As Mejía (2002, pp. 7–8) argues, there is a clear subject of knowledge that such epistemological logics aim at creating, which is a docile and competent worker who "sees education only as the obtention of technical skills, and is the subject of homo economicus, only interested in their salary" and capacity to consume.

This neoliberal version of education is manifested in the reconceptualization from the Uribe governments of education as contributing to the development of human capital in which as Salcedo describes (2013, pp. 117–118) "capital is human development and in education is a product... a type of capital that actualises capitalist production in education, and is sold." As such the importance of education is not the amount of studies undertaken but the quality of such studies, measured by standards that focus on the acquisition of cognitive skills and their impact on the productivity of the economic system.

The role of the state changes from guarantor and provider of free education to regulator of a competitive market in education in which consumers choose the best quality education. Such decisions are made on the basis of external rankings that focus on quantitative measurements and marketized criterion and the socioeconomic conditions of students and their families. As Salcedo continues (2013, p. 116) this converts education from a public good "into an economic issue which results in the development of academic capitalism."

As part of the educational revolution, the Uribe government developed a discourse of access to high-quality education and of a neoliberal version of the objectives of education in which success or failure was the responsibility of individuals and teachers. This individualization of social ills is a quintessential move in the construction of neoliberal hegemony in which structural causes of exclusion, inequality, and poverty are mystified and placed on the shoulders of individuals. This acts to disarticulate the subjective and social epistemologies able to develop a critical reading of such hegemonic representations and leads to individual self-blame, competition, and fragmentation of communities of resistance.

Such a framing of the importance of education in the possibility of success, inclusion, and modernity enters into the very desires and affective attachments of Colombia's poor. Access to education becomes a route to dignity and inclusion in consumer society. The desire for such a good becomes a motor force of their activities, horizons, and choices. This ties the poor more deeply into the political economy of financialization characteristic of neoliberalism in which they become debtors to access educational services, often offered by private providers of low-quality and technical education.

Such neoliberalization of desire augments the inequalities and exclusion of neoliberal development as the wealthy are able to access the internationally renowned and ranked public universities, while the poor are relegated to the poor-quality private institutions, which offer diplomas based on short, online, and technical courses. As Salcedo (2013, p. 123) describes the impact of this

> is to expand educational hope into the intimacy of society... stimulating cultural consumerism free from the right to education, making this seem like the immediate and obvious answer for the individual... Bringing this into relationships, affectivity, citizenship and politics... this brings the mark of modernity into the everyday in which to improve life chances; one must learn to educate oneself.

These logics reproduce the dependent insertion of Colombia in the international division of labor and epistemological logics of capitalist coloniality. Colombia produces the workers and the consumers for the benefit of transnational capital, both in terms of outsourced labor and massification of consumption. Capitalist coloniality is exercised by international centers of power such as the IMF, World Bank,

European Union, and transnational capital determining the meanings of quality, professionalism, and modernization in this culture of neoliberal education reform. This became institutionalized during the Uribe governments through inclusion of private entities and organizations in the evaluation of educational quality. Thus, the demands of the private sector became key in the development of pedagogy and curriculum as evidenced in the Estrategia de Gestión Del Recurso Humano en Colombia (EGERH). As Pinilla (2012, p. 7) argues, this moves the framework underlying Colombian education reform in a direction in which

> it is the private sector that should define and evaluate education of workers, in line with the work positions available, orientating students to labour demand and determining the conditions of training offered in a way that results in the total correspondence in the training given and the work to be performed, without recourse to the emblematic frameworks of integral education.

The underlying politics of knowledge and educational praxis of the Uribe and Santos governments reproduce a neoliberal understanding of knowledge as a consumer good accessed through individual choice in a regulated educational market. This inserts Colombia into the international division of labor and politics of knowledge reproducing them as the passive receiver of the knowledge and expertise of the West and provider of labor for multinational profitability. A monological closure toward other epistemological logics, pedagogical traditions, and educational practices is enacted in which the ideal educated subject is a trained yet docile worker and consumer. The neoliberal disciplinary state develops a discourse of inclusion, development, and possibility that become a form of regulating society and constructing the conditions of hegemonic consent in the very contours of affective desire of the poor, resulting in the creation of the ideal neoliberal subject who internalizes the individualization of social ills and so therefore blames themselves or others for their exclusion and poverty.

Neoliberalization of Schooling

At the heart of the education plan of 2002–2006, and then the 2006–2016 plan of education, is a political economy discourse that naturalizes and neutralizes the neoliberal economic strategy of development and its relationship to education, democracy, and peace. As the National Plan of Development states,

> Stability and peace will come with a country's increasing productivity...this is based on three factors: educational advances; enhanced abilities of the labour force and technological development. (Departmento Nacional Planeacion, 2003, p. 5)

Interestingly the restructuring of education implemented by the Uribe and then Santos governments has been held up as an ideal model to follow by international experts and institutions (Light et al., 2009, pp. 7–8). The epistemological logics that frame the plans are those of capitalist coloniality in which an external model is implemented that silences, delegitimizes, and invisibilizes local knowledges, pedagogies, and epistemologies. It also reproduces the epistemological international divisions of labor in which the North is the producer of knowledge and the South the passive recipient.

A deconstruction of the ten-year educational plan, introduced during Uribe's second term in office, uncovers the hegemonic logics, practices, and subjectivities the plan seeks to foster. Also revealed are the ways in which this delegitimizes and excludes possibilities for alternative counterhegemonic articulations of radical pedagogy and educational subjects and practices. There are six key areas of reform: local capacity building, enrollment and efficiency, new technologies, curriculum reform, teacher and professional training, and assessment.

The reform is framed within the language of modernization, excellence, internationalization, competitiveness, professionalism, efficiency, and democratization of choice. All these terms are articulated in a form that is compatible with globalized processes of neoliberalization of education in which the possibilities for alternative epistemological, ontological, and political educational paradigms are silenced and excluded. In the name of democratization, a monologue of educational technification and depoliticization is constructed through institutional mechanisms of control enacted through externally imposed standards of quality and excellence that discipline and (mis) name educators, schools, and students (Garces and Jaramillo, 2008).

Colombia implemented educational decentralization, which was institutionalized in the 1991 constitution and, not surprisingly, in line with the dictates of World Bank second generation neoliberal reform (Meade and Gershberg, 2008, p. 7). Educational responsibility was decentralized to provinces and municipalities and at intermediate levels to schools themselves. The ten-year educational plan focuses one of its reform initiatives in the area of local capacity building. While recognizing the progress of decentralization, it highlights continued inefficiencies and lack of professional and managerial capacity and coverage, being unable to administer the system in line with national educational policy objectives of quality and excellence.

The reform focuses on a strengthening of leadership through the development of Ciclos de Calidad (Quality Circles). These institutional spaces are legitimized as promoting a "shared vision of quality" (Light et al., 2009, p. 9) through fostering an improvement process that takes place in school, municipal, and departmental secretariats in control of identifying problem areas and devising strategies of improvement. The model is composed of three stages: (a) defining shared standards of skills and competencies that can be aligned across the education system; (b) assessing student, teacher, and school performance on those standards to evaluate progress; and (c) designing and implementing a plan of institutional improvements. The expectations are that plans "expect schools to strive to help students meet or exceed the new basic standards" (Light et al., 2009, p. 9).

In the name of quality, standards, and excellence, the reform suggests a system of educational surveillance and standardization. Within this educational failure and success is reabsorbed into a discourse that removes it from its structural moorings in inequality, exclusion, reduced public expenditure, and increased privatization, and places it on the shoulders of families, students, and educators. This individualization and depoliticization of social ills necessitates particular subjectivities and practices of institutional management in which these logics become naturalized. Thus, the reform supports the development of epistemic communities of managers, trained in the logics and mechanisms of externally imposed and measurable standards of quality and performance. The quality circles are an attempt to produce hegemonic subjectivities that can enact such individualized performance policies on schools and teacher communities. This is fostered through a particular embodied and affective subject who feels little sympathy for schools or educators and can separate culturally and affectively from such subjects. He is thus able to legitimize acts of discipline in the name of efficiency. Through this micromanagement, the impersonal, cold efficiency of neoliberal practice is reinforced.

In the area of enrollment and efficiency the plan notes improvements in primary school attendance and completion. Yet also observed is that only 47 percent of teenagers finished tenth grade (legally mandated at age 15). Rates of desertion and repetition in the early 2000s remained high in upper-primary and secondary school, particularly in rural areas where school coverage was uneven. As in the area of local capacity building, much of this failure was blamed on the school, teachers, and the inefficiencies in management and distribution of resources (Cadavid et al., 2010, pp. 118–119).

The reform aimed to (Light et al., 2009, p. 10) "modernize the system's institutional structures, processes, incentives, and supervision schemes to boost enrollment and to promote a more effective use and allocation of resources." It supported partnerships between public and private schools, particularly in relation to ensuring educational coverage in rural areas and the tendering of educational services to private sector institutions. A national monitoring system was set up to collect statistics in relation to attendance, repetition, and enrollment. This system allows national, provincial, and local administers to track attendance and enrollment issues, and to provide educators, parents, and communities with data about the performance of students and schools.

The divisive discourse of success and failure also underlies this area of reform, which develops the national infrastructure to enact a disciplinary depoliticization of education. The focus remains on quantitative pedagogy of results, as opposed to qualitative pedagogies of integral learning that develop critical thinking for transformation and agency of Colombia's majority. Thus, the key objectives underlying the evaluation criterion are whether they provide the skills and competencies for Colombians to compete in the globalized economy and to ensure the development of a particular type of compliant citizenry who do not question the confines and contours of the neoliberal development model (Cadavid et al., 2010, pp. 118–121).

In the area of curriculum reform and teacher development, the plan built on the first national evaluation of teachers' and school principals' performance undertaken in 2003. The plan institutionalized a national pedagogic evaluation in which teams of educators visit schools as a means to redefine the curriculum and expected student outcomes, using quantifiable measures. Three broad standards were established: basic competencies in subject areas (mathematics, language, social sciences, and natural sciences), citizenship competencies, and work-related competences (Light et al., 2009, pp. 13–14).

The educational revolution, as epitomized by the Uribe regime, placed heavy rhetorical emphasis on teachers to take the lead in implementing many of these curriculum changes. Yet ironically the top-down technocratic approach to the design of the educational paradigm had shaped its contours and contents in a way that excluded the voices and perspectives of educators (Meade and Gershberg, 2008, pp. 10–12). Teachers were expected to change their practices and improve their content knowledge, with evaluations of their performance implemented as part of school improvement plans and executed by these new educational managers. This undermines the professionalism of teachers and their autonomy to make decisions regarding ways to teach or improve their teaching practice. Evaluations were linked to pay and working conditions—clearly a means of creating insecurity and fear in workers, thereby ensuring their compliance with the reforms.

In 2007 as part of the national survey of school desertion, private sector groups were involved in developing with the national educational ministry, the implementation of a system of teacher evaluations and variable compensations based on performance. However, the national teachers' union, FECODE (Federación Colombiana de Educadores), resisted and blocked its implementation. The government used a discourse that sought to delegitimize teachers' protests as outdated, enemies of educational modernization, and as self-interested groups. This discourse of othering is a central mechanism to eradicate alternative educational and political horizons. The government has since tried to circumvent their resistance by adopting two models of school administration: concessions and partnerships. Under the former the government outsources management of the school's infrastructure to a private institution and under the latter the government pays tuition costs at a privately owned school (Whalton, 2013, p. 2).

As Valencia argues (2013), through developing a discourse that overplays the flaws and failings in the public educational system the government can continue the erosion of financing of public education, particularly of those schools deemed failing with failing teachers, while subsidizing private education that augments inequalities in educational access. This is combined with the privatization of courses of teacher training and a reduction in funding for basic resources and infrastructural needs in schools. A discourse and set of disciplinary practices aimed at controlling and fracturing educators is an attempt to disarticulate the conditions for counterhegemonic educational practices, subjectivities, and relationships. It also undermines the relationships between educators and communities, particularly impoverished communities, in which many of the failing schools are found, and in this way breaks the linkages between the oppressed and critical educators and thus fosters the conditions for the construction of hegemonic neoliberalism. As Martinez explains (cited in Salcedo, 2013, p. 127),

> The subject of knowledge becomes the subject of normalisation...enabling the multiplication of institutional mechanisms and juridical controls that enclose, surveil and punish, which are socially accepted and in which the educator becomes trapped in the role of a functionary worker.

Teachers: Coercion and Consensus in Constructing Neoliberal Educational Subjectivities

Teacher-research and improvements in professional training are proposed strategies of diverse perspectives that emerged from the Pedagogical Movement. What is searched for is that the teacher improves their relationship with pedagogy that they are intellectuals who recognise their pedagogical knowledges and who teach in a critical reflexive manner embedded in their praxis. (Garces and Jaramillo, 2008, p. 176)

The neoliberal historic bloc of Uribe and Santos developed an educational reform that is represented as contributing to modernity, peace, and democracy. However, the nexus of violence, exclusion, silencing, and coercion at the heart of the neoliberal educational and epistemological project becomes clearest in the case of teachers. The use of coercion to silence dissent exposes the inability of the neoliberal historic bloc to achieve stable hegemonic consent and disarticulation of dissent. Critical researchers such as Novelli demonstrate how critical teachers have been at the forefront of struggles for social justice and democracy in education, developing (2010, p. 272) "popular education, education for democracy and human right, justice in education, raising awareness of processes of marginalisation and non-violent activism." This has led them to be the targets of the government, which actively vilified all opposition as terrorist guerrillas threatening the democratic stability agenda, and therefore, Colombia's entrance into the globalized world.

·Thus, educators, and particularly those who are organized in unions and who work with social movements, have become key targets of political violence. As part of the expansion of counterguerrilla military operations many political opponents have been targeted and represented as terrorists thus legitimizing their criminalization. This has involved high levels of murder, disappearance, forced displacement, detention, and death threats (Novelli, 2009, pp. 30–33). As

Novelli argues, this is not a national phenomenon but rather, linked to the international epistemological and political logics of neoliberal capitalist coloniality, which is premised upon the eradication of the other and the end of politics.

The nexus between political violence enacted by and with the consent of the Colombian state and political elites to silence potential opposition, and the mechanisms of creating the hegemonic subjectivities of neoliberalism and disarticulation of counterhegemonic subjectivities is also paradigmatically illustrated in the case of teachers. The dominant educational discourse of the government has been to blame teachers for educational failures as a means to break their political, social, and epistemological power (Cadavid et al., 2010, pp. 124–126). This is illustrated in the process of passing and implementing Law 715 of 2001, despite strong opposition by teacher's union. The law placed rules around funding to prevent cost overruns in the name of efficiency. Departments and municipalities were prohibited from acquiring deficits in education spending and strict limits were placed on hiring and pay increases for teachers. A national assessment of teachers registered on the payroll was undertaken to detect fraudsters. Private contractors (who were exempt from public sector wage and other labor agreements) were allowed to provide educational services, particularly in secondary schools, rural education, and to vulnerable groups.

Uribe blamed increased hiring and wages of teachers for the lack of resources available for the rest of the education system. He thus legitimized this educational reform, which involved the flexibilization of working conditions and breaking of the labor power of teachers in the name of equity and inclusion in the education system, and presenting teachers as a corrupt special interest group opposed to the interests of ordinary Colombians (Meade and Gershberg, 2008, p. 12). Such processes aim to produce docile and depoliticized teachers.

These mechanisms of disarticulation of the political, social, and epistemological power of teachers and fragmentation of their relationships with oppressed communities are also manifested in the training programs and evaluations that are developed as part of the educational revolution. As I have demonstrated, curriculum is externally imposed from above, in the process silencing and delegitimizing local knowledges and alternative pedagogies and epistemologies. The objectives of education are to create a particular type of citizen subject whose desires and subjectivities normalize a commodification of social relationships and practice of education as a means of ensuring productivity and competitiveness in the worker. As Cadavid et al. (2010, pp. 124–125) comment, teachers are pressurized to "not think...[they are] pressurised in terms of content and what they can and cannot embed in their curriculum and no attention is given to research and investigation as training." Training models do not advocate the need for autonomous reflective educational practitioners and fail to recognize and value teachers' expertise and knowledge outside of this dominant discourse. Indeed, such knowledges are actively delegitimized as outdated, undemocratic, and barriers to modernization (Mejía, 2002; Novelli, 2010). Teachers are presented as instructors (tellingly, not as educators) and their needs as workers or as learners are sidelined: first, to ensure flexibilization and labor control and second, to undermine the conditions for the creation of critical educators able to foster the intellectual and epistemological conditions for dissent and counterhegemonic alternatives to militarized neoliberalism.

Privatization of Higher Education (HE)

From the 1980s until the early 2000s, there was little change in opportunities of access to HE in Colombia. HE remained a choice of a few and with partial state funding. The lack of regulation of HE institutions by the state and the definancing of public HE through proposals and public politics in the name of modernization resulted in a situation of increasing privatization of HE over the past three decades. This is founded in the 1981 constitution in which HE is not conceived as a public service that is free and accessible. As Morales (2010, p. 217) describes, by the time Uribe came to power "the general level institutions of public higher education represented 32%, and of these public universities represented 14%. The private sectors represented 67% of HE institutions, with private universities representing 12% of these."

Uribe's attempt at education reform was to implement modernization and democratization of access to HE through the development of external standards and institutions of evaluation and reliance on the private sector and international actors due to the proclaimed lack of state capacity. It was argued that this would enable the development of international-level quality HE and increase in consumer choice for Colombian students and their families (Marrero and Hernandez, 2005, pp. 1–10). As part of this, new transnational actors become determinant in the international politics of knowledge in which Colombia becomes a passive receiver of the expertise and epistemology of the North, consequentially widening the division of labor in the international development of knowledge.

The first group of transnational actors is international organizations such as the IMF and the World Bank, which focus increasingly on educational development and modernization within a neoliberal pedagogy of results focus. In addition there is increasing internationalization of educational debates and centers to produce epistemic communities of neoliberal knowing subjects who define what is valid and invalid in terms of education reform (Marrero and Hernandez, 2005, p. 3). The second group is from the private sector, both transnational and national, who become key actors that relate with the Colombian state and its officials in the government to determine the logics that structure HE educational reform (Hernandez, 2004).

The neoliberal logics of HE reform result in the intensification of the internal inequalities of access to education and the epistemological conditions of transformation, through a system that fragments poor communities and inserts them into the hands of financial capital through the development of educational credit. This is illustrated in reforms related to educational credit that were supported by the World Bank, who argued that due to increased demand for access to HE, particularly from poor sectors of society and the limited capacity of the Colombian state, policies of educational credit financed by the private sector should be designed and implemented (Campo and Giraldo, 2009, pp. 107–108).

Thus in 2002 the Uribe government launched a new project called Accesso con Calidad a la Educacion Superior (Access with Quality to Higher Education, ACCES), which was specifically targeted to young people from low socioeconomic groups through access to subsidized educational credit. For young people from the lowest-two socioeconomic sectors, 25 percent of fees would be paid. There was a high uptake from students from these socioeconomic backgrounds. Of the credits given between 2003 and 2008, 80 percent went to those studying in private institutions and only 20 percent to those studying in public institutions. The government further institutionalized educational credit in 2005 through Law 2002, which transformed the Instituto Colombiano para los Estudios Tecnicos (The Colombian Institute of Technical Studies, ICETEX) into an autonomous financial entity with legal, personal and financial autonomy to work with private sector financiers. Credit for enrollment in HE studies was conditional upon career choice. Thus for students from the two lowest socioeconomic strata, 100 percent was lent for technical and technology courses but only 75 percent for university courses. The conditions of loans include that in the case of student nonrepayment, the family becomes legally responsible and financiers are able to order payment (for further details, see Ossa, 2011, pp. 24–34).

The epistemological logics of neoliberalism enter into the structures of desire of excluded communities who are presented with the myth that access to education and their individual ability to obtain this access is the way to dignity and modernity. Thus, the poorest become indebted to obtain access to often low-quality diplomas and short courses, as they are unable to compete for the highly prestigious and competitive public university places, which in their majority go the upper-middle classes and elites. An internal epistemological division of labor that mirrors the international division of labor is constructed in which the poorest become indebted in order to access education as training for flexibilized labor. Meanwhile, the elites have access to internationally recognized degrees that enable them to become part of the transnational elites.

The lack of commitment to the democratization of public education is illustrated in the almost nonexistence of affirmative action programs, which only exist in 50 universities, with 68 percent in the private sector. The majority of institutions of HE haven't developed such programs. Importantly, as there is no national and governmental commitment to the implementation of such programs, it remains the "autonomous choice" of institutions. The nature of the programs that are offered demonstrate how these do not favor disadvantaged groups but rather reinforce their exclusion from high-quality public universities. There are three types of affirmative action programs in place. The first provides total or partial grants to students to finance their studies. However, to be eligible a student must have reached a particular academic level. This automatically excludes many young people from disadvantaged backgrounds. The second is academic and includes extra support for students to facilitate their completion. However, these are open to all students. The third type of program grants subsidies for transport, childcare, and food at a minimal level. This does not facilitate registration or completion for those who lack additional economic support. As Campo and Giraldo (2009, p. 115) argue,

> In this way the poor student, with poor quality basic education, as opposed to having better opportunities to public education, is obliged to finance their private education through educative credit, which creates a situation of extreme inequity; they are unable to compete for

the few places at public universities...Access is a mechanism to privatise the costs of higher education on the shoulders of the poorest students.

Uribe's successor in 2010, Santos, placed the reform of HE at the center of the National Development Plan of 2010–2014. This model of education has deepened the neoliberal epistemological logics of Uribe's education reforms in its conceptualization of education, pedagogy, teaching, quality, relevance, and organization with the development of human capital at its core (Pacheco, 2011, p. 128). Law 1450 introduced in June 2011 introduced a new model of national evaluation of the HE sector, which would include the participation of productive sectors, associations, and business groups as well as the academia in the design and implementation of national evaluations. The logics behind such a new system of evaluation, clear in the original institutional recommendation from this law, emerged. This argues for the need to develop

> a national framework of qualifications that can facilitate permanent learning, helps the private sector to regulate demand with the supply of competencies, orientates people to professional training and facilitates recognition of the training, professional skills and experiences acquired; such a framework should be adapted to technological changes and the evolution of the labour market.

This augments the power of transnational and national capital to determine the logics, values, and contents of HE and foster the conditions that support neoliberal hegemony and the disarticulation of dissent through devaluation of counterhegemonic pedagogies, philosophies of education, and critical educators.

The Santos government also signed the Free Trade Agreement with the United States on October 21, 2011, which reinforces the epistemological politics of capitalist coloniality and created incentives for the further marketization of HE. In the area of education three key areas were included in the agreement. The first key area was transborder commerce that included the sale of educational services from one nation to the other without passing borders, such as virtual and distance learning favoring North American multinational providers. The second was transborder consumption that promotes the transference of students, professors, and researchers between the two countries with the principal flows being from Colombia to the United States. The third was commercial presence that included the establishment of offices, and campuses of institutions of HE from one nation in the other, again favoring the establishment of US institutions of HE in Colombia. These were underpinned by four conditions. The first condition was that an institute of HE from the United States was to be treated as if it were a Colombian institution implying that private institutions could receive state subsidies. The second was the treaty of the most favored nation in which favorable treaties that one nation had with others were also applicable to the United States. The third was transparency in which there would be free and open access to information in relation to all educational services that were being negotiated. Fourth was access to educational markets (Ossa, 2011, pp. 24–34).

The realization of these conditions that overall favored the US private transnational providers of education necessitated the reform of Law 30, which regulates the financing of public universities. This is the broader epistemological-political economy logic that contextualizes Santos's attempt to reform Law 30. Santos justified the reform through a discourse that focuses on the promotion of quality and research, an increase in the resources available for HE, the development of a national HE system relevant for Colombia and competitive globally, and guaranteeing of educational management based in good governance, as defined by the World Bank (Rodas, 2012, p. 7).

Santos called for open debate in regional workshops and working groups. He argued that these "enrich the discussion of public policies and above all for a policy with such importance, which is transcendental for the future of our country" (cited in Rodas, 2012, pp. 4–5). However, the reality behind the rhetoric was very different. The actors consulted were political and economic elites while the most important educational actors who participated in HE were excluded (Zapata, 2012, p. 2). As a result the educational reform proposed to deepen the definancing of public education and the growth of private sector providers of HE. The reforms proposed opening the educational market to private institutions (thus enabling the realization of the statues of the free trade agreement with the United States) through permitting private investment via public-private alliances in the creation of profit-making HE institutions. They also proposed the strengthening of the national evaluative framework of the quality of programs and institutions of HE. As Marrero and Hernandez (2005, p. 2) argue, this deepens a change in the logics of HE to

> an individualistic and differentiated model, orientated to the formation of workers-producers and centred on the role of the market as the guarantor of the freedom of choice for consumers of educational services.

This process of reform is an attempt to deepen the disarticulation of epistemological dissent and the conditions of critical educational praxis able to deconstruct and transform the militarized and marketized exclusions of Colombian neoliberalism. However, as we shall see in chapter 6, counterhegemonic subjects of critical education and local epistemologies rose up to defeat the proposed reform and open the horizons of political change and social transformation.

Conclusion

In this chapter I have demonstrated the violent and coercive epistemological and ontological logics of militarized neoliberalism in Colombia, particularly under the governments of Uribe and Santos. Such a politics of knowledge has sought to disarticulate through coercive, discursive, and institutional mechanisms the possibilities of critical educator subjectivities, pedagogical-political projects as articulated in radical teacher training courses, critical formal educational spaces, and informal movement and community spaces. This project proletarianizes, deprofessionalizes, and deintellectualizes educators in an attempt to produce teachers complicit in the pedagogical construction of consent for neoliberalism.

Through the privatization of education via definancing of public education and opening up to national and transnational educational providers, Colombia is more deeply inserted into the uneven and unequal epistemological and material international division of labor. Again its people become interpolated as uneducated, underdeveloped, and empty to be filled with the universal and neutral knowledges of elites in the global North. This enacts ontological and symbolic violence against indigenous pedagogies, epistemologies, and ways of producing community and social relationships. Through enacting such a monological closure, access to education becomes ever more fragmented and unequal.

For the Colombian student, particularly of the subaltern, the politics of knowledge seeks to construct an individualized, depoliticized, and docile consumer of educational services. This subject internalizes a discourse that individualizes social ills and therefore tends to (self-)blame for their conditions of exclusion and poverty. Entering into the structures of emotions of Colombia's poor, such processes of subjectification and technologies of governance reproduce in a pernicious way the self-disciplining practices constitutive of neoliberal hegemony. These hook the subaltern into the webs of parasitic transnational financial capital as consumers and precarious laborers.

Yet the discourse of educational revolution is highly contradictory. It has been unable to fulfill its promise that access to quality education would lead to success in terms of social mobility and consumer possibility. It is here that those who have been excluded by the militarized logics of neoliberal capitalist coloniality in Colombia have ruptured the myth of the educational revolution by politicizing its faultlines and exposing its unfulfilled promises.

Chapter 2

Brazil and the PT as the Popular Face of Neoliberalism: A Contradictory Terrain for Education and the Politics of Knowledge

Sara C. Motta

Under the emblematic leadership of Luiz Ignacio "Lula" Da Silva, the election of the Workers' Party (PT) to national government in late 2002 represented hopes that neoliberalism would be challenged and a new more popular, participatory, and inclusive model of development and democracy fostered. However, the Lula governments, and now that of his chosen successor Dilma Roussef, held a trump political card; their relationship with Brazil's organized popular classes, which their predecessors from the traditional political elites had lacked. Their was their historic emergence from within the popular classes in the late 1970s had created relationships of trust, history, and loyalty between sections of the organized popular classes and the PT. This has enabled the PT to stabilize neoliberalism in Brazil by becoming the popular democratic face of the neoliberal historic bloc.

In this role they have developed political, ideological, and epistemological practices and mechanisms that have continued and deepened the neoliberal development strategy through reproducing the fragmented and divided sociopolitical conditions of Brazil's popular classes. However, their leadership of the neoliberal historic bloc has faced barriers and tensions in its implementation. This is particularly evident in relation to social policy where the traditions, legacies, and relative levels of political articulation of sectors of the popular classes linked, but not bound, to the PT have enabled movements to appropriate in popular and democratic ways these reforms. These counterhegemonic practices, horizons, and traditions have arguably worked in, against, and beyond the PT governments to open up spaces of possibility for emancipatory action. This is the case in the education sector. The generic shift to marketization in primary, secondary, and further education is thus marked by fault lines and contradictions from which have emerged pedagogical practices of resistance and transformation (to be explored in chap. 5).

In this chapter I begin by contextualizing and outlining the anatomy of the PT's leadership of the neoliberal historic bloc, with a particular focus on its political, ideological, and epistemological articulation with the popular sectors. I demonstrate how they have deepened processes that articulate consent and disarticulate dissent to neoliberalism in the subaltern. However, these processes of hegemonic construction are contradictory and fraught with fault lines. I then move on to analyze how these logics have impacted upon the education sector with a focus on the politics of knowledge of neoliberalism. I demonstrate the logics and rationalities of this epistemological project, which seeks to enact a monological closure toward all others through disarticulating indigenous educational heritages, epistemological horizons, and pedagogical-political projects. I then briefly visibilize the fault lines, contradictions, and tensions in this project from above. I end by suggesting that by turning our analytic lens on its head to focus on the politics of knowledge and pedagogical-political projects from below we visibilize another epistemological-political reality. Here we can find the contours and possibilities of other epistemological logics and counterhegemonic pedagogical practices that contest and transgress neoliberalism.

The PT in Power: Anatomy of the "Popular" Face of the Neoliberal Historic Bloc

The first key element in the anatomy of the PT's ability to create the conditions of hegemonic consent and disarticulation of dissent in the subaltern to neoliberalism is its relationship with the organized popular sectors. To understand this dynamic it is important to briefly outline key elements of the social and political history of the PT.

The PT emerged from the popular democratization and union struggles of the late 1970s and 1980s (Alves, 1985, p. 263; Keck, 1995, p. 106). It distinguished itself as a democratic popular and leftist party that combined the majority of the social and political organizations, movements, and groupings of the organized popular classes. Thus, many members (both leadership and militant) were both party members and movement organizers.

Yet throughout the 1980s and 1990s, as the party increasingly won electoral power in local and regional elections, it reorientated much of its strategic practice toward the gaining of institutional power and the logics of governance. Thus, even by the early 1990s a leftist critical intellectual linked to the union movement could argue that,

> as far as the PT is concerned since its creation in 1980, it has gradually separated itself from the trade union movement and lost many of the characteristics of a mass party...Today it is closer to the model of a quadro, or figurehead party devoid of grass roots organisation, with only seasonal party activity, linked to elections, and featuring the decisive influence of elected officials. It does fight for a reformist program advocating the creation of a welfare state, but less as the political instrument of a mass labour movement organised into unions and party that make up an articulated and conscious social movement than as a figurehead electoral party with few ties to the populace. (Boito, 1994, p. 15)

Additionally, democratic unionism, which was an important actor in the emergence of the PT, went through a process of bureaucratization and oligarchization. Union leaderships became increasingly driven by logics of power and self-interest as opposed to logics of social organization and political articulation (Boito, 1994, p. 21).

However, elected local and regional governments associated with leftist tendencies such as Democracia Socialista and Articulação de Esquerda attempted to maintain their popular and democratic identity against this majoritarian practice of moderation and delinking from popular struggle. This is paradigmatically represented in the development of innovative and participatory forms of local government such as participatory budgeting. This ambiguous and contradictory relationship between the PT and the organized popular sectors fostered historic, symbolic, and affective relationships with those organized popular sectors traditionally associated with the Left.

The second key element in the anatomy of the PT's ability to create the conditions of hegemonic consent and disarticulation of dissent in the subaltern to neoliberalism is its relationship with the informal popular sectors. True to the dominant (but not only) ideological moorings of the PT in the hegemonic traditions of the twentieth-century Left politics, they have historically focused their political attentions on the formal popular classes (Motta, 2013a). In the context of dependent development, in which the informal working classes in most regions made up the majority of the working classes, this strategy reproduced the historic political fragmentation of, and divisions within, Brazil's popular classes. This undercut the party's ability to come to power on a counterhegemonic antineoliberal agenda in the elections of 1989, 1994, and 1998.

It also meant that the PT increasingly mirrored the individualized and depoliticized relationships of traditional political elites with these social sectors. Thus, the party tended to relate to these sectors not through political organizing and educational work in communities but rather through election campaigns designed and molded by marketing strategists. As Bianchi and Braga (2005, p. 1750) describe,

> The PT's rise within the state apparatus was accompanied by the strengthening of a party bureaucracy increasingly removed from the Party's bases. By the mid-1980s the groups that should have organised the base militants had shown clear signs of atrophy... In the beginning of the 1990s, they simply no longer existed, having been substituted by the candidates supported by electoral committees, thus reproducing the personalisation of Brazilian politics, dictated by votes for a name and not for a party.

This reproduced instrumental and conditional relationships with the informal sectors and undercut the political and institutional conditions through which they might become collectively and socially articulated as a political force.

These political practices created a fragmented and contradictory set of relationships between the PT and the popular sectors. The organized sectors were often collectively and institutionally embedded within the PT's political sphere. The informal sectors were in much more traditional individualized and deinstitutionalized conditional relationships with the party. Thus, the party throughout the 1990s and until its election to national power in 2002 in some localized cases played a role in articulating popular class agency. While at a national level and in many of its electoral experiences reproduced their disarticulation and fragmentation. As Sabadini (2005, p. 9) argues, "The interference of the Lula government in social movements, unions and popular organisation is nefarious... it has fragmented even further the working classes."

It is from this contradictory terrain that we can interpret Lula's election to power and the ambiguous impacts this would have on the popular classes. When Lula issued his Carta ao Povo Brasileiro (Letter to the Brazilian People) during the 2002 election campaign, which committed any future PT government to maintaining the macroeconomic framework of neoliberalism, many PT militants, Left organizations, and movements such as the movimento dos trabalhadores rurais sem terra (Landless Rural Workers' Movement, MST), were torn between feelings of betrayal and loyalty. As Oliveira (2007, p. 6) illustrates, "The PT's switchover from opposition to government insider produces an immediate paralysis of the existing social movements." Yet his electoral victory was not the result of popular-class political power and social autonomy but rather expressed the disarticulation of a counterhegemonic popular politics reinforced by PT political agency. As Oliveira (2007, p. 12) astutely describes,

> The paradox of Lula's electoral victory is that it is simultaneous with the sinking of his own social class into disastrous levels of disorganization. His electoral campaign's lack of specificity—everything reduced to the level of "Lulinha for Peace and Love"—is the perverse and contradictory proof that his legendary class base had ceased to matter. Perhaps Lula and his marketing analyst alone had understood that his electoral sleight-of-hand was only made possible by the fact that the veto-power once exercised by his working-class constituency had been reduced to almost nil.

Predictably, once elected, and despite formal concessions to the solidarity economy movement, the MST and in sectors such as education, the overall economic, political, and social strategy of the government was marked by continuity and deepening of the neoliberal model of development (Oliveira, 2007). While some in the PT had understood A Carta ao Povo as a tactical move to ensure his election, indications that this represented a substantive commitment became evident in the appointments Lula made to his ministerial team (Guimarães, 2004). Figures from the international neoliberal elite such as Palocci and Meirelles were appointed to key economic ministers. "Expert" economic policy-making advisory teams were created that were populated by representatives of international capital and international organizations. As Oliveira continues (2007, p. 17),

> The offices charged with the formulation of economic policy, the chairmanship and the board of directors of the Central Bank and of the Bank of Brazil, which were turned over to major players from the finance and capital markets. In this sense, Lula and the PT have gone one better than even Cardoso himself, who filled these posts with intellectuals and economists affiliated with his own party. After their time in power, the latter, in most cases, moved on to head large consulting firms or to become bankers, occupying the right flank assuming it is possible to say what that is!—of the new "duckbilled

platypus" class. In Lula's government not one of the above mentioned high-ranking economic or financial officials is or was a PT cadre, nor do any of them have any intellectual credentials to speak of.

The government developed and deepened a model of development in which the market is the primary motor of development with minimal intervention in production, distribution, and exchange. The main objectives underlying economic policy decisions are increase in profit and intensification of processes of capitalization of agriculture and low-value-added products. The resultant exponential growth of multinational investment in agroindustry is described by Breilh (2011, p. 26) as resulting in,

> the de-capitalisation and destruction of peasant small economies, ending this form of family agriculture, the sovereign production of food and the possibilities for the consolidation agro-ecological mechanisms.

An alliance was formed between the state, government, and multinational capital, which consolidated a model of accumulation centered on agribusiness exports to the detriment of nationally orientated small- and medium-sized production (Braga, Vicente da Silva, and Paz Feitoso, 2011, p. 436).

The government has fostered processes of primitive accumulation in rural areas, particularly intense in the states of Rio Grande do Norte, Bahia, Pernambuca, and Ceará (all in the northeast poorer states) as part of the expansion of the Política Nacional de Irrigação no Nordeste Brasileiro. Incentives for agribusiness including relative deregulation of investment, development of production, and unregulated use of technology and agrotoxins have fostered the increasing production of monoculture with a focus on crops such as soya across these regions (Breilh, 2011, p. 26). These policy and investment processes have resulted in peasants and communities being thrown off their land, the destruction of ways of life and the possibilities of autonomous social reproduction, the destruction of biodiversity and ecosystems, and increase in social inequalities (Breilh, 2011; Elias, 2003, p. 63). This has created a new actor in the rural context: the agroindustry worker often working in unregulated and precarious working conditions (Pequeno Marinho et al., 2011). The socioeconomic conditions of production, which are characterized by temporal, decentralized, and precarious working conditions undercut the formation of the sociopolitical conditions for the development of collective organization and identity.

In Ceará, for example, public policies led by a PT administration based in Fortaleza have strengthened the agroexport agricultural sector through fiscal incentives and loop holes that have resulted in monocultivated lands, an increasing concentration of wealth, and the extensive use of agrotoxins. This has come at the expense of public policies and projects that privilege social development, or respect the culture of communities, their history and their concerns (Pequeno Marinho, Ferreira Carneiro, and Almeida, 2011, p. 273).

The situation in Ceará is not an exception; rather, it is paradigmatic of the growth of agribusiness incentivized by PT government's federal, state, and municipal incentives and concessions, and the consequences of this for the consolidation of the neoliberal project of capitalist development, which is antipopular in nature (Oliveira, 2007; Braga et al., 2011). Not surprisingly, in 2008 Brazil became the foremost global consumer of agrotoxins (Ferreira Rosa, Matos Pessoa, and Rigotto, 2011, p. 210).

This model of development deepens social/environmental risks and negative consequences for rural communities through a class project formed by the neoliberal capitalist state, politicians from the PT, and other parties, all interacting with transnational capitalist forces (Boito, 2012). As Acselrad, Mello, and Bezerra (2009, p. 138) observe,

> [This] results in large business becoming almost the subjects that decide the policies that regulate the land and what are acceptable limits of risks for the local population, thus the process of construction by the population of what they understand to be risky or intolerable is constrained by the conditions imposed by those with the greatest investment capacity.

And despite historic ties between the PT and the MST, agrarian reform remained a promise as opposed to a reality. Yet because of these histories of struggles and solidarities, the MST refrained from intensifying oppositionary mobilization. Sandra Gadelha (interview February 2013), activist academic and popular educator, expresses some of the complexity of this popular political terrain when she reflects that "Lula and the PT governments have represented themselves as the 'father of the MST' whilst acting as the 'mother of agrobusiness.'"

Another consequence of this export-orientated strategy focused on agrobusiness was the continued weakening of a national manufacturing sector, thereby undercutting the sociopolitical conditions favorable to the political articulation of labor. The creation of the new agroindustry worker in conditions of precarious and decentralized work also produced fractured and fragmented structural conditions that undercut the formation of a new labor organization in the countryside. Yet the relationship of the organized working class with the PT resulted in the relative acquiescence of union leaderships and the demobilization and disorientation of combative social movements such as the MST (Oliveira, 2007).

In the realm of the state, the PT leadership governed more with the traditional political classes, through informal political bargaining, than with its own party and militancy. They actively disarticulated potential internal dissent by, for example, expelling dissident senators who voted against the neoliberal reform of public sector pensions. The PT's governing practices reproduced the historic dedemocratization of the Brazilian state and political elite and the exclusion of the popular sectors from political power, particularly noticeable in ministries related to economic policy making. As Oliveira (2007, p. 15) describes,

> To the decomposition of his class Lula responds with a presidential style that some have termed a new populism or "lulismo-petismo." Whatever it is, the president displays it in his communication with the masses, bypassing political institutions themselves and even his own party, especially when what is at stake is the political functionalizing of poverty. The erosion of class as a basis for politics and the breaking down of any representational bond between society, parties, and other political organizations, including the trade unions themselves, produce a short circuit fatal for politics and the exercise of government.

These processes were also mirrored in internal party politics. The bureaucratized leadership and dominant tendencies such as Articulação concentrated political power in terms of appointments of candidates and the making of significant political decisions. They also hollowed out party education and organizing in the grassroots (Bianchi and Braga, 2005). The logics of dedemocratization and pursuit of power meant that no consistent political work was done to connect the party with the new generations of youth who were promised democracy, development, and a say in politics, and yet were surrounded by continuing inequalities, deteriorating public services, and a continent in multiple uprisings.

Paradoxically the party was able to govern but at the expense of the consolidation of an institutionalized party apparatus and militancy. Dominated by the logics of power, they undercut the institutional moorings of their historical Left identities and practices. Some of this delinking from its historic roots expressed itself in disillusionment and disarticulation. Yet it was also responded to with an attempt at political rearticulation through the public split from the party in 2005 of intellectuals, Left militants, and tendencies to form Partido Socialismo e Liberdade (PSOL). Thus, as a party in government and political institution the PT in power continued a process of dedemocratization and disarticulation of dissent in its organized political and social base.

The PT's relationship with the informal working classes is the second key axis along which they managed to consolidate the relative stability of neoliberal hegemony until the 2013 uprisings. While in government the PT developed a strategy that depoliticized and individualized social policy to the Brazilian poor. Key to this is Bolsa Familia—a targeted conditional transfer of funds—highly praised by the World Bank that has its greatest distribution in the northeast (Bianchi and Braga, 2005; Oliveira, 2007). While reducing absolute poverty this had no intention of creating universal public services, but rather disciplinary social policy mechanisms that maintain the fragmented and individualized relationships of the informal popular classes with the state (and the PT as the democratic face of a neoliberal disciplinary state). Yet here perhaps is the Achilles's heel of the story of the PT's marriage with neoliberalism. Targeted, conditional money transfers do not create the cultural, institutional, or affective relationships of loyalty, solidarity, and commitment that do sustained political organizing and articulation. While enabling the winning of votes, this support is conditional and does not provide a guaranteed popular base for the continued stability of PT governments and the neoliberal coalition of economic and political elites.

Thus, the losers of the PT's marriage with neoliberalism are multiple: the organized working class, public sector workers, Left militants, peasant and indigenous communities, youth, and despite Bolsa Familia, the informal sectors. The PT governments have consolidated their marriage with neoliberalism, deepened their separation from their historic support base, and developed social and economic policy that disarticulates the conditions for the development of a new popular Left politics. Through exploration of social policy, particularly education, a deeper understanding of the neoliberalization of social relationships and societal projects fostered by the epistemological politics of the PT governments can be developed. However, it is also from this understanding that we can make visible contradictions and possibilities for popular counterhegemonic epistemological and political-pedagogical articulation in, against, and beyond the

PT's marriage with neoliberalism (to be explored in greater depth in Chapter Five).

The Marketization of Education under the PT Governments
Primary- and Secondary-Level Schooling

Bolsa Familia

Brazil has historically had poor indicators for primary and secondary schooling with low rates of enrollment and completion. This is explicable through the classed and raced orientations to education that shaped political elites. Particularly from the push to intensify industrialization under the military governments (1964–1985), the focus was on investment in higher education (HE). As Denes describes (2003, p. 138), "While the children of middle and upper-class Brazilians were able to attend some of Latin America's finest universities free of charge, primary and secondary public schools were left to deteriorate."

However, since the implementation of neoliberal reforms during the Cardoso governments and continuing with the PT governments, targeted and conditional monetary assistance has been given to incentivize enrollment and completion of primary and early secondary school level. This type of social policy design is supported by the World Bank as part of the second stage of neoliberal reform and constitutes an attempt to legitimize and institutionalize the neoliberal development strategy (World Bank, 2013). The Bolsa Escola program was introduced on a national scale in 2001 under Cardoso. By late 2003, Bolsa Escola had been implemented in almost all of Brazil's 5,561 municipalities, providing nearly US$500 million in total stipends paid to over 8.6 million children from 5.06 million families. In October 2003, Bolsa Escola was merged with three other transfer programs to collectively form the Bolsa Familia program.

Both the prereform Bolsa Escola program and the current Bolsa Familia program belong to a class of programs called "conditional cash transfers" that provide cash transfers to beneficiary families in exchange for meeting prespecified conditionalities (de Janvry et al., 2005). Eligibility is based on a "means-tested" and "scoring" system. Means-tested programs set the parameters for beneficiaries by establishing a mean income level. The scoring system is based on a number of variables, including housing status, presence of durable goods, and number of parents in the household (De Ferranti et al., 2004).

Many aspects of program implementation for Bolsa Escola were devolved to the municipal governments. As of October 2005, Bolsa

Familia had expanded to reach over 8 million households throughout Brazil, targeting in particular two groups: households with a monthly per capita income of less than R$50 (*extremely poor*) and households with a monthly per capita income between R$50 and R$100 (*moderately poor*). These households receive monthly payments ranging from R$15 to R$95.

Unlike the Bolsa Escola program, which placed requirements on the individual children, the conditionality emphasis of the Bolsa Familia program is at the family level. All relevant family members must comply with a set of key human development requirements that include the following: (i) children ages 6–15 years old be enrolled and attend at least 85 percent of their classes; (ii) children under the age of 7 years visit health clinics to have their growth monitored and immunizations updated; and (iii) pregnant women conduct prenatal care.

The federal government specified three criteria for eligibility to the program. First, the child must come from a household that earns not more than R$90 per capita per month. Second, the child must be enrolled in primary or lower-secondary school. And finally, the child must be between the ages of 6 to 15. Many municipalities used other criteria in addition to the three federal ones, suggesting that these municipalities screened eligible (by the federal standards) households prior to the actual *selection* process. According to a cross-municipal study carried out by a World Bank team (de Janvry et al., 2005), 33 percent of municipalities surveyed required that parents either attend school meetings (30%) or maintain and clean the school (3%). Four percent of the municipalities made other demands such as to provide receipts for how the money was spent, to have vaccination cards up to date, or to require parents to attend school and learn how to read.

There are several steps involved in monitoring and enforcement of conditionalities, each with its own institutional arrangements under the Bolsa Escola program: (a) monitoring of compliance at the school level (responsibility of municipalities to compile reports of school directors); (b) forwarding of information by municipalities to the Ministry of Education (MEC) and the Caixa Economica Federal (Caixa); and (c) linking of noncompliance information to payments for eventual penalties (MEC, Caixa).

Bolsa Familia undoubtedly marks a historic transfer of funds to some of the most impoverished families in Brazil and is an improvement in the absolute living standards of recipients. Yet in relative terms inequalities between the richest and poorest in Brazilian society have deepened, while the program is not institutionalized or universal but rather dependent on the decision of the president to continue its implementation. Indeed, as Miguel Székely (2001) argues, while programs such as Bolsa Escola and Bolsa Familia may have positive effects on educational attainment and income in the short to medium term, they do not change the "elements in the underlying economic structures" that create poverty. Indeed the policy logics that underlie the educational aspect of the policy are economistic based in quantitative statistics and measurable results and not focused upon the creation of a sustainable and democratizing quality public education or other public services (see also Marques, 2005; Halls, 2006).

The decentralized nature of the program again is in line with neoliberal "second generation institutional reform," which seeks to devolve social policy to the local level as a means of a reduction in overall public expenditure and in the name of democratization and participation. However, localization of policy implementation and oversight does not result by necessity in democratization but rather in the politicization by local interests of social policy, as observed in mayoral intervention in the creation of social councils and in the selection of recipients and distribution of funds (de Janvry et al., 2005, p. 4).

Social and educational policy—when organized with and by communities—as in the case, for example, of Venezuela, can indeed act as a means of sociopolitical articulation of subaltern communities (see chaps. 3 and 4). However, in the case of Bolsa Familia, its individualized distribution and the conditionalities embedded in its very logics work to maintain the political and social disarticulation of subaltern informal working-class communities. In the process a popular support base for the PT governments is assured while the possibilities of subaltern articulation eroded.

In line with the policy discourse of neoliberal government, there is a clear individualization of social ills in which the problems of poverty, exclusion from education, and noncompletion of schooling are placed on the shoulders of poor families. The placement of conditionalities on poor families to comply with certain requirements develops new forms of micromanagement and disciplinary institutional techniques of power, which attempt to foster a societal understanding of poverty that blames the poor.

The social councils institutionalize such practices of microdisciplinary governance between state and the poor and between acceptable representatives of civil society and their poor neighbors.

Importantly, organized women's movements, for example, have on the whole not been invited to participate on such social councils, reinforcing an analysis in which Bolsa Familia is a hegemonic strategy of continued depoliticization of poverty and inequality. Here a clear gendered hegemonic strategy is at play in which woman as victim is an acceptable citizen subject, whereas organized women who might contest the logics of such social and educational policy are excluded and become the unacceptable non-citizen subject.

Reform of Public Schooling

When we look to the reform of public schooling that has been consolidated during the PT governments, then the analysis of Bolsa Familia as a hegemonic strategy of subaltern disarticulation becomes even clearer.

Historically the reform of the education system, including curriculum, teacher training, and the distribution of educational resources, has been conceived under either a political or a bureaucratic model. Since the consolidation of the neoliberal historic bloc under the PT governments, the orientation that guides educational reform is economistic (Libâneo, 2008, pp. 168–170). This involves a logic of measurable results, external evaluation, competition for funding, a productivist pedagogical orientation, and the increasing growth of the private sector as provider and organizer of education. Thus, the societal project underlying the current supposed technical and expert restructuring of education is the neoliberal strategy of development. None of these orientations is pedagogical, in the sense of strategic thinking and action related to how to foster the conditions for an inclusive and democratizing pedagogical practice that enables the development of autonomous, critical thinking citizens.

Educational restructuring has come from above, and particularly from the guidance and prescription of international experts and technocrats to the detriment of nationally orientated and designed programs. As Laval demonstrates (2005), many of the educational reforms across the globe are linked to an international discourse preferred by international organizations such as the World Bank, OECD, and European Commission. As he argues this is a political project with particular epistemological politics and practices that attempt to homogenize educational systems in line with the needs of the global economy and economic elites (Laval, 2005, p. xiv). In postcolonial terms there is thus a clear politics of knowledge and global epistemological design underlying neoliberal globalization. As Teivanen (2002) argues this is a common characteristic of the neoliberal historic bloc, which results in the dedemocratization of policy making and the formation of a neoliberal disciplinary state. In the Brazilian case this is based upon a historic bloc of transnational alliances made between the governing political bloc, nonaccountable national actors, and international representatives of the epistemological logics of global neoliberalism (Oliveira, 2009, p. 198).

As Libâneo (2008, p. 169) demonstrates, this policy from above has resulted in an educational policy orientation that has undermined the consolidation of an articulated national education system and presided over the continual underfunding of the public educational sector, deepened the deterioration of the working conditions and salary of public school teachers, and increased the devaluing and precarity of educational institutions that could think strategically about a relevant and democratizing educational reform. As Ernandi Mendes (interview February 2013) explained, "Despite having a PT major who has made promises to invest in education, our public schools in the city (Fortaleza) lack books, desks, basic materials."

Teacher training is in a process of massification as means of servicing the massification of public education as a result of Bolsa Familia. However, the formal democratization of education does not mean the real democratization of public education. The pedagogical quality of this training has been highly criticized because of its focus on quantity as opposed to quality. The logics underlying such training are a productivist reading of the objectives of education. Thus, a key principle is the training of a globally competitive and skilled workforce able to support the globalizing objectives of the PT governments. This is primarily organized through distance learning, which saves money and enables faster graduation (for a detailed analysis of this policy shift see Frigotto, Ciavatta, and Ramos, 2005). However, it results in an instrumentalized conceptualization and practice of teaching. This creates a closure to other conceptualizations of the pedagogical and political role of the educator, thereby undercutting the conditions that would enable the educator to be a critical participant in democratizing educational practice and development of pedagogical-political projects committed to social emancipation. Indeed such training produces epistemological communities and marketized education subjects who naturalize a marketized conceptualization of education in their practice. As Lopes illustrates (2004, p. 114), "Training in the name of autonomy and creativity is put at the service of the insertion of this subject into the globalised world maintaining the submission of education to a productivist model." This disarticulates the intellectual, cultural, and epistemological possibilities of counterhegemonic resistances (Lopes, 2004, p. 112). Such "training for results" to produce neoliberal education subjects is a common facet of the epistemological politics of global neoliberalism (Laval, 2004). A reorientation of curriculum, funding, and school organization has been intensified in line with the logics of marketization and commodification and justified in terms of modernization and development. In continuity with the Cardoso governments the underlying principles guiding reform have been as follows: the improvement of the national economy through a strengthening of the links between schooling, employment, and productivity; an improvement in student performance particularly related to labor-related skills and abilities; a reduction of public costs of education; more direct control of curriculum and evaluation; and more local participation in schooling decisions particularly through the concept of choice of schooling through the logics of the free market (Oliveira, 2009, p. 200). Again this orientation is in line with global educational orthodoxy and the epistemological logics of colonial capitalism in which Brazil is inserted as a dependent developed Southern state into the international division of labor (Ball, 2002).

In terms of schooling, for example, curriculum organization has been restructured to be organized by cycles of schooling (ciclos de escolarização) as a means to ensure higher rates of completion and lower rates of repetition. The system was introduced without consultation with teachers and therefore without an understanding of the actual pedagogical practices of teachers. It was also introduced without provision of the materials (infrastructure, resources) and funding to ensure its implementation (Libâneo, 2008, pp. 175–176). External quantitative measures of evaluation were introduced to evaluate schools for their successful implementation of the curriculum reform through the rates of children finishing primary and early secondary school. Through the concept of performativity, responsibility for education is moved away from central government to the individual school and family, individualizing and depoliticizing social ills (Oliveira, 2009, p. 201).

Through a universally imposed standard the design of schooling and curriculum is distanced from its local context and community needs. As a curriculum orientation embedded within an education of results, it has done little to improve the quality of education received. As Ernandi describes in the case of Ceará, "Children may be completing school but they continue to leave without knowing how to read and write which reproduces social exclusion and inequalities in the name of inclusion." It has also set up an external disciplinary measure of ranking to blame underfunded schools for the problems they face in the implementation of new measures. The installation of regimes of performativity as noted comparatively, induce a stressful and uncertain environment for educators that also tends to undercut and fragment collectivity and therefore the possibilities for the articulation of counterhegemonic practices, horizons, and understandings (for a comparative discussion of this, see Ball, 2002; for Brazil, see Lopes, 2004, 2006). As Libâneo (2008, p. 176) describes,

> Educational policy is identified with an economistic vision. External evaluation is transformed into a motor of educational reform. The objectives are quantitative, much more about the reduction of teaching costs than about a solid educational preparation for students. The numbers appear positive in the statistics, yet those approved don't know how to read and write. We are effectively, faced with a pedagogy of results.

However, there have been ambiguities in the discourse of the PT governments, with the education minister of the second Lula government, Fernando Haddad, using a discourse that framed public sector educational reform in terms of the development of a republican and democratizing education that would realize the stipulations and guarantees of the 1988 constitution in which education was guaranteed as a constitutional right. While the overall educational policy of the government is in line with neoliberal educational orthodoxy, these ambiguities reflect the existence of competing interests and forces within the government and in its social base (for examples of such ambiguities and hybridities in curriculum reform, see Lopes, 2004, 2006). The consequences of such ambiguities will be explored in greater depth in chapter 5.

HE-Sector Reform: Marketization in the Name of Democratization

The democratization of access to HE and the development of a high-quality HE system have been a defining discourse of the PT governments. However, as in the case of public schooling, their strategy has demonstrated continuity with the epistemological logics of marketized education, undercut the conditions of possibility for a democratic and public HE for all, and fostered processes of restructuring that erode the possibilities for the formation of counterhegemonic subjects, practices, and projects.

A Programa Universidade para Todos (PROUNI) was one of the central policy commitments during the Lula governments developed in the name of democratizing access to HE through enabling access for the poorest sectors of society. The financing of the program can be contextualized in the broader political economy of the government, the strategy being to reduce public expenditure, foster private sector engagement in education (and social policy more generally) and to create the second-generation institutional structure for successful neoliberal economic strategy. Private sector providers of HE were offered fiscal incentives (in terms of a reduction in taxation) if they offered subsidized places for disadvantaged students. Here we see not the removal of the state from intervention in education but rather its restructuring to favor the privatization of HE. As Almeida de Carvalho (2006, p. 180) describes, "Fiscal exceptions become a mechanism of public policy to support the private higher education sector."

This support for the private sector is also connected to the privatization of HE that intensified in the second Cardoso government. This resulted in the multiplication, fragmentation, and specialization of the HE sector with numerous courses (short as well as long), institutes, and universities emerging. As De Paula (2009a, p. 255) describes,

> From the internationalisation of higher education we pass to the commercialisation of educational services. In other words, higher education is no longer seen as a state responsibility and citizen right and instead is conceived as a consumer good...In this context, there is a definancing of state support for public institutions of higher education, which promotes on the other hand, the indiscriminate expansion of private institutions of higher education.

By the time of the first Lula government, these private sector providers of HE were suffering from oversupply with many places in their courses remaining empty due partly to increases in unemployment and underemployment. The private sector therefore needed this governmental support to ensure their reproduction (Almeida de Carvalho, 2006, pp. 984–985) while the government could legitimize the program in the name of social justice and democratization. The Central Única dos Trabalhadores (Unified Workers' Central, CUT) close allies of the government and representatives of organized labor, through their president, came out in public support of the program. As Almeida de Carvalho (2006, p. 996) describes, "They were sympathisers of the program, demonstrating this in the media, arguing that at last the hour had come in which the worker would have access to higher education."

The results of the program have favored profit-orientated institutions of further education and have not resulted in the democratization of education as professed by politicians and policy makers, despite the big increase in students enrolled in HE. Due to the high rates of socioeconomic inequality reproduced in primary and secondary education, the majority of students from disadvantaged backgrounds are not in a position to apply for HE places. For many who are in lower socioeconomic strata, the stringent conditions and limitations of the financial support offered in the program mean that participating in HE is not a financially viable alternative. For those who are able to study and afford it, they are in the majority entering private sector HE, which is renowned for its lower quality and pedagogical content and the absence of research or extension projects. Conversely, the public universities of excellent quality remain the preserve of the middle classes and elites. The HE sector in Brazil remains one of the most elitist in Latin America and the world, with 73 percent of registered students in the private sector and only 27 percent in the state sector (De Paula, 2009b, p. 157). Thus, as Mencebo (2004, p. 86) argues, "Far from resolving or correcting the unequal distribution of educational goods, privatisation promoted by the policy has tended to deepen the historic discrimination and denial of the right to higher education for the popular sectors. The allocation of poor students to private institutions crystallises even more the dynamics of segmentation and differentiation in the school system, resulting in the strongest academic schools for those that enter public institutions and the weaker academic schools, save exceptions, for the poor."

The government made an admission of these weaknesses in the program when in 2006 they introduced special support for entry into public universities. However, the support was targeted and conditional, covering a small percentage of the overall subsidized places, reflecting targeted conditional transfers characteristic of second-generation neoliberal reforms (Davies, 2004, p. 251). As Catani and Gilioli (2005) argue, PROUNI "promotes a public policy of access to, but not one of permanence or conclusion of courses. It is orientated to an ameliorative conceptualisation in the mold of the recommendations of the World Bank that offers benefits and not rights to recipients."

The strategies of the PT governments have resulted in increasing fragmentation and distortion of HE with a group of elite public universities that combine teaching, research, and extension and numerous teaching-only universities. This strategy is in line with World Bank recommendation from the 1990s which argued that Brazil needed to diversify the HE sector and move away from HE institutions which mainly undertake research as these are (cited in Otranto, 2006, p. 20) "too expensive and not necessary for the labour market needs of poor countries." Rather, countries like Brazil needed few research-orientated institutions and more teaching-only institutions that offered shorter vocational courses. This results in the banalization and devaluation of the key areas of university practice through the separation of teaching, research, and extension. This, as De Paula (2009b, p. 155) argues, turns university education into a role of "training…increasingly and strictly for the needs of the labour market, losing its meaning as the integral education of society and individuals for their life and for the construction of participatory citizenship."

The marketization of HE is represented not only in the growth of private sector institutions and increasing fragmentation and disarticulation of their pedagogical quality, including the production of knowledge, but also in internal processes of privatization within the university. From the late 1990s in pursuit of international competiveness and excellence in research, key elements in university practice have been increasingly opened to private sector participation. The PT governments have deepened these processes through a strategy of university autonomy, which meant financial autonomy to capture resources from the private sector (Otranto, 2006, p. 20). Accordingly, research is increasingly funded in partnership with the private sector and carried out in terms of its contribution to the logics and needs of private capital. Public universities are able to open courses for which they charge. This is particularly prevalent at the postgraduate level. This has fostered practices of corruption and clientelism through the personalized use of funds received by course coordinators and has deepened the entry of privatization into the public university space. This is increasingly naturalized and normalized by the institutions themselves that support and value the development of such courses (De Paula and Avezedo, 2006). Many extension projects have also become orientated to partnerships with private organizations to augment the salaries of university workers and bring in finance. This fosters relationships between university and community that reproduce the epistemological logics of neoliberal capitalism in community work. As De Paula (2009b, p. 155) argues this "disfigures the concept of extensions as a form of socialising the knowledge and practices of the university for society. Which ultimately means privatisation, inside and by public institutions, of knowledges socially produced by the academic community." This is also a key part of the recommendations of the World Bank as to how Brazil can reduce its external debt and restructure the state in line with the neoliberal economic model (Davies, 2004, p. 246; Otranto, 2006, p. 21). This strategy is thus a key hegemonic strategy to reproduce the epistemological logics of neoliberal capitalism in which education is naturalized as an uncritical instrumental acquisition of skills whose value is orientated to the profit motivations of the private sector.

The Lula governments also introduced policy that resulted in internal shifts for academics through external evaluation mechanisms. O Sistema Nacional de Avaliação da Educação Superior (SINAES) was instituted in April 2004 with the objective of institutionalizing processes of evaluation of HE, which would include evaluation of individual universities, of graduate courses, and of student performance. The PT governments in this way have strengthened mechanisms of control and surveillance over institutions of HE at the same time as reducing public financing. The demands and criterion against which Brazilian HE are evaluated are those stemming from the recommendation of international organizations with a strong focus on quantitative results that foster competition and ranking between institutions (Otranto, 2006, p. 27). Like in the schooling sector, such external evaluations embedded in quantifying and ranking education outcomes undermines the creation of a democratic and critical education linked to the concrete needs of the communities of which it forms a part. It also fosters internal disciplinary mechanisms that seek to create the neoliberal education subject who is infinitely flexible, always on call, and practices an instrumental and competitive educational practice. There is increasing use of differential salaries determined by "performance" and "productivity," which fosters competition among academics and the search for individual solutions to deteriorating working conditions and pay (De Paula, 2009b, p. 155). Such a strategy attempts to create internal conditions of insecurity, instrumentality, and uncertainty, which undercut the formation of communities of resistance within university spaces and foster the hegemonic reproduction of neoliberalism.

However, representative of the contradictory relationship of the PT with the subaltern are the programs for affirmative action developed and implemented by the government. Particularly, Law 3627/04, in which public federal HE institutions must reserve 50 percent of places on all its courses for students graduating from public schools and must include quotas for economically disadvantaged students, indigenous, and Afro-Brazilians in accordance with their proportion of the population in the state of which the university is a part (De Paula, 2009b, p. 160). Of course, this does not overcome the fact that many students from these social groupings face numerous barriers to the completion of their education. Even if they complete a university course, multiple resources are needed, including meeting living expenses which means that many students must take up part- or fulltime employment. Yet as Ernandi Mendes explains, "This represents an important opening towards democratising access to public HE."

Conclusion

Under the PT governments the conditions for the articulation of consent and disarticulation of dissent to neoliberalism in the subaltern have been constructed. This has deepened processes of subjectification, which produce instrumental rationalities and commodified social relationships. It has been constructed through mechanisms that reproduce and augment the historical political and social fragmentation of the popular classes undercutting the possibilities through which they can become agents of social emancipation.

At the schooling level the flagship social policy organized around Bolsa Familia has (re)created a state and political relationship with the informal popular classes that reproduces their individualization and social fragmentation through a practice of conditional cash transfers and a discourse of the individualization of social ills. This is implemented through new disciplinary mechanisms of state surveillance and regulation in the lives of poor families and their children. Such practices reinforce the political disarticulation and social dependency of the Brazilian poor fostering a new third-way populist politics, which helps bring stability and governmentality to neoliberalism.

In educational policy, practices, and representations the implementation of external systems of ranking have been implemented in ways that seek to standardize curriculum, teacher training, and pedagogical practices in line with the dictates and needs of the political and economic elites of the neoliberal historic bloc. Thus, an education of results that is framed as providing the services and skills to enable successful entrance into the competitive labor market and consumer opportunities is fostered.

These logics are implemented on the educational ground through multiple processes of bureaucratization and micromanagement that seek to disarticulate critical educator subjectivities, collective and critical pedagogical practices, and cultures of solidarity among academics.

They instead seek to foster educator subjectivities that are instrumental, competitive, and (self-)disciplining and reproduce a pedagogical practice deeply imbricated in naturalizing and normalizing neoliberalism. This is done through producing feelings of insecurity and fear as performance-related pay, flexibilization, and proletarianization of academic labor are implemented.

Public HE has been definanced and increasingly privatized through the legalization of private investment in educational services and institutions. Poor students who have internalized the dominant discourse of education in which it is presented as the panacea for overcoming social and economic exclusion are now willing to take private loans to finance their studies. The elite public university places remain the preserve of the children of Brazilian elites while poor-quality technical and technological courses and diplomas of the masses. This augments in ever more pernicious ways historic inequalities in access and opportunity to education while at the same time linking the poorest students into the web of transnationalized finance capital.

However, the contradictory and uneven terrain of popular class social and cultural articulation and their historic relationships with the PT have also created spaces of tension and possibility within the practices and process of implementation of social and educational policies. Switching our analytic lens in chapter 5 to pedagogical politics and epistemological practices from below will enable an analysis of the struggles over education and social projects that politicize these tensions and contradictions and open possibilities for an epistemological counterhegemonic politics to develop and consolidate.

Chapter 3

The Bolivarian Republic of Venezuela: Education and Twenty-First Century Socialism

Mike Cole

This chapter is in two sections. In "Section One," I begin with a historical analysis of the origins of twenty-first century socialism in Venezuela, prior to the first presidency in 1999 of the late Hugo Chávez. I concentrate on three turning points in the counterhegemonic struggle against (neoliberal) capitalism and imperialism: the 1958 uprising; the 1989 Caracazo; and the 1992 coup, led by Chávez. I then address the issue of twenty-first century socialism and the Chávez years, beginning with a discussion of the social democratic reforms enacted under the 14 years of Chávez's presidency. After looking at the 2002 coup that momentarily interrupted that presidency, I examine in the next section the dialectical relationship between the people and Chávez, concentrating on the communal councils, communes, workplace democracy, and the militias.

Having laid the historical and contemporaneous framework of twenty-first century socialism, in the first section of the chapter, in "Section Two," I focus on education, specifically the self-education of the people (of which the account in the first section is a major feature); mass intellectuality in the public sphere; and the formal education system. As far as formal education is concerned, I consider both the intentions and successes of the revolutionary government and some of the shortcomings in practice.

I conclude the chapter with a consideration of opposition to the Bolivarian Revolution, both external and internal, before ending with some thoughts on the new presidency of Nicolás Maduro.

In chapter 4, I return to an analysis of education in the Bolivarian Republic of Venezuela, this time venturing outside the formal system to view revolutionary educational processes taking place in an alternative school in Barrio[1] Pueblo Neuvo, Merida.

Section One

The Origins of Twenty-First Century Socialism

1958: The Uprising and the Punto Fijo

In order to understand the origins of twenty-first century socialism, we need to go back briefly to the overthrow of US-backed dictator Marcos Pérez Jiménez in 1958 by a unified civilian-military uprising. Just before the uprising, leaders of the three main parties—Democratic Action (AD), the Christian Democratic Party (COPEI), and the Democratic Republican Union (URD)—had signed a deal in the presence of the US state department chief of Latin American affairs, to establish a government of national unity. The Punto Fijo Pact, named after the residence of the leader of COPEI, where it was signed, in actuality meant the sharing of power by the two hegemonic parties (AD and COPEI), and, beginning with the election of Rómulo Betancourt, lasted for 30 years until the Caracazo in 1989. Punto Fijo's political ideology was summed up by Ojeda, elected to congress in the 1958 general elections as a member of the URD, when he resigned in 1962, as follows:

> The 23 of January was only this; a change of names. The exploiting oligarchy, the servers of imperialism were immediately accommodated into the new government. Political power remains in the hands of the same interests. (Cited in Janicke, 2008)

After his resignation, Ojeda joined the guerrilla struggle, which was a prominent feature of the 1960s; the various groups being drawn together by vanguardism, a strategy based on the belief that workers need to be led by a small group of the most class-conscious and politically advanced members of the working class. By the late 1960s, as a clear precursor to the current Bolivarian Revolution, which started with the Chávez years, there was clear evidence of a large degree of self-education among the people. In the words of former guerrilla commander Douglas Bravo, this entailed a rediscovery and a reclaiming of the "spiritual and religious matrix" of the indigenous and enslaved African populations (cited in Ciccariello-Maher, 2013, p. 48). Another revolutionary, Isidro Ramírez, tells Ciccariello-Maher of the importance of both liberation theology and the various cultural histories that make up Venezuela that "we had to accept that part of our reality and part of our cosmovision, besides the Catholic and Christian, also includes the African and indigenous contributions, a plurality of spiritualities," so long forgotten and erased by Eurocentrism. In this context, Ciccariello-Maher refers to "a spiritualization of Marxism itself" (2013, pp. 49–50). Some 40 years later, Chávez was to assert that, as well as a Christian, he was also a Marxist (Chávez, 2010), describing Marxism as "the most advanced proposal toward the world that Christ came to announce more than 2,000 years ago" (Suggett, 2010). At about the same time, he declared that "the people are the voice of God" (cited in Sheehan, 2010).

By 1970, Ciccariello-Maher points out, as another foretaste of twenty-first century socialism, the Party of the Venezuelan Revolution (PRV), founded by Bravo in 1966, had defined itself as a Marxist-Leninist-*Bolivarian* party (2013, p. 48), with leading member of the PRV Cornelio Alvaredo publishing the newspaper, *El Bolivariano* (2013, pp. 48–49).

Another member of the PRV at the time, Rafael Uzcátegui, reminds us again of the central place of education in the revolutionary process. He describes the PRV as "one of the parties with the greatest theoretical structure," which "allowed us to get to know the various socialisms that existed in the world," and whose members made an effort to learn Venezuela's history, including the potential of the traditional armed forces (at this point, he mentions Chávez's 1992 coup). Explicitly tracing his own youthful intellectual enquiry to the oratory of Chávez, Uzcátegui relates to Ciccariello-Maher the effects it has on him:

> When I listen to Chávez now, his speeches, his anguish, his way of expressing things, I see a portrait of my young militancy during those times, jumping from a quote by Mao Tse-Tung to a quote by Gramsci, to a quote by Toni Negri, to a quote by Rosa Luxemburg, to a thought of Che Guevara, or that of a Latin American patriot. (2013, p. 49)

The 1958 uprising, which spawned the guerrilla wars of the 1960s, was a qualitative leap forward in popular struggle. The next momentary rupture and breakthrough was the Caracazo of 1989.

1989: The Caracazo
Carlos Andrés Pérez Rodríguez was inaugurated for a second term on February 2, 1989. In the course of the 1988 election campaign, he had promised reforms to protect living standards. His attempts to

evoke memories of the boom years of his five-year presidency in the 1970s worked. Once elected, however, Pérez reneged on his promises and initiated a number of policies formulated in the United States, which became known as the "Washington Consensus." These were based squarely on neoliberal capitalist principles, and were foisted on Latin American and Caribbean governments as a condition for their obtaining international loans; and also by threats (Victor, 2009). The country worst effected, Maria Paez Victor (2009) goes on, was the country that most thoroughly applied them—Venezuela.

In a very short space of time, gas prices doubled, and public transportation prices rose by 30 percent (Martinez et al., 2010, p. 17). As a result, the first popular uprising against the measures took place in the barrios of Caracas and surrounding towns on February 27, 1989, with people reappropriating goods from the stores. The response from the state was intense, with about three thousand people killed by armed troops. Gildifredo Solzana, or "Coco," a member of the Coordinadora Simón Bolívar and Che Guevara Collective, based in the 23 de Enero, a notoriously revolutionary area of west Caracas (Ciccariello-Maher, 2013, p. 2), describes how the police attacked the people, shooting to kill, shoved bodies in plastic bags, and threw them from apartments into a truck below. The uprising in 23 de Enero lasted for about 15 days, and Coco explains how afterward, in a combination of repair and repression, the state rebuilt the buildings and raided the Coordinadora Simón Bolívar a number of times to seize all the evidence of police machine gun fire and destruction (cited in Martinez et al., 2010, p. 276).

The Caracazo, as the uprisings became known, seemed to intuit that in reaction to the adjustment measures imposed by the Pérez government, a new future was possible. This was a key moment in the events leading up to the election of Chávez as president of Venezuela in 1998. As Ciccariello-Maher (2013, p. 89) puts it,

> Neither completely spontaneous nor fully organized, the Caracazo was an instant in which widespread disgust and revolutionary capacity met on the streets, generating historical agency by emboldening the faithful and converting the waverers: it was 1989 that enabled 1992, and 1992 that enabled 1998.

1992: Chávez Arrives

According to former guerrilla and women's leader, Nora Castañeda, the repression that followed the Caracazo was "the pueblo against the pueblo," with poor dark-skinned military recruits sent into the barrios to slaughter their brothers and sisters. Unsurprisingly, some refused to fire, including members of the Bolivarian Revolutionary Movement (MBR) (a clandestine revolutionary organization within the army forces) (cited in Ciccariello-Maher, 2013, pp. 98–99). The MBR was founded by lieutenant colonel Hugo Chávez Frías, who on February 4, 1992, three years after the Caracazo, led a military coup d'etat against President Pérez. While the attempted coup was unsuccessful, it captured the people's attention not only because Chávez claimed sole responsibility but because he told his troops that "*for now*" the mission had been accomplished (Martinez et al., 2010, p. 18).

When Chávez was jailed (during which time there was another unsuccessful coup in November, 1992), a movement was organized for his release, and two years later, he was pardoned by incoming President Rafael Caldera Rodríguez, who had recently split from COPEI and had formed a coalition of leftist and Center-Right parties with the name of "Convergence." Chávez traveled across Venezuela and visited Cuba where he was met on the runway tarmac by Fidel Castro. MBR turned its attention to state politics and created the Movement for a Fifth Republic (MVR), with the aim of getting Chávez elected, ending the Punto Fijo, and rewriting the constitution (Martinez et al., 2010, p. 18).

By 1998, as a result of neoliberalism, Victor (2009) describes Venezuela as follows: "This oil-rich country's economy was in ruins, schools and hospitals were almost derelict, and almost 80 per cent of the population was impoverished." In that year, Hugo Chávez won the presidential elections in Venezuela by a landslide.

Victor (2009) concisely summarizes Chávez's impact on the racist oligarchy on the one hand, and on the people on the other:

> Immediately the elites and middle classes opposed him as an upstart, an Indian who does not know his place, a Black who is a disgrace to the position. Hugo Chávez established a new Constitution that reset the rules of a government that had been putty in the hands of the elites. Ratified in overwhelming numbers, the Constitution gave indigenous peoples, for the first time, the constitutional right to their language, religion, culture and lands. It established Human Rights, civil and social, like the right to food, a clean environment, education, jobs, and health care, binding the government to provide them. It declared the country a participatory democracy with direct input of people into political decision making through their communal councils and it asserted government control of oil revenues: Oil belongs to the people.

Twenty-First Century Socialism and the Chávez Years

1999–2013: The Social Democratic Reforms of the Chávez Governments
The massive social progress that has occurred in Venezuela since Chávez assumed office in 1999 has been well documented (e.g., Bruce, 2008; Dominguez, 2013). The Economic Commission for Latin America and the Caribbean (ECLAC) indicates that Venezuela now has the lowest percentage of social inequality in Latin America, while the United Nations Development Programme (UNDP, 2011) shows that it has the lowest gender inequality index in the region (cited in Dominguez, 2013, p. 124). Major reforms under Chávez's governments include laws enabling land reform, a number of nationalizations, the elimination of Venezuela's large estates, bringing justice to the rural poor and to indigenous and Afro-descendant Venezuelans, and boosting the country's ability to grow its own food. To understand the full impact of the changes in Venezuelan society since Chávez first took office in 1999, however, it is necessary to look to the misiones.

The Misiones Consisting of tens of social programs targeted at the poor, the misiones provide food and nutrition, in the form of high-quality cheap products, and healthcare, which is comprehensive and free. They also ensure adequate housing—legitimating the dwellings in the barrios, as well as building new homes. The misiones give subsidies to low-income women and retirement benefits for the poor. In addition, the environment is protected; and there has been substantial rural development. Indigenous rights are secured, though there is still much work to be done, as there is with Afro-Venezuelans. All these innovations have taken place in the context of socioeconomic transformation (the promotion of production for social needs rather than profit) and the expropriation and redistribution of land.

Those misiones dealing specifically with education, all free of charge, include Mision Ribas, which provides evening remedial classes to high school dropouts; Mision Sucre, where ongoing higher education (HE) courses are given to adults; and Mision Robinson, where volunteers teach reading, writing, and arithmetic, also to adults. As a direct result of these education misiones, in 2005 UNESCO recognized Venezuela as country free of illiteracy. Mision Sucre caters for the university sector at the center of which is UBV (the Bolivarian University).

Clifford Young and Julio Franco (2013) document the immense scope and reach of the misiones, pointing out that, just before the presidential election in April 2013, 88 percent of Venezuelans "reported that they personally, someone in their family or someone else they know has benefited from at least one of these programs."

Regional Integration As Victor (2009) points out, the Bolivarian Republic of Venezuela has also brokered the beginning of solid, true integration of the Latin American continent and the Caribbean in the creation of the following:

- TeleSUR, a TV channel fed by the state TV stations of the continent, so that people learn from one another and enjoy Latin American news, art, and music, directly, and not through the mediation of CNN
- ALBA (Alianza Bolivariana para los Pueblos de Nuestra América), an association of solidarity where economic projects are geared toward social justice and human development
- PETROSUR, a consortium of the state oil companies of Latin America to make sure that the oil and gas is used not just to fuel the growth of richer nations, but to help the infrastructure needed at home
- Petrocaribe, an initiative to provide much-needed fuel to the smaller Caribbean nations with preferential financial arrangements and a fund for joint projects
- The Banco del Sur, representing the liberation of Latin America from the high interest rates and hegemony of the International Monetary Fund (IMF), World Bank, and other international banks and organizations, the loans of which have imposed neoliberal capitalist policies on governments
- UNASUR (Unión de Naciones Suramericanas), a defense organization of Latin America, that asserts that it alone assumes the defense of the region. UNASUR has an energy council to put in place safeguards for the supply of energy for the region to protect the natural environment. UNASUR rejects the Monroe Doctrine of 1823, which effectively asserted the United States' sole right to defend the region.

As a further bulwark against US imperial hegemony, Chávez also created CELAC (Community of Latin American and Caribbean States), which includes all 33 states in the region.

The misiones and the regional integrative programs represent fundamental quantitative and qualitative improvements in the lives of the people. They also entail a massive educational project for Venezuela, and for other peoples in the region, and indeed the world. As such they are a major challenge to US neoliberal capitalism and imperial hegemony, and the ideological and repressive apparatuses that sustain what Chávez, Maduro, and others in Venezuela refer to as "the empire." If the misiones are essentially *social democratic* in nature in the sense that they exist in a society that is still a capitalist one, they need to be contextualized in the overall project of twenty-first century socialism, with its promotion of participatory democracy and communal ways of decision making and living which, as we have seen, began before the presidency of Hugo Chávez, and, as we shall see, intensified under his presidency, and continues after his untimely death.

2002: Chávez's Presidency Interrupted, and Reinstated by the People

The Royal Spanish Academy offers five definitions of "*el pueblo*" (the people), four of which refer to the inhabitants of a particular space or territory, while the fifth denotes the "common and poor" members of the population—the oppressed, the people in struggle. These include guerrillas', students', women's, and Afro-indigenous movements as well as the traditional working class, the peasantry and the informal urban poor, and peoples' militias and, at times, state military forces. Of course, there is overlap between them (Ciccariello-Maher, 2013, pp. 8, 20). It is this fifth usage of *el pueblo* that I employ most often in the chapter as a whole, and that I have particularly in mind in this subsection and the last subsection of "Section One" of this chapter.

In November 2001, frustrated at opposition sabotage of his social reforms and factionalism among his own supporters, Chávez used presidential decree to issue enabling laws to reform agriculture and urban property in favor of the people, as well as support for cooperatives and the creation of a new fisheries law, thus signaling his seriousness about challenging the Venezuelan oligarchy. In the following months Chávez dismissed a minister working with the opposition and also disloyal members of the board of the public oil company, PDVSA (Petróleos de Venezuela, S.A.). These events, along with some public declarations calling for Chávez's resignation by senior military figures, led to the signing of an anti-Chávez pact by the Federation of Chambers of Commerce (Fedecámaras), the Venezuelan Labour Confederation (CTV), and the Catholic church among others. On April 11, 2002, a rally was held "to save the PDVSA." The rally was suddenly diverted by the organizers and the anti-Chávez demonstrators moved off in the direction of the presidential Miraflores Palace (Raby, 2006, pp. 166–167). The Venezuelan opposition activated snipers who opened fire on a largely Chavista crowd of people who had gathered near the palace to defend Chávez from the approaching aggressive mob. Some 20 people were killed (Ciccariello-Maher, 2013, p. 167; Raby, 2006, p. 167).

There followed a coup, staged by military officers, and abetted by the mainstream media, after which Chávez was jailed and Pedro Carmona, head of Fedecámaras, swore himself in on the morning of April 12, as de facto president of the Republic of Venezuela—no longer the "Bolivarian Republic" (Martinez et al., 2010, p. 20; Raby, 2006, p. 167). Chavista leaders were publicly flogged in the streets, dozens were shot dead, and Carmona abolished the 1999 Constitution, which embodied the aspirations of decades of revolutionary movements and had been ratified by nearly 72 percent of the electorate soon after Chávez's first election victory (Ciccariello-Maher, 2013, p. 170).

On the same day (April 12, 2002), opposition media journalist, Napoleón Bravo had opened his program *24 Hours* as follows: "Good morning, it is 6.14 am. Thanks to society and the armed forces, today we awake differently. Good morning, we have a new president." Bravo then read a false letter of resignation from Chávez, and engaged in a discussion with some of the coup leaders who expressed their debt to "all the private media" for making the coup possible! (Ciccariello-Maher, 2013, p. 168).

Less than two days after Chávez was taken from office, *el pueblo* responded. Descending from the poor barrios around Caracas and the major cities, they surrounded the Miraflores Palace and demanded their president be returned to office. Within a few hours Chávez was rushed back to the palace (Martinez et al., 2010, p. 20). Recounting how the spontaneous actions of the people need to be seen in the context of the small percentage of die-hard revolutionaries who were part of the descent from the hills and who had "a far more radical vision than the mere return of Chávez to his predetermined position of state power," Ciccariello-Maher (2013, pp. 172–173) describes April 13, 2013, as an "explosive dialectic between spontaneity and organization." Moreover, as he puts it, "mass spontaneity, while fundamental in its importance, is often the result of serious organizing that, in the case of Venezuela, spans decades." This brief episode succinctly illustrates the nature of counterhegemonic politics in Venezuela and the crucial role of informal revolutionary pedagogy in the barrios.

Socialist Revolution: The Process and the President
With respect to the Bolivarian Revolution, Ciccariello-Maher (2013, p. 6) makes a distinction between *el proceso* (the process) and *el presidente* (the president), the former of which he describes as "the

deepening, radicalization, and autonomy of the revolutionary movements that constitute the 'base' of the Bolivarian Revolution." He emphasizes (2013, p. 274) that almost everyone he interviewed, as well as all those appearing in the book *Venezuela Speaks!* (Martinez et al., 2010), spontaneously made this distinction. Through the eyes and voices of the revolutionaries in the decades that preceded the election of Chávez, and through his own incisive analysis, Ciccariello-Maher demonstrates with great skill and clarity the fact that the origins of the revolution predated Chávez, that there is a dialectical relationship between *el pueblo* (the people) and Chávez, and that the key to understanding the apparent synthesis of revolution from above and below can be best explained by the formula "the people created Chávez" (the title of his book). However, in so doing, while he talks of "a complex and dynamic interplay and mutual determination between the two: movements and state: 'the people' and Chávez" (2013, p. 6), and while he notes "the undeniable importance of Chávez to the *contemporary* moment and his relationship with the revolutionary social movements that created him" (2013, p. 21), for me, the whole thrust of his analysis has the effect of underemphasizing the supreme historical importance of the insertion of Chávez into the history of Bolivarian socialism. For example, Ciccariello-Maher (2013, p. 21) places the election of Chávez in 1998 (he assumed his presidency early in 1999) in a subordinate historical position. Chávez's central role in the revolution, I would argue, is witnessed by the aforementioned social reforms, and as we shall see, by the acceleration of the communal council movement and communes and the militias (noted by Ciccariello-Maher himself in the last chapter of his book) and by workplace democracy. Not least, Chávez's central role was also as a figurehead constantly urging *el pueblo* forward to twenty-first century socialism. As we shall see in "Section Two" of this chapter, Chávez's charisma was a key element in mass intellectuality in the public sphere, as well as in the overall ethos guiding the Bolivarian educational project.

Dario Azzellini (2013) describes the dual process at work in the revolution as follows:

> The particular character of what Hugo Chávez called the Bolivarian process lies in the understanding that social transformation can be constructed from two directions, 'from above' and 'from below'. Bolivarianism...includes among its participants both traditional organizations and new autonomous groups; it encompasses both state-centric and anti-systemic currents. The process thus differs from

traditional Leninist or social democratic approaches, both of which see the state as the central agent of change; it differs as well from movement-based approaches that conceive of no role whatsoever for the state in a process of revolutionary change.

This strategy, that entails a fundamental reconsideration of Marxist theories of the state (see the last subsection of "Section One" of this chapter) has been described as the "state for revolution" strategy (e.g., Artz, 2012, p. 2), as part of a strategy of "parallelism"—the creating of parallel institutions—which not only provide basic social democratic reforms, but in tandem with the existing capitalist state, build a "self-government of workers" (Artz, 2012, p. 2). The communal councils, which discuss and decide on local spending and development plans, are key in the Bolivarian process. It is the view of Roland Dennis, a grassroots organizer in the 1980s and vice-minister of Planning and Development from 2002–2003 in Chávez's government (he resigned after ten months because of lack of grassroots involvement in the planning process; Spronk and Webber, 2012), that communal councils provide a historic opportunity to do away with the capitalist state (cited in Piper, 2007).

Communal Councils

> We have to go beyond the local. We have to begin creating...a kind of confederation, local, regional and national, of communal councils. We have to head towards the creation of a communal state. And the old bourgeois state, which is still alive and kicking—this we have to progressively dismantle, at the same time as we build up the communal state, the socialist state, the Bolivarian state, a state that is capable of carrying through a revolution. (Hugo Chávez, cited in Socialist Outlook Editorial, 2007)

As Azzellini (2013) explains, communal councils began forming, in different parts of Venezuela on their own in 2005 as an initiative "from below," as rank-and-file organizations' promoted forms of local self-administration called "local government" or "communitarian governments." Following Chávez's landslide victory in the 2006 elections, and as the revolution intensified, "official" communal councils were created, consisting of small self-governing units throughout the country that "allow the organized people to directly manage public policy and projects oriented toward responding to the needs and aspirations of communities in the construction of a society of equity and social justice" (Article 2 of the 2006 Law on Communal Councils, cited in Ciccariello-Maher, 2013, p. 244).

In urban areas, they encompass 150–400 families; in rural zones, a minimum of 20; and in indigenous zones, at least 10 families. The councils build up a nonrepresentative structure of direct participation that exists parallel to the elected representative bodies of constituted power. They are financed directly by national state institutions (Azzellini, 2013). Within a year 18,320 councils had been established (Ciccariello-Maher, 2013, p. 244), and in 2013, there are approximately 44,000 (Azzellini, 2013). Their objective is to submit the bureaucracy to the will of the people through direct participation at the local level. Committee members are elected by the community for two-year revocable terms and are unpaid. Ciccariello-Maher (2013, pp. 245–246) concludes, having noted that every council elects a five-person committee to oversee other levels of government at municipal, regional, and national level, that this is a powerful weapon against corrupt state and local bureaucracies that many hope they will eventually replace. According to the *National Plan for Economic and Social Development 2007–2013*, "Since sovereignty resides absolutely in the people, the people can itself direct the state, without needing to delegate its sovereignty as it does in indirect or representative democracy" (cited in Azzellini, 2013). The government also created the Federal Council of the Government (CFG), which is a link between the government and the councils, and where the two can decide budget allocation together.

Communes At a higher level of self-government, socialist communes are being created. These are formed by combining various communal councils in a specific territory. The councils themselves decide about the geography of these communes. The communes are able to develop medium- and long-term projects of greater impact than the communal councils, while decisions continue to be made in the assemblies of the communal councils. As of 2013, there are more than two hundred communes being constructed. Communes can, in turn, form communal cities, again with administration and planning from below if the entire territory is organized in communal councils and communes. The communal cities that have begun to be formed so far are rural, since it is easier in the countryside than in metropolitan areas, because there is less distraction and less oppositional presence. Moreover, common interests are easier to define (Azzellini, 2013).

Workplace Democracy The most successful attempt at the democratization of ownership and control of the means of production is the Enterprises of Communal Social Property (EPSC), which consists of local production units and community services enterprises. The EPSCs are collective property of the communities, who decide on the organizational structures, the workers employed, and the eventual use of profits. Government enterprises and institutions have promoted the communal enterprises since 2009, and since 2013 several thousand EPSCs have been formed (Azzellini, 2013).

In June 2013, labor movement activists from all over Venezuela met for the country's first "workers' congress" to discuss workplace democracy and the construction of socialism. The aim of the meeting was to "promote, strengthen and consolidate the self-organisation of the working class, based on an analysis of its labour and an evaluation of its struggles, to allow for the generation of its unity around a common plan of struggle" (Robertson, 2013a). As Ewan Robertson (2013a) explains, as part of resistance to factory closures and management lockouts by bosses opposed to Chávez, dozens of workplaces came under whole or part worker management in the last decade. However, the workers' control movement, which had the support of Chávez, has tended to stagnate because of opposition from management bureaucrats and reformist politicians within the Bolivarian process.

The congress, the result of a year of meetings between workers in different parts of the country, took up the slogan of the Venezuelan radical Left, "Neither capitalists nor bureaucrats, all power to the working class." The main themes of the congress were "the self organisation of the working class"; "the class struggle and the state; legality and legitimacy"; "workers' councils, worker control and management for the transformation of the capitalist economy"; and the "formation and socialisation of knowledge." The main goal of the congress was to draft a final declaration on the national political situation and on the labor movement, and to draw up a manifesto and plan of struggle. At the time of writing, the manifesto and declarations from the workplace democracy congress are to be made public and handed to President Maduro for his consideration (Robertson, 2013a). Given Maduro's clear and obvious commitment to the continuation of the revolution, discussed in the second and last section of the "Conclusion" to this chapter, it is highly likely they will meet with his approval.

Militias In October 2009, a reformed Organic Law of the Armed Forces came into effect and established Bolivarian militias. This law was passed a month before the reformed Law of Communal Councils, which gave the councils "security and integral defence" and linked them directly with the militias (Ciccariello-Maher, 2013, p. 249). As Ciccariello-Maher points out, this relationship was strengthened by the aforementioned government-sanctioned communes, which Chávez described as the "building blocks" of a new Venezuelan state (cited in Ciccariello-Maher, 2013, p. 249). The Chávez government also formally established peasant battalions as a component of the Bolivarian Militia to protect them from the wave of violence from the landed oligarchs (Janicke, 2010a). Chávez proclaimed that the "militia is the people and the people are the militia, the armed people and the armed forces are one" (Janicke, 2010b, cited in Ciccariello-Maher, 2013, pp. 249–250). Quoting a former PRV guerrilla, Chávez asserted,

> The time has come for communities to assume the powers of state, which will lead administratively to the total transformation of the Venezuelan state and socially to the real exercise of sovereignty by society through communal powers. (Cited in Ciccariello-Maher, 2013, p. 250)

Chávez and Orthodox Marxist Theories of the State

It should be stressed that Chávez had no illusions about the nature of the actually existing state in Venezuela. In his socialist plan for 2013–2019, presented during the electoral campaign for the 2012 presidential elections, he stated clearly, "We should not betray ourselves: the still dominant socio-economic formation in Venezuela is of capitalist and rentist character." In order to move more toward socialism, Chávez underlined the necessity to advance in the construction of communal councils, communes, and communal cities, and, as he put it, the "development of social property on the basic and strategic factors and means of production" (cited in Azzellini, 2013).

While Chávez was right, this does not detract from the extraordinary phenomenon of the Bolivarian state, which places a square challenge to orthodox Marxist theories of the state (see Cole, 2009, pp. 229–233; Cole, 2011, pp. 151–153). While the nature of the capitalist state has been the subject of considerable debate among Marxists (e.g., Jessop, 1990, 2002, 2014), there has been a general agreement that the state in capitalist societies works directly or indirectly in the interests of the capitalist class, and that it comprises not just the government. Louis Althusser (1971, pp. 142–144) makes a formal distinction between what he calls the repressive state apparatuses (RSAs) (government, administration, army, police, courts, prisons) and the ideological state apparatuses (ISAs) (religion, education, family, law, politics, trade unions, communication, culture). In Venezuela within all of these apparatuses, along with reactionaries and bureaucrats, there are sizeable numbers of revolutionary socialists. The Bolivarian state's unique character is summarized by Ciccariello-Maher (2013, p. 252): "The traditional state apparatus houses an explosive combination of guerrillas and opportunists, authentic decentralizers and a new, power-hungry elite dressed in red." This state of affairs underlines the crucial importance of confronting the opportunists and the bureaucracy, which, as we shall see, was central for Chávez, and continues to be a priority for Maduro. However, it also provides grounds for optimism in that revolutionaries are at the heart of the Bolivarian state apparatuses.

Section Two

Education

The Self-Education of the People

In many ways, much of the first section of this chapter is in essence an account of the self-education of the Venezuelan people. Revolutionaries constantly need to relate theory to practice, and this involves serious academic study. For example, when, as revealed in the first section, Douglas Bravo tells Ciccariello-Maher about the rediscovery of the spiritual and religious matrix of the indigenous and enslaved African populations, or when Isidro Ramírez, tells him of the importance of both liberation theology and the various cultural histories that make up Venezuela—a "plurality of spiritualities" erased by Eurocentrism, this is, of course, quintessentially educational. Similarly, Rafael Uzcátegui's recollection of how the PRV had a great "theoretical structure" reads like a university course on socialist thinking and imperialism. PRV's members learned not just Venezuelan history, but a wide spectrum of theory ranging from Maoism, through humanist neo-Marxism and autonomist Marxism, taking on Spartacus League Marxism and *foquismo* to traditional historical Latin American anti-imperialist struggle. Reading Carlos Martinez, Michael Fox, and Jojo Farrel's (2010) book, *Venezuela Speaks!* and George Ciccariello-Maher's (2013) volume *We Created Chávez* further substantiates the massive self-educative processes at work in Venezuela. What differentiated these pedagogical processes from similar Marxist reading groups popular at about the same time in the United Kingdom (I was a member of one) were the real possibilities in Venezuela for putting theory into practice outside of academia.

Mass Intellectuality in the Public Sphere: Chávez's "Giant School"

Education, as a liberatory process from birth to death, a process of human emancipation and socialism was articulated in 2010 by Chávez in describing the (peaceful) nature of the Bolivarian Revolution, and the role of knowledge and education as the first of three forms of power in the revolutionary process, the others being political power and economic power:

> When we talk about power, what are we talking about...The first power that we all have is knowledge. So we've made efforts first in education, against illiteracy, for the development of thinking, studying, analysis. In a way, that has never happened before. Today, Venezuela is a giant school, it's all a school. From children of one year old until old age, all of us are studying and learning. And then political power, the capacity to make decisions, the community councils, communes, the people's power, the popular assemblies. And then there is the economic power. Transferring economic power to the people, the wealth of the people distributed throughout the nation. I believe that is the principal force that precisely guarantees that the Bolivarian revolution continues to be peaceful. (Cited in Sheehan, 2010)

Venezuela as "a giant school" and "education for socialism" is exemplified by the Revolutionary Reading Plan launched by Chávez in 2009 (Pearson, 2009). "A change in spirit hasn't been achieved yet," Chávez suggested, and argued that the plan will be the "base for the injection of consciousness through reading, with which our revolution will be strengthened even more" (cited in Pearson, 2009).

The plan involves the distribution by the government of 2.5 million books to develop the communal libraries. Chávez said that part of the plan was a "rescuing of our true history for our youth," explaining that many standard textbooks do not acknowledge the European imperialist genocide of the indigenous peoples and their resistance (Pearson, 2009). Chávez went on to recommend that people do collective reading and exchange knowledge, mainly through the communal councils and the popular libraries. He called on communal councils as well as "factory workers, farmers, and neighbors, to form revolutionary reading squadrons," one of whose tasks is to have discussions in order to "unmask the psychological war...of the oligarchy" (cited in Pearson, 2009).

"Read, read and read, that is the task of every day. Reading to form conscious and minds," Chávez noted, "everyday we must inject the counter revolution a dose of liberation through reading" (cited in MercoPress, 2009). Moreover, the revolutionary reading plan is intended to reaffirm values leading to "the consolidation of the new man and the new woman, as the foundations for the construction of a Socialist motherland, unravelling the capitalist imaginary" (MercoPress, 2009).

A second example of mass intellectuality in the public sphere is the establishment by the government of *Infocentros* for the poor so that they could have access to modern telecommunications technologies. There are 820 of these in nearly 86 percent of the municipalities of Venezuela and they played a central role between 2006 and 2011 in the eradication of illiteracy (Dominguez, 2013, p. 128). As well as making telecommunication technology available to masses of people, *Infocentros* also provide free online training programs. These include text processing; multimedia; use of calculations and data in excel; surfing the Internet; social networking; computer-generated presentations; and a program for the visually impaired. There are also guides to create communicational and photographic products. Help is given for creating websites. It is possible to learn computer-generated drawing; multimedia resources for video forums; and how to look after a computer. In addition advice is given on how to learn from people's own experiences of participation in communal councils. It is also possible to learn how to generate specialist websites such as for tourism, communal socialist commercial exchange, and polls. How to improve writing, public speaking, and spelling is also available (Fundacion Infocentro, Logros del Proyecto Infocentro 2011, Ministerio para Ciencia y Tecnologia, December 14, 2011, pp. 18–22, cited in Dominguez, 2013, p. 130).

The total number of visits to use the *Infocentros* in 2011 alone was nearly 12.5 million, compared to less than 1.5 million in 2001 (Ministerio para Ciencia y Tecnologia, December 14, 2011, p. 15, cited in Dominguez, 2013, p. 128?)

The Formal Education System

The Bolivarian Government's Educational Project for Schools
As far as more "formal" education is concerned, after the election of Chávez, there was a massive increase in funding for primary, secondary, and HE. With respect to the curriculum, the Venezuelan Ministry of Culture stated on its website that there is a need to help school children get rid of "capitalist thinking" and better understand the ideals and values "necessary to build a Socialist country and

society" (cited in MercoPress, 2009). Education is increasingly put forward by the state as a social good, and a central factor in shaping the system of production (Griffiths and Williams, 2009, p. 37).

Tom Griffiths and Jo Williams (2009) outline the essential factors in the Bolivarian Revolution's approach to education that make it truly counterhegemonic. The Venezuelan approach, they argue, draws on concepts of critical and popular education within the framework of a participatory model of endogenous socialist development (Griffiths and Williams, 2009, p. 41). In representative democracies such as the United Kingdom and the United States, political participation is by and large limited to parliamentary politics—which represent the imperatives of capitalism, rather than the real needs and interests of the people.[2] Participatory democracy, a cornerstone of the Bolivarian Revolution on the other hand, involves direct decision making by the people. At the forefront, they note, is "the struggle to translate policy into practice in ways that are authentically democratic, that promote critical reflection and participation over formalistic and uncritical learning" (Griffiths and Williams, 2009).

As in the United Kingdom and the United States, formal school education in Venezuela is based on an explicit, politicized conception of education and its role in society (Griffiths and Williams, 2009, pp. 41–42). However, whereas in the United Kingdom and the United States, the capitalist state increasingly uses formal education merely as a vehicle to promote capitalism (e.g., Hill, 2013), in the Bolivarian Republic of Venezuela, "the political" in education is articulated *against* capitalism and imperialism and *for* socialism. In 2008, a draft national curriculum framework for the Bolivarian Republic was released. It stated that the system is "oriented toward the consolidation of a humanistic, democratic, protagonistic, participatory, multi-ethnic, pluri-cultural, pluri-lingual and intercultural society" (Ministerio del Poder Popular Para la Educación, 2007, p. 11, cited in Griffiths and Williams, 2009, p. 42). It went on to critique the former system for reinforcing "the fundamental values of the capitalist system: individualism, egotism, intolerance, consumerism and ferocious competition...[which also] promoted the privatisation of education" (Ministerio del Poder Popular Para la Educación, 2007, p. 12, cited in Griffiths and Williams, 2009, p. 42).

It should be stressed at this stage that, in terms of actual practice in the schools and universities, education based on the above revolutionary principles is by no means universal. Indeed, as Griffiths and Williams (2009, p. 44) point out, discussions with education academics and activists during fieldwork in Caracas in 2007, 2008, and 2009, repeatedly raised the challenge of the political and pedagogical conservatism of existing teachers, often in opposition to the government's Bolivarian socialist project (e.g., Griffiths, 2008). With respect to this project, Tamara Pearson (2011) has pointed out that, "so far such a vision for education is limited to a number of 'model' schools and the majority of Venezuelan children continue to be educated in the conventional way." She goes on to argue that, while education in Venezuela is now accessible to almost everyone, illiteracy has been eradicated, the working conditions and wages of teachers are much improved, and education is more linked to the outside world, mainly through community service and the communal councils, "structural changes in terms of teaching methods and democratic organising of schools and education have been very limited" (Pearson, 2011).

She concludes,

> Building a new education system is an important prong to building a new economic and political system, because the education system is where we form many of our values, where we learn how to relate to people, where we learn our identity and history, and how to participate in society. Hence we need an alternative to the conventional education systems that train us to be workers more than anything else, to be competitive, to operate under almost army-like discipline, to focus only on individual results not collective outcomes, and to not really understand our history, or the more emotional aspects of life...The effort to change Venezuela's education system is intricately connected to its larger political project. (Pearson, 2011)

Pearson (2012) has commented on one of the latest government documents. In a generally extremely positive account of Chávez's 39-page proposed plan for the 2013–2019 period of the Bolivarian Revolution, she notes that with respect to education, while the plan mentions increasing enrollment, the building of new schools, the introduction or improvement of certain elements of the curriculum content—such as "the people's and indigenous history of Venezuela," as well as strengthening research into the educative process, there are "no structural or methodology changes." There have hardly been any changes, she argues, in the last 12 years. She concludes,

> The achievement of literacy and enrolment of the poorest sectors is important, but the teaching methods are still traditional authoritarian, competitive ones, and while some schools have become more involved

in their community life, many are still merely producers of obedient workers and a source of income for the teachers. More radical change than what has been proposed is needed. (Pearson, 2012)

Bearing Pearson's prescriptions in mind, there is much to learn from alternative schools, such as the one in Barrio Pueblo Neuvo, Merida (see chap. 4 of this volume). The creation of a parallel set of popular educational institutions may be viewed as a process of construction—as part of a longer-term process of anticapitalist struggle, which can eventually serve as a model and help to free the official state schools from the stranglehold of the long-standing bureaucracy, created in part before the presidency of Chávez.

HE in the Bolivarian Republic

Tom Griffiths (2013, p. 92) notes how massification of HE in Venezuela since Chávez's first election victory is evidenced by frequent references to its now being ranked second in Latin America (behind Cuba) and fifth worldwide in university enrollment rates, as reported by UNESCO in September 2010 (Ramírez, 2010, cited in Griffiths, 2013). This expansion has resulted in a nearly 200 percent increase from 1999 to 2009, from under 900,000 to over 2 million students (Ramírez, 2010, cited in Griffiths, 2013). Griffiths explains the specific nature of the massification project,

> A particular feature of the envisaged transformation is the intent to directly link higher education to the project of national endogenous development, under the banner of reconnecting universities to local communities, and to concrete social problems and their resolution, thus connecting theory with social practice. (Griffiths, 2013, p. 92)

The intending transformation, he points out, following Muhr (2010), seeks to build students' social and political consciousness in order to undertake work in the interests of the local community, the society, and the Bolivarian Republic (Griffiths, 2013, p. 92).

Griffiths and Williams (2009, p. 43) give the example of the UBV. Founded in 2003 as part of a major attempt to extend access to HE, UBV is free to all students and "seeks to fundamentally challenge the elitism of many of the traditional universities." Social justice and equality are "at the core of all educational content and delivery," and all courses taken there use Participatory Action Research (PAR) methodology, "described as a multidisciplinary approach linking practice and theory." PAR methodology bases UBV students in their local communities, working alongside a mentor on a community project, which is a core part of their formal studies (Griffiths and Williams, 2009). Griffiths and Williams (2009, p. 43) give the examples of "Community Health students working with doctors within the *Barrio Adentro* health mission"; "legal studies students establishing a community legal centre to advise and support families with civil law issues"; and education students working with a teacher/mentor in schools in their local community.

All UBV students relate theory to their experiences in the project. As Griffiths and Williams (2009, pp. 43–44) explain,

> The approach is designed to place day-to-day decision-making and problem solving in the hands of local communities, as part of the broader societal reconstruction underway, with all participants gaining skills through the process. The intent is that the PAR methodology places researchers in positions of political leadership, but with the projects being democratically controlled and driven by the communities themselves and their own leaders, and aimed at realising the objectives of the community based organisations.

Griffiths and Williams (2009, p. 44) conclude that while the discussions are interesting, what is most important is *who* is taking part in them. This is not only "social and economic inclusion" but also *political* inclusion, with educational decision making in the hands of staff, students, parents/carers, *and the community at large*. I had the privilege of teaching at UBV for a short while in 2006.

Just as with education in schools, in the realms of HE in general, there are serious shortcomings that need addressing. Griffiths (2013, p. 105), for example, cites "the prevalence of passive, transmission pedagogical practices; top-down and highly centralised governance structures and practices including the appointment (rather than election) of university authorities." He also refers to "high levels of casualisation of the academic workforce; and extremely high attrition rates accompanying the expanded enrolments in some universities, caused partly by inadequate funding and resources to support these expanded numbers."

Bolivarian Education: Some Conclusions

One central message of the Bolivarian Revolution tells us is that a fundamental counterhegemonic shift in the political economy toward socialism, including *universal* free access to education, with a high degree of equity in terms of opportunity and outcomes, can be achieved quite quickly (Griffiths and Williams, 2009, p. 34). As Griffiths and Williams conclude, the Bolivarian system consistently refers these back to the underlying project to promote the formation of new republicans, with creative and transformational autonomy, with revolutionary ideas, and with a positive attitude toward learning in order to put into practice new and original solutions for the endogenous transformation of the country (Ministerio del Poder Popular Para la Educación 2007, p. 16, cited in Griffiths and Williams, 2009, pp. 42–43).

Another obvious message, as Griffiths (personal correspondence, 2013) points out, is that the expansion reinforces and further promotes the counterhegemonic view of education at all levels as being a human right (and obligation), thus contributing to heightened anticipations among the people. As he puts it, Bolivarian education "has politicised people and has generated/awoken in the most marginalised a new sense of identity, power and expectation."

Conclusion

Opposition to the Bolivarian Revolution

If capitalist structures and epistemologies abound in education, as they do in the society in general, the Bolivarian Revolution has demonstrated that another world is possible, and has unsurprisingly generated fierce and intense opposition from the United States and its procapitalist proimperialist allies throughout the world. For example, Ed Vulliamy (2002), writing in the *Observer* newspaper, argued that his newspaper established, shortly after the 2002 coup that momentarily ousted Chávez, that the coup "was closely tied to senior officials in the US government... [who] have long histories in the 'dirty wars' of the 1980s, and links to death squads working in Central America at that time." According to officials at the Organization of American States "and other diplomatic sources," Vulliamy goes on, "the US administration was not only aware the coup was about to take place, but had sanctioned it, presuming it to be destined for success." Moreover, "the visits [to the White House] by Venezuelans plotting a coup, including Carmona himself, began... several months ago," and went on until weeks before the coup. The "crucial figure around the coup," Vulliamy states, was Elliot Abrams who was senior director of the National Security Council for "democracy, human rights and international operations," a leading theoretician of "Hemispherism," which "put a priority on combating Marxism in the Americas." It led to the coup in Chile in 1973, Vulliamy concludes, and sponsored regimes and death squads elsewhere in Latin America.

As its figurehead, Chávez, rather than twenty-first century socialism *per se*, was consistently demonized. The ideological apparatuses of the state, in particular the media, in the capitalist heartlands were also adept at denigrating him. To take the case of the United Kingdom as a typical example, a quick search for "Chávez" on the website of the United Kingdom's best-selling newspaper, the *Sun*—circulation, nearly 2.5 million—immediately threw up the facetious and discourteous headline, "Sick Prez Chavez Dies at 58." The article, not much more than hundred words, states, "Dictator Chavez, who ruled for 14 years, outraged Brits by claiming the Falklands should be returned to Argentina. He hated the U.S. and ordered American diplomats out after accusing them of trying to destabilise the country" (Royston, 2013). The accusation of "dictator" is a common one (in reality, there were 16 elections and referenda since 1998, almost all won by the government. Moreover, ex–US president Jimmy Carter described the Venezuelan democratic process as "the best in the world").

While the *Sun* makes no attempt to hide its very right-wing conservative ideological position, embedded in interpellative claims that what it says is straightforward "common sense," the supposedly liberal *Guardian* newspaper, sister publication of the *Observer* that published the story about US involvement in the 2002 coup, has been predominantly and regularly anti-Chávez (its Latin American correspondent, Rory Carroll, regularly wrote anti-Chávez articles). Moreover, the *nominally* neutral BBC has a history of similar anti-Chàvez bias (Salter and Weltman, 2011).

This demonization has also, of course, come from the internal political opposition whose credentials and abuses have been paraded throughout this chapter. They consistently racially abused Chávez, referring to him, for example, as "*mico mandante*" (monkey in charge) rather than the Chavista term of respect, "*mi Comandante*" (Ciccariello-Maher, 2013, p. 159).

The damnation and denigration of Chávez also served the purpose of mystifying the relationship between Chávez and *el pueblo* (in reality, as has been argued, a dialectic made possible by decades of struggle prior to Chávez) and in so doing, also defaming the people: "It is just a case of a communist dictator hoodwinking the gullible and easily-led people in the barrios with bribes from the sale of oil to keep himself in power."

While all of this anti-Chávez and antisocialist action and rhetoric is to be expected from the world capitalist system, including the homegrown opposition, perhaps the biggest obstacle to change comes from within the Bolivarian Revolution itself. As high profile indigenous leader José Poyo argues,

> At present, we are accompanying a revolutionary *government*, but one which is slowed by a bureaucratic *state*... and as a result, while the law is progressive, it lacks implementation...We agree with the President, his political will, his discourse, and efforts to turn that will into practice. We disagree with the functionaries that surround him and their vision. (Cited in Ciccariello-Maher, 2013, p. 161; emphasis original)

Others have referred to "the endogenous right," "the Fourth Republic within *Chavismo*," "the Boli-bourgeoisie" (Martinez et al., 2010, p. 23). As Luis Perdomo has argued, many government officials, on becoming ministers or heads of a department in an institution, act as if they own that institution. As he puts it,

> Being a revolutionary is modelled by the attention given to the people...We don't want to be a deck of cards shuffled by someone else...we want to shuffle the deck. We want to construct along with the president and the assembly representatives, and the ministers as well. (Cited in Martinez et al., 2010, pp. 230–231)

Greg Wilpert (2007, 2010, p. viii) has also made reference to the practices of "clientelism-patronage" and "personalism," the former referring to politicians' use of government resources such as jobs or material benefits to favor their own supporters against political opponents; the latter to the tendency among both citizens and political leaders to place greater importance on loyalty to politicians than to political programs.

There is also a notorious degree of corruption within the Bolivarian process, with those claiming to be Chavistas, showing more interest in lining their own pockets, or in obtaining positions of power within the revolution, not to forward it, but to exert that power to forward their own interests and agendas.

It should be pointed out that Chávez showed awareness of, chided, and attempted to undermine this reactionary bureaucracy on a number of occasions. For example, noting that some of the delegates present at his call for a Fifth Socialist International in November 2009 had been elected by irregular means and that some people were only interested in getting elected to parliament or becoming mayors and governors. He described this as unacceptable (Woods, 2009).

Into the Future

Despite these considerable obstacles, I have stressed throughout this chapter that the revolution is in the hands of the people (in the sense of *el pueblo*). I have also insisted on the huge historical importance of Hugo Chávez. At the time of writing (summer 2013), it is too early to make an accurate political assessment of the presidency of Chávez's favored successor, Nicolás Maduro. However, there are a large number of grounds for optimism, for thinking that, like his predecessor, Maduro will make a significant contribution to twenty-first century socialism in the Bolivarian Republic of Venezuela. Maduro's socialism dates back to his childhood. When he was 12 years old and a high school student, he began to participate, unbeknown to his parents, in the revolutionary project of Douglas Bravo (mentioned earlier in this chapter). From then he has participated without interruption in socialist struggles (Navarro, 2013). Luis Hernández Navarro (2013) describes Maduro as self-taught in the classics of Marxism, and "a brilliant organiser and political agitator of the masses."

Maduro has promised to maintain Chávez's "revolutionary, anti-imperialist and socialist legacy" (Ellner, 2013), and has also promised "zero poverty" in Venezuela by 2019 (Robertson, 2013b). On being sworn in on April 19, 2013, he pledged a "revolution of the revolution," saying he would reduce crime, improve government efficiency, and tackle corruption (Robertson, 2013b). The following examples of the actions taken in the first months of his presidency are a testimony to Maduro's commitment to the continuation and reinforcement of mass intellectuality in the public sphere, and to the continued promotion of Chávez's giant school.

A Government of the Streets

On April 2, 2013, the first day of the presidential campaign, Maduro committed himself to "breaking with bureaucratism," which plagued the Chávez years, and which he labeled "the mode of the petty bourgeoisie." In its place, Maduro said that he would create a "government of the streets." Since then he and his cabinet have started to travel to all states to meet with grassroots organization and regional officials. The program has resulted in the approval of numerous projects ranging from environmental issues to crime, and has included Maduro's first expropriation of land to build public housing for 213 families (Bercovitch, 2013a, 2013b).

Tackling Corruption

After over a hundred arrests had been made in a month, the majority of which are from within the government itself, Maduro declared, "Anyone who is corrupt is a counter revolutionary, anti-Chavista and anti-Bolivarian." Venezuelan authorities are currently investigating the offices of the opposition leader Henrique Capriles Radonski (Mallett-Outtrim, 2013a).

LGBT Rights

As far as Lesbian, Gay, Bisexual, and Transgender (LGBT) rights are concerned, holding a rainbow flag at an LGBT rally, Maduro stated that the ruling United Socialist Party of Venezuela (PSUV) "will never be homophobic...[because the]...revolution claims freedom, equality and respect for human beings." "To you," he went on, "all my respect and our support." Given that, according to head of the opposition-aligned *Proinclusion de Voluntad Popular* Tamara Adrian, Venezuela is the only country in Latin America where the National Assembly has never discussed issues such as same-sex marriage, and in the context of recent homophobic and transphobic remarks from one of Maduro's government members, Maduro's intervention is significant (cited in Mallett-Outtrim, 2013a).

A Multicultural Nation

After seven years of planning and public consultation, Venezuela's National Assembly (AN) has passed a new law aimed to promote Venezuelan culture. According to a summary of the new law on the AN website, it aims to "develop the guiding principles, obligations, guarantees and cultural rights enshrined in the constitution of the Bolivarian Republic of Venezuela." It also mandates the ministries of education and youth to work alongside the ministry of culture to promote the development of a "national identity" based on "decolonisation thought." The law will "promote and guarantee the exercise of cultural creativity, the pre-eminence of the values of culture as a fundamental human right...recognising the national identity of cultural and ethnic diversity, multiculturalism and respecting the principle of cultural equality." The statement also affirms an obligation on the government, the private sector, and social organizations to preserve not only the Spanish language and Hispanic culture, but also Venezuela's indigenous and Afro-Venezuelan population. Maduro stated that an "ethical-cultural revolution" is needed to counter corruption. "I'm more and more certain that we must build new political ethics to overcome capitalism's evil power," he concluded (Mallett-Outtrim, 2013b).

A Democratic Socialist Revolution

Maduro has also committed Venezuela to a "democratic revolution" by working to promote community councils and communes and moving toward a "socialist mode of living," which must be done not by the government but "by the people" (Robertson, 2013b). He has called on his government to give greater support to the construction of communes in the country, proposing some initiatives by which this could be done (Robertson, 2013c). "Let's make the issue of the communes into a central issue for the construction of territorial socialism, concrete socialism, where we all contribute to the construction of the communes, [and] support and consolidate those communes already established," Maduro proclaimed (Robertson, 2013c). "Established and consolidated communes must be transformed," he concluded, "into a vanguard which goes out to construct, and with their example, educate, motivate, form and support the construction of new communes" (Robertson, 2013c).

Another proposal was for the formation of a national television channel for communes, which will be dedicated to sharing information about the work and daily life of communes and community councils, with Maduro arguing, "Every communal council and every commune should aim to be an organised [group of] people, that develops an economically productive socialism" (Robertson, 2013c).

At the time of writing (summer 2013), it has just been announced that 20 new communes will be created in Caracas, and a mass grassroots electoral operation is being organized to elect spokespersons for them and for the communal councils. The councils, through their own electoral commissions, will conduct the elections, with the first elections taking place in the aforementioned radical 23 de Enero district of the city (Robertson, 2013d).

Maduro also proposed "a complete restructuring" of the government so as to optimize its functioning and better achieve its objectives. "We've inherited the structure of the bourgeois government, the bourgeois state. We need to erect a new structure," he declared. Part of this restructuring will be a greater focus by ministries on mechanisms of grassroots power. "We call ourselves ministries of people's power. We have to be ministries of peoples' power," Maduro concluded (Robertson 2013c).

Anti-imperialism

As far as anti-imperialism is concerned, he initially offered "relations [with the United States] within the framework of equality and respect." However, following several incidents, including remarks in July 2013 by President Barack Obama's nominee for US envoy to the United Nations that she would fight against what she called a "crackdown on civil society being carried out in countries like Cuba, Iran, Russia, and Venezuela," Maduro dramatically changed his mind. As he put it, "My policy is zero tolerance to gringo aggression against Venezuela. I'm not going to accept any aggression, whether it be verbal, political, or diplomatic. Enough is enough. Stay over there with your empire, don't involve yourselves anymore in Venezuela" (Bercovitch, 2013c). Maduro recently announced that Venezuela and other Latin American governments are going to officially invite Puerto Rico, an "unincorporated territory" of the United States, to be a member of CELAC (CB Online, 2013).

Formal Education

With respect to the formal education system, in August 2013, the Maduro government started the delivery of free computers to a further 2.5 million young people attending secondary school nationwide under the Canaima program, started by Chávez in 2009 (about the same number are already in schools). The program has themes such as "Indigenous Resistance"; "Independence Bicentennial"; "Educators and Democracy"; "The Protection of the Environment"; and "Friendship, Solidarity and Love" (Dominguez, 2013, p. 131). Secondary school students can take the machines home and teach the new technologies to family members. Maduro has stated that the program will also be extended to "all universities and barrios" (http://www.democraticunderground.com/110818114).

El pueblo

As Chávez's successor, Maduro is faced with a task of great magnitude. It is symptomatic of Chávez's extraordinary effect on the Venezuelan people that crowds gathered outside the Caracas military hospital where he died, chanting, "We are all Chávez." Nevertheless, to underline once again one of the central themes of this chapter—the primacy of the Venezuelan people in the overall Bolivarian project—Pearson (2013) has noted their role in securing Maduro's narrow election victory. As she explains, the choice for socialists was not about

Maduro or individual candidates, but about "revolution v capitalism and imperialism" [with Capriles representing the latter]:

> We should recognise the problems and challenges, but also feel some comfort that this time, 7 million people largely voted for the revolution of the poor to continue. And they did that, despite most media being against us, despite the distortions and lies, despite the minor, but real, economic hardships, despite 14 years of marching and voting again and again, despite the bureaucracy in the government. As one comrade of mine said, "Chavez got us used to victories that were marvellously planned and masterfully lead by him. This time it was up to us to do it alone, and we won." We can only learn from here. (Pearson, 2013)

I will leave the last words (spoken before Chávez's death) to a woman, resident in the Caracas barrio of Baruta, who joined the hundreds of thousands of people, maybe a million, descending from the barrios around Caracas, successfully demanding the reinstatement of Chávez after the military coup in 2002 (Blough, 2010):

> We love our president, but this is not his revolution. This is our revolution and it will always be the revolution of the people. If President Chávez goes, we will miss him dearly but we will still be here. We are revolutionaries and we will always be here. We will never go back! (Cited in Blough, 2010)

Part II

Counterhegemonic Epistemologies and Decolonizing Pedagogies from Below

Chapter 4

The Alternative School of Community Organization and Communicational Development, Barrio Pueblo Nuevo, Mérida, Venezuela

Mike Cole

In this chapter, I trace revolutionary developments in an alternative school in Barrio Pueblo Nuevo, Mérida. I begin by recounting some fieldwork done at the school on my behalf by Edward Ellis in 2010. I go on to discuss a video made at the school by the children in 2011. I then update Ellis's fieldwork by summarizing an interview in 2012 with the school's cofounder, Miguel Cortez, also carried out by Ellis. I conclude the chapter with a 2013 e-interview I conducted with Tamara Pearson, a teacher at the school, and a writer for venezuelanalysis.com.

Introduction

Myriam Anzola, formerly head of the Universidad Politecnica territorial del Estado Merida "Kleber Ramirez" (UPTM), and currently the coordinator of the open studies program at the university, defines Venezuela's alternative schools as,

> informal educative spaces that are guided by the national Bolivarian curriculum, but apply it with a more open and flexible methodology, without prerequisites or ranking students, and allowing them to advance at their own speed. (Anzola and Pearson, 2013)

She points out that there are 20 alternative schools in Mérida, the capital of Mérida state in western Venezuela, one of the country's 23 states. Nestled in a valley formed between the Sierra Nevada de

Mérida and the Sierra's Head, two of Venezuela's Andean mountain chains, the city has a population of about 330,000 people. Only seven of the alternative schools, created by the education ministry and the state government, are operating because the ministry has not maintained the necessary technical support. The schools represent a diverse range of projects, including "an agro-ecological school that encourages children to study and learn within a conservationist and environmentally friendly dynamic"; a science school; a school for artistic development, which stimulates children through creative activity; and one that is "centred around a project of interpretive systemology [a philosophical theory based on antireductionist thinking, centered around the work of Fuenmayor (1989)] and develops an interest in building meaning through reading." There is also a school that has children with disabilities, and functions as an example of integration "in order to increase the sensitivity of the school population towards differences" (Anzola and Pearson, 2013).

Finally, there is the school in Barrio Pueblo Neuvo, which is the subject of this chapter. The Alternative School of Community Organisation and Communicational Development "promotes an awareness of community surroundings and develops means of social integration in the children" (Anzola and Pearson, 2013). Elsewhere Anzola has stated the reason for the other part of the name of the school:

> Since in the activities that they were doing there were many things that had to do with communication, and the radio is here, and also they like theatre, dance and other activities that had to do with communication, we thought we could call it the "Alternative School for Communicational Development." (Soundtrack to Fundación CAYAPA, 2011)

The school also "encourages self-management in all school based and non-school based activities" (Anzola and Pearson, 2013).

Although the experiences in each school are different, what they have in common is a break with routine study and a set curriculum. All pursue an "environment of freedom and of active participation by the children in their own learning" and the development of school projects. They all prioritize capacities for thinking over memorizing and repeating content. This model of education promotes "the creation of spaces where students are involved in their surrounding reality," which generates social consciousness (Anzola and Pearson, 2013).

The schools practice alternative pedagogy that Anzola defines as centering "on the empowering of students within their socio-cultural context." "It allows them," she goes on, "to develop their individual talents within a shared project that has a theme that interests all the participants and which responds to the idiosyncrasy of the locality" (Anzola and Pearson, 2013).

Pueblo Neuvo, 2010

Creating Space[1]

The Alternative School of Community Organisation and Communicational Development is a small project, started about five years ago by committed socialist revolutionary residents and activists of Barrio Pueblo Nuevo, perhaps the poorest community in the city of Mérida in western Venezuela. It caters to students aged between 4 and 14, and since, at the time of this research in 2010, it had been operating for only 6 months, it was very much in its initiatory phase. The teachers (known as "cooperative educational facilitators") want to create an alternative for young people who have been left behind in the public (state) school system and reengage them in participatory pedagogy consistent with socialist and democratic values. The school is currently linked to the Ministry of Education under the title of "alternative school" and receives some state funding.

Reflecting on the overall context of his fieldwork at the school, Edward Ellis (2010) points out that the fact that the school is the exception rather than the rule as far as education in the country as a whole is concerned "need not be understood as distressing. It can be seen...as a great opportunity to empower and encourage new forms of change." He underlines the spaces that the Chávez government opened up—in this case for "independent and autonomous...new projects to grow and develop." As Gerardo, a part-time collaborator at the school, a longtime community activist from the barrio, and an organic intellectual of the working class par excellence states, recalling the pre-Chávez years, "This wouldn't have been possible. This would have been called 'terrorist' and would have to be underground." As he puts it, revolutionary teachers, unlike before, can advance faster, no longer having "to worry about being hunted down."

Gerardo points out that the school has opened many doors for people and that there are "a lot of expectations" from the Ministry of Education, which is hoping that the school might work as "a model for other schools."

Twenty First Century Socialist Praxis

Gerardo is committed to socialist praxis, noting that "socialism is done, not decreed." Given that the words "revolution" and "socialism" are omnipresent in Venezuelan society, and can be used "without much thought," Gerardo is working on the *construction* of socialism in the school, being "a bit more responsible in this sense." As he explains, "Here we practice socialism with concrete elements from everyday life...sharing, working in a collective way, friendship, getting along, the fundamental bases of socialism with praxis." Having seen societies torn apart in a capitalist system based on consumption, and underlining twenty-first century socialism's stress on participatory democracy, Gerardo notes that the teachers are trying to teach the children to be "critical and proactive"—"not just criticism but how things can be changed," "we are trying to show that the children have a participatory role in society, and that this role can be transformative." Communication tools are crucial in this process—"the radio, the television, the written word...these things can lead to the transformation of society."

Lisbeida Rangel, at the time of this research a university student studying criminology, and a dance instructor ("dance" being, of course, one of the ways the school students are encouraged to communicate), working at the school and in the community as a volunteer, says of twenty-first century socialism, it "is being redefined, something that is flexible. I believe there are new understandings of what socialism is and how it can be implemented":

> But basically, the core concepts are the same: equality, social justice, elimination of class differences, more horizontal processes, all of this inside our school is an intrinsic part of what we are doing. It's our base...So we are trying to transmit these values of equality, solidarity, cooperation, collective work.

James Suggett, a writer for venezuelanalysis.com[2] who is also a community activist and a volunteer at the school, reflects Freireian analysis when he says he is critical of those teachers who view socialism as being authoritarian, those who believe they should be getting students into line.[3] For Suggett, "Socialism means creating a democratic space in the classroom," encouraging people "to recognize oppression and overcome it."[4]

Communal, Cooperative, and Democratic Living and Learning

At the Alternative School of Community Organisation and Communicational Development, each day starts with a communal breakfast, after which students are brought together to discuss what will take place that day. Sometimes communal cleaning of the community center where the classes are held ensues; sometimes the day starts with group activities, focused on reading, writing, or mathematics, depending on what students wish to work on, or need to improve.

Addressing the socialist roots of Venezuela's indigenous communities, Gerardo illustrates Freire's process of conscientization (the pedagogical process by which counterhegemonic awareness is achieved) as he points out that indigenous peoples have a tradition of companionship, solidarity, respect, and sharing, and that private property did not exist, and how the teachers are trying to break the paradigms of Western society that value "capital more than people," and that prioritize individualism and competition. The school aims to provide the children with a point of departure so that they can all advance together toward socialism. Gerardo points to the use of a pedagogy that "involves the children in collective work and thinking" and includes cooperative games. When the teachers meet with the children, as Jeaneth Lopez explains, the teachers try to emphasize "that we are a collective and if something happens to the group it affects us all."

Learning at the school is in line with Freire's advocacy of "dialogic education," which entails a democratic learning environment and the *absence* of authoritarianism, of "banking education" (where teachers deposit "facts" into empty minds) and of grades (Freire, 1993). As Jeaneth puts it,

> We plan activities and then ask the children which they would like to work on. They choose the area. We have some basic parameters that they need to work in but they choose. Also, when we leave the school for a trip, we propose the idea to them and they take part in the discussion about how to plan the trip.

Tamara Pearson, like Suggett, is a writer for venezuelanalysis.com, and also a volunteer teacher of reading at the school, points out that

> no one is forced to do anything and there are no punishments. If they don't want to participate in an activity, they can simply go somewhere else, or sit and watch. Hence, the weight is on the teacher to properly motivate the students and draw them in through the activity rather than discipline and threats of lower grades or whatever.

"There is no grading or competition," Pearson explains, "there's simply no sense of them competing with others." "The idea of the school," she believes, "is to teach using more creative and dynamic methods, without the usual competition and grades and failure and passing and who is first etc, with teachers who are very supportive and friendly, while also involving the community in school life, and vice versa."

Socialism and the Community

As Edward Ellis (2010) states, "There is a real emphasis on trying to increase students' participation in all activities." He gives the example of how "the students watched a movie and then discussed how to organize a screening of that same film in their community. A group conversation was held to identify what the steps necessary would be to put on this screening." As Ellis (2010) explains, "There is a lot of collaboration on the part of the community and different activities are led by different folks...It is quite common for the students to leave the classroom to attend an event in the community." In addition, as Lisbeida points out, the school's "activities [are] open to the entire community so that the community is a protagonist in what happens in the school. In that way, the dance group which is part of the school is also part of the community." Emphasizing how Participatory Action Research (PAR)[5] works in the community and school, Lisbeida explains,

> The idea is that the children have an impact in their community, carrying with them this experience to their homes and to their families so that their families also become integrated in the educational process that the school is trying to carry out. So there's a kind of feedback that we are trying to accomplish between the community and the school. And school-community means family, workers, etc. There is an important interaction which is very relevant to the educational process in the school.

This is not to glamorize the students' community. As Gerardo explains, some of the students come from homes where there are problems of violence, alcohol, or drugs, or unemployment and *its* attendant problems. However, as Lisbeida believes, this can also be a source of strength for the students:

> As these students come from backgrounds that are very difficult, I think that this gives them the ability to see certain social realities with more clarity: justice, the marked differences between violence and love. I see this as a potential to create criticisms and questions with more meaning. Because they have experienced very difficult things, they are not going to be afraid and they are going to have a very strong base to be critical of things.

Gerardo points out that there is help from some government misiones, such as Mision Barrio Adentro (literally "mision inside the barrio"), which provides comprehensive publicly funded health care, and sports training to poor and marginalized communities. Barrio Adentro delivers de facto universal health care from cradle to grave. In addition, the teachers are trying to improve human relations, not only with cooperative games, from which the teachers are also learning, but there are physical spaces "with a community vision," such as a community library and a community radio station. As Lisbeida puts it,

> We've noticed that the children are arriving at their house with new attitudes, and although we don't have a way to scientifically measure it, we can feel a difference in the attitude of the parents as well...how they treat their children. Something very interesting is happening. Things are changing...[the children] learn things based on what they already know and live. In this way, they can also learn that they have the potential to change the reality that surrounds them.

The students at the alternative school in Barrio Pueblo Nuevo are in a process of self-liberation, and already, at the time of this research, there were signs of progress. As Lisbeida enthuses, "One of the things that we have seen with this process in the school is that the ones who were thought to be completely without potential or capacity to learn are making people turn their heads. They are doing some incredible things." As Gerardo concludes,

> We've only had a short time operating but I have noticed a change in the way the children see things. Before, their world was just the barrio, but now they are looking a little bit beyond this. And I have seen that the children are speaking now, they are conversing...Before everything was resolved through violence. Now there is more talking. There are still some very sharp words, but we are working on it. This has opened many doors for people. There are a lot of expectations...And there are many things that we have learned about ourselves due to the students.

Thus, in launching the school and in teaching there, the teachers are learning too. James Suggett concludes that this empowerment arises from the challenge of teaching the students in the school every day. As he puts it, "The revolution is there in what they're doing and in their transformation process."

Pueblo Nuevo, 2011[6]

Communication and Play: The Students Speak

Many of the students at the Alternative School of Community Organisation and Communicational Development emphasize how the freedom to communicate and the promotion of "play" aids the learning process. As Carlos Sosa López puts it,

> I feel like in this school I have learned in a freer way, with group work. In other schools you were always really quiet because the teacher didn't let you speak, because we had to do whatever they said, we couldn't do anything else. The teachers give us the opportunity to talk with them and to express ourselves, what we want to do, how we feel...here you learn more than in other schools. Even though you hear people say, "no, in that school they don't learn anything because the children spend all day playing," but when we play, we're learning new things.

Responding in a similar vein, when asked whether she likes the school, Hellen Contreras replies,

> Yes!...I like it because there are more playmates here. Because here they give us the freedom that they didn't give us in the regular school, because here they don't scold you and make you copy from the blackboard like they did every single day.

Further underlining the authoritarian and didactic methods of the traditional schools, Hellen notes that, "they just say, 'Repeat this! Repeat that!' And Jeaneth taught me a way that I don't have to repeat, I just use my fingers."

Emmanuel Sánchez also recognizes the connection between enjoyment and learning, stating that "it's fun, you love it, playing, doing assignments...all of that," while Isamar Izarra and Ruby Contreras appear to recognize the atmosphere of Freireian authoritativeness as opposed to authoritarianism: "Here they don't scold so much! There's something that's so...so...so different...lots of things are different, the books...everything here is different." And, Wilber Flores says simply, "It's beautiful, I've enjoyed it a lot now I've been here for six months and I've learned to play a little more Cuatro [a Venezuelan small guitar]."

Ruby Contreras, showing awareness of the ways in which various forms of communication and play all aid in the learning process, and therefore perceiving no need to make a distinction between assignments, play, and dance, comments, "Here what they teach me is to do assignments. I like this school a lot because they let us play here and we can dance here too. We study for a while and then we can go to recess." Carlos Sosa López widens the discussion to encompass further aspects of play and communication and the positive effect it has had on him:

> I used to be very quiet, very lonely, I was bored all the time because I had gotten used to copying into a notebook and not going out and playing. Not anymore, now I'm in Dance, Soccer, Singing and that's helped me because there I have friends and teachers that I can talk to and express myself and that's helped me a lot.

The students' views on the interconnectedness of play, communication, and effective learning are corroborated by teacher Gerson Zambrano who points out that "what they learn in Dance the children show in Physical Education, what they learn in Physical Education they reinforce in the classroom."

One of the students, Hellen Contreras, makes a similar point to Zambrano with respect to communication and play, but in the context of collective planning. When asked what the students collectively plan, she replies, "The field trips, cleaning up, breakfasts, classes...and dance."

Video footage shows the students choosing what they want to do first: computing, English, or PE and a student is heard to exclaim, connecting the role participatory choice has on communication, "when we plan we talk to each other without yelling...ok sometimes we yell because some want this and some want that." Carlos articulates the advantages of participatory planning:

> If you don't want to read you can do math and the teachers give us options to do different things each day and not follow the same pattern every day because that's really boring for us kids, if you ask me.

Teacher Luis Díaz contrasts traditional schooling with participatory democracy at Pueblo Neuvo:

> We're talking about a school where the children construct knowledge for themselves according to their needs. The majority of us grew up in schools where beatings, punishments, and recognition were what dominated. Here no, here a child isn't going to compete to be recognized and the child is going to decide what he or she wants to learn.

Myriam Anzola adds,

> It makes the learning more pleasant, much more participative because the children decide what they want to do, how they want to do it, but in the end they learn everything that they would learn in a regular school and, I believe, a little more.

Revolutionary Love

Che Guevara (1965) once wrote, "At the risk of seeming ridiculous, let me say that the true revolutionary is guided by great feelings of love. It is impossible to think of a genuine revolutionary lacking this quality." He also warned against "cold scholasticism, or an isolation from the masses," and argued that "we must strive every day so that this love of living humanity is transformed into actual deeds, into acts that serve as examples, as a moving force."

This form of revolutionary love is clearly abundant in the Alternative School of Community Organisation and Communicational Development, as is apparent throughout the video. For example, when asked by one of the students how he believes the school has helped the children, teacher Joshua Wilson replies,

> I think that we all want to be loved and here...those of us that work here love you all very much and that's very good for us and it's also very good for you and it makes you feel good and it makes you understand how special you all are.

Lilibeth Sánchez, one of the mothers of the students, concurred with this view, when she stated, "They're very affectionate...there's always unity between the teachers and the students...my kids are very happy. Because they don't seem like teachers, they seem like parents," a view supported by one of the students, who said of one of the teachers, "He's like my dad...Because he's given me the things that my dad hasn't been able to give me...Spend time with me like a father."

Teacher Lisbeida talks of the love also emanating from the students, as well as a passion for life:

> They're very restless, they're very curious, they're always looking for something beyond what you tell them or what you show them, they're also very difficult sometimes a little intense, their character is a little harsh and at the same time they're very affectionate and very loving. So I feel like we've changed them a little and they've changed us too.

The reciprocal relationship of respect between the teachers and the students is also recognized by Gerardo who says, "They came here and we started learning and unlearning things with them."

Education in an atmosphere of revolutionary love extends to local health care. As teacher Joshua explains,

> Some of the things that we do in the health clinic to coordinate with the school are things like when we take [the children] to get...vaccines, we do checkups to make sure that everyone is growing normally, when somebody gets sick we treat [them] here in the clinic. We've done things like the campaigns about dengue, the one against smoking things that are educational around health.

Pueblo Nuevo, 2012

In mid-2012, Edward Ellis revisited the school, and talked to its cofounder, Miguel Cortez. Miguel describes how someone from the Ministry of Education described the school as the concretization of the Bolivarian curriculum, so that in one sense the school is not an *alternative* school. However, in another sense, because no one is actually implementing the Bolivarian curriculum to the same extent elsewhere, it *is* an alternative school. He repeated what was discussed in chapter 3 of this volume, namely, the central contradiction between the very progressive ideas in government documents, and the difficulty of translating them into practice in the day-to-day curriculum.

What is happening in School of Community Organisation and Communicational Development serves as an example of the radical change that is needed to create educative practices along the lines of the features of a truly anticapitalist prosocialist pedagogy as outlined by Rikowski (2012). The processes involve a lived critique of capitalist society, both educationally and socially, the forefronting of social justice, and socially productive labor with revolutionary socialism at the core. All this is in direct opposition to schooling to produce obedient workers. Miguel states that when the alternative school was started, the staff decided not to be indifferent to the needs of the students, and soon found out, as we have seen above, that the students wanted to participate, that they needed to be a part of everything happening in the school. He describes how the staff proceeded to give the students more and more responsibility, and how the relationship between them and staff is one of mutual respect. In Venezuela, he argues, there is now a generation who understand what is going on—and who need to be subjects of social transformation. "We are building a community," he stresses, that realizes it has an impact on the barrio.

He gives the example of a money-raising initiative, initiated by the students whereby, they made pizza to sell from scratch. In so doing, he argues, they were acting as true researchers. Everyone got a chance to be involved, to write, to look after the money, and so on. The students provide a model for participatory democracy, and, as Cortez notes, "they are more democratic than us." Everyone has access to the money and the treasurer was at the time of the interview a five-year-old girl. Crucially, the students take their activities to the central location of the street. Indeed, Miguel talks of "taking the streets," which would otherwise be under the control of gangs and narco-traffickers. In a very real sense, the students are helping to foster democratic socialism in the community.

In tandem with the 2013–2019 Socialist Plan, initiated by Chávez (and continuing to be implemented under Maduro), Miguel concludes by stressing the importance of democratizing history, of the centrality of local history to bridge the gaps between generations. All histories are important, he concludes, because they occur in the context of life in the barrio. For the development of participatory democracy and twenty-first century socialism, the barrios need to be organized, and a discourse has to be constructed. The students at the alternative school in Barrio Pueblo Nuevo are actively involved in this construction, thus providing an exemplar for the resolution of the major contradiction between the progressive policies of the government, and schooling as practiced in Venezuelan schools.

Pueblo Nuevo, 2013

Some of the teachers in the School of Community Organisation and Communicational Development are among the first to have graduated in July 2013 under the alternative pedagogy plan based at the UPTM, and the school has become a research center in alternative pedagogy. Tamara Pearson is one of the recent graduates and is still a teacher at the school, as well as a writer for venezuelanalysis.com. The following e-interview took place in September 2013.

> MIKE COLE: Thank you for agreeing to do this interview. First of all, I would like to ask you, given that the school has been in existence for about five years, what do you consider to be its main achievements?

TAMARA PEARSON: I think our work is ongoing and nothing has been finished so to speak, but we have definitely created a space in Pueblo Nuevo where children and adults can come, feel safe, get support, socialize, and organize. Capitalism is violent, and our kids especially have mostly grown up in violent homes, and I've seen most of them change over the years from violent children, even drug selling or violent adults, to confident, happy, affectionate, and creative beings, who know how to organize together without even our help, to solve their problems, to raise money, or put together a cultural event. As I said, things aren't perfect yet, sometimes they argue, or insult each other or us, but they have a huge and alternative kind of family in the school and they are proactive there.

Second, I feel that we've played an important role in putting alternative education on the map—we've started with one small project, but we hope to multiply it. Both the above point and promoting alternative education is part of creating a new human being, one that knows how to relate well to other human beings, who is solidarious, and cooperative. As we teach we learn a lot ourselves. We want to make our school a center of investigation as well, and as we teach and learn and study alternative pedagogy, we can also teach others.

There are other concrete achievements: Wilbur learning to play cuatro; Katy learning to read; the youth group performing in other communities; the kids getting out to Caracas and seeing the beach for the first time in their life; a photo exhibition of photos the kids and one teacher took; the video [discussed earlier in this chapter]; Joelys not attacking the other kids any more; toothpaste making workshops; the mothers, instead of feeling unconfident and intimidated by us and the project, becoming involved in it; introducing the kids to traditional and protest music and them loving it; class meetings where the kids and teachers sit in a circle and discuss a fight that just happened or decide what they want to study together; street health campaigns; a high school program, and so on—but I think the two main ones are helping to create community and to create and promote alternative education.

MIKE COLE: If one were to read many accounts of the Bolivarian Revolution, one might get the impression that barrios are hives of revolutionary activity, yet the children, *at least when they enter* the school, seem, in many ways, from what some of the teachers say, like young economically deprived young people in the capitalist heartlands. I know that Venezuela remains a capitalist country, something recognized by Chávez just before he died. Nevertheless, I would welcome your comments on this?

TAMARA PEARSON: Well it's hard for me to really say, as my experience has been limited to one Bolivarian primary school in my old community, and to the alternative school—but just going by those two experiences, and I guess what other teachers have commented to me, it seems that most of the very young kids are often Chavista—they would call themselves that, or agree with many of the values, and rather it's their parents who are often opposition supporters. In the Bolivarian school (Rivas Davila it's called, in Belen, Mérida), most of the teachers were opposition, including one teacher who I had taught when she was a student in Mision Sucre. That is, they were hostile to the communal council, hostile to the idea of working with community, and hostile to anything "political." When, as the communal council, we were campaigning to get PAE (Programa de Alimentacion escolar; the free breakfast and lunch provided in primary schools), the teachers, and especially the director, were hostile to the idea of meeting with the parents and organizing actions. Nevertheless we did, but only ten parents accompanied us to the Zona Educativa—the state education offices, where we spoke to the person in charge of the PAE for Mérida. In the end we won that small battle, and the school now has breakfast, a snack, and lunch every day, but it was more through community organizing and pressure than through support from the schoolteachers, board, and parents.

The reasons for these dynamics are complicated: it very much depends where you are—rural schools, for example, would be very different. Most teachers have been educated under the traditional system and their teaching methods and their educational philosophy is fairly conservative (i.e., capitalist) and they aren't very open to changing.

Yet its also true, that when many of our kids started with us, they were also pro-opposition. We think they just went with what their parents did, or against what their parents supported (to rebel against them), went with what they saw on television, and so on. Many weren't opposition though, and now, though of course we don't harass them about it, we know most of our kids are Chavista, identifying that with their school, their "poor" status, their community, but also having picked up the ideology from JPSUV (the youth wing of the United Socialist Party of Venezuela) activists organizing in the area, and from discussions we've had in the school. Those discussions have always been initiated by them—we don't believe in imposing our political views or religion in the classroom, but we do openly answer what we as individuals believe, and we promote values that are very clearly socialist or revolutionary or communist.

MIKE COLE: Throughout this chapter, I have documented how the ideals of twenty-first century socialism are incorporated into the way the school is operated—its revolutionary pedagogy, for example, how participatory democracy is promoted at the school; how the teachers are authoritative rather than authoritarian; how play is incorporated in all the activities; and how children choose their learning. I would be interested to know if socialism is part of the content of the curriculum too? I mean, do you actually teach them socialist concepts *per se*? Put another way, the students must hear the word "socialism" all the time, do they know what it means, and do the teachers encourage an understanding of twenty-first century socialism, and how this differs from capitalism and imperialism? In Edward Ellis's interview, Miguel Cortez argues there is now a generation who understands what is going on—and who needs to be subject of social transformation. How does this transformative role manifest itself in the school in the sense of anticapitalist, anti-imperialist, and prosocialist *content*?

TAMARA PEARSON: Ah well I touched on this above. Here in Venezuela, in the press, by politicians, the words socialism and capitalism and empire are mentioned a lot. They are part of everyday speech, yet I'd argue some of the politicians—for example, our Mérida governor—don't know what they mean. Others do, but more important than the words, is their substance. So, in terms of anti-imperialism we teach history from the perspective of the indigenous nations, of the workers, the fighters, of liberation, of African descendance, of Latin American identity, rather than the old history of "Columbus discovered America" and of "Mother Spain." Likewise, as you said, we teach solidarity, cooperation, self-management and production, agroecology, participation, and so on—the substance of socialism. And if the children want to talk about Chávez, or George Bush, or Maduro, we have no problems at all in doing so. But it's about practicing rather than preaching.

Also, many of the children are 5 and 6 years old, and children at that age usually haven't developed mentally enough to be able to understand abstract concepts. They know they love someone, but they can't explain what love is. So we focus on their basic skills, and we also foster socialist type habits right from the start, such as sharing in the preparation of breakfast, no gender division of labor in terms of cleaning, for example, cooperation, caring for others, listening to them and valuing their input, planning classes, organization, active thought and active learning, involvement in the community, and so on.

The school and the community also organize other extracurricular, or nonclassroom activities. For example, we recently organized a "song debate." Two trova singers (a political music movement which originated in Cuba)—comrades, revolutionaries—from Lara State, came to the school on our invitation, and with some organization help from the JPSUV, and they played trova, and discussed the political situation. They talked about socialist values, about corruption within the government, about Jesus as a revolutionary, about the important role of youth in social change—through their songs, and through discussion held between the songs. It was lovely, and many of the school's children came along, many teachers, parents, and some of our older kids who are now teenagers and attending our high school classes or going to high school elsewhere. The high school classes are run in the afternoon, by the same collective—CAYAPA—which runs the primary school classes in the morning. Likewise, sometimes we hold street cinema screenings of movies and documentaries with very radical and pedagogical content—about Venezuela's history, Latin America, Chávez, the environment, women's rights, and so on.

The Community

The concept of "community" is an essential element of the Bolivarian process, and a dialectical relationship with the community in the Alternative School of Community Organisation and Communicational Development has been demonstrated throughout this chapter by the number of times community is referred to by the teachers. In the video, Lisbeida states that everything that is done in the school is an open space where the parents or people in the community can show up and take an interest in something and they can participate, while Luis stresses the importance of "sensitivity towards the problems that they have around them in the barrio."

Without a mutually supportive relationship between school and barrio, education for twenty-first century socialism is meaningless. Joshua underlines the dialectic between school, community, and society:

> What happens in the community is just as important as what happens in the school. And for us make the school better also means make the community better and make the society in which we live better.

Empowerment

Empowerment is, of course, fundamental to revolutionary socialist education. In one scene in the video, the camera hovers on these words on the flip chart: "How can we inculcate empowerment in everything that we do?" This is also taken up by James who states,

> This alternative school focuses on the empowerment of the children and the teachers too. Anytime there is something that the children

can do for themselves without the teachers, we, the teachers, make it a priority to put the job in their hands so that the kids learn not to be managed by others but to manage themselves.

Lisbeida makes a similar point when, as noted earlier, she declares, "They're always looking for something beyond what you tell them or what you show them," while Tamara Pearson argues, when asked why it is important for the children to learn reading, writing, and English,

> We want to create people who think. If we don't think, those who have power can dominate us, but if we can read and we can write, we can read the news to know what's happening, we can write and express ourselves, we can confront the powers that exist and we're not so vulnerable.

Conclusion

In this chapter I have examined in some detail revolutionary processes in one school in the Barrio Pueblo Neuvo in Mérida, and found considerable grounds for optimism that the school can serve as a model for the Bolivarian education system as a whole in the longer term transition to twenty-first century socialism in Venezuela. In chapter 3 of this volume, I argued that "if the misiones are essentially *social democratic* in nature in the sense that they exist in a society that is still a capitalist one, they need to be contextualized in the overall project of twenty-first century socialism, with its promotion of participatory democracy and communal ways of decision-making and living." The same line of argument can be applied to Venezuelan alternative schools. In *themselves* alternative schools in Venezuela seem very similar to schools associated with the "free school movement" in the United Kingdom (e.g., Neill, 1960) and to some of the progressive practices enacted under the Inner London Education Authority (ILEA), which either took place in the school as a whole, or within specific units within a school—I worked in the latter scenario in the early 1970s.[7] However, whereas these UK schools existed under Labour or Conservative governments, committed to various models of capitalism (although there were revolutionary socialists who were members of the Labour Party), alternative schools in Venezuela operate under the auspices of a state, which although it contains a mix of bureaucrats and opportunists, as well as revolutionary socialists, it is a state that is committed to socialist transformation (see chap. 3 of this volume). This is the crucial difference between the two models. Whereas, in the United Kingdom, the schools were under varying degrees of assault by the state (Margaret Thatcher abolished ILEA in 1990), in Venezuela the schools have a chance of being adopted as mainstream models of practice, and of continuing to be part of a revolutionary process.

Alternative schools also have a specific role to play in undermining the corruption endemic within the Bolivarian process (see chap. 3 for a discussion). As Anzola argues, "Corruption is a consequence of the need individuals have to accumulate material goods in the short term, and is also a product of greed." "Traditional education," she goes on, "is competitive and individualistic" and "teaches people to stand out above their peers, and seek personal benefits" (Anzola and Pearson, 2013).

"Cooperative learning," on the other hand, Anzola maintains, can challenge corruption and greed in that it "encourages solidarity, understanding of others, and mutuality in the exchange of knowledge between all the members of the school community." "This breaks," she goes on, "with the selfish model of only achieving personal goals through education, and it deepens the real mission of educating, which is based on the socialisation of human beings for the common good" (Anzola and Pearson, 2013).

With respect to combating corruption in adults, she points to the open studies courses program university at UPTM, of which, as noted earlier, Anzola is coordinator, where adults who were educated through the traditional system have begun to view education in a different light, as they learn to share responsibilities, and to research in order to resolve mutual problems, rather than seeing university as a place to gain grades and benefit only themselves (Anzola and Pearson, 2013).

George Ciccariello-Maher (2013, p. 243) refers to the privileges that the recipients of traditional education, the intermediate layer of the state, holds, the layer that needs confronting. As he puts it,

> The enemy—the utmost expression of state power that becomes the target of revolutionary transformation—is *not* the executive, *not* the president himself, but rather a vast middle sector, a broad swath of the midlevel bureaucracy (as well as local executives on the state and municipal levels) that, by dint of its tendencies toward inertia and the power-sharing privileges it enjoys, has proven the most resistant to change.

While the campaign that Maduro is conducting against corruption (see chap. 3 of this volume for a discussion), Anzola believes, is having some success, what is needed in the long term, she insists is "humanist education...which promotes new values from an early age." She also advocates similar educative processes in the various grassroots organizations, many of which I examined in chapter 3 of this volume.

The open studies program provides students who have a project in mind with renowned academic researchers in their chosen fields who will help them in their work in public or endogenous development centers, organized communities, barrios, or rural areas (UPTM, 2013).

Some of the obstacles to a national system of alternative education, Anzola goes on, are the training of teachers in traditional universities, which "promotes competition and personal success based on a misunderstood meritocracy, the administrative system of primary education which is bureaucratised and sectioned into grades...a pre-established and dogmatised curriculum, and lastly, families which hope to see their children do better than their companions, without worrying what they learn" (Anzola and Pearson, 2013).

Educational change, Anzola concludes, "requires a collective consciousness regarding the importance of learning in a meaningful way in order to: reflect on reality, seek answers, and construct concepts within the logic of solidarity." This collective consciousness is also needed to resolve the objectives of humanity: to save the planet; to create a peaceful culture; to seek solutions to the social problems in the cities and rural areas; for food productivity; and for technological development according to the needs of the times, without attacking the dignity of the peoples (Anzola and Pearson, 2013).

In "Section One" of chapter 3 of this volume, I looked at twenty-first-century socialism in Venezuela more generally, before examining in "Section Two" of that chapter the task of education—the self-education of the people; mass intellectuality in the public sphere; and the formal education system—in the revolutionary process. In this chapter, I have discussed the specific role that alternative education can play, concentrating on the Alternative School of Community Organisation and Communicational Development in Barrio Pueblo Nuevo in western Venezuela.

I argued in chapter 3 that it is primarily *el pueblo* (the oppressed people) who are the revolution's driving force, but that Hugo Chávez was a figure of great historical importance in the Bolivarian process. I concluded that Nicolás Maduro looks set to follow the path set by Chávez. Education, broadly conceived, has been, and will continue to be, a significant factor in the transition to twenty-first century socialism.

Chapter 5

Epistemological Counterhegemonies from Below: Radical Educators in/ and the MST and Solidarity Economy Movements

Sara C. Motta

To fully understand and evaluate the pedagogical and educational possibilities of counterhegemonic struggle in the Brazilian context, it is not enough to limit our analytic lenses to the realms of education policy and the practices of formal and informal elites. Rather we need to reorientate our analysis to focus on the practices, horizons, and subjects of counterhegemonic educational praxis from below. Thus, in this chapter I focus on the struggles, histories, and pedagogical practices of subaltern actors, including popular educators, communities, and social movements with reference to the pedagogies of the Solidarity Economy Movement (SE) and the development of educação do campo (countryside education) as part of the movimento dos trabalhadores rurais sem terra (Landless Rural Workers' Movement, MST) practice of social and political change and transformation.

The pedagogical is taking central stage in the emergence, consolidation, and sustainability of counterhegemonic movements across Latin America (Motta, 2013c). In the Brazilian case heritages of popular education, liberation theology, and indigenous cosmologies have shaped the histories of struggles, relationships of solidarity, and moral economies of subaltern educators, communities, and movements. This has created a cultural terrain of collective practices and moral economies inflected with beliefs and practices in which all are given the right to speak as all (including in some cases the land) are divine and all assumed to be able to play a part in realizing their faith and self-liberation. These culture terrains, beliefs, and practices have been shaped by and shape Brazil's Left history. There are historic, affective, and political connections and relationships with the Workers' Party (PT). Thus, the relationships between movements and educators, and the PT is complex, encompassing what we can term a politics in, against, and beyond the limitations of the PT government's marriage with neoliberalism. It is in the cracks of contradictions of the PT's marriage with neoliberalism that we can find the emergence, development, and consolidation of pedagogies of resistance and transformation.

SE

Many traditional Left intellectuals view the SE as an ameliorative practice and support from the government as policies of co-optation and individualization of the popular classes. As Plinio Sampaio suggested in an interview, "They (SE) are not a political movement. The only popular political movement about which we can have hope is the MST." Yet the SE is not homogenous but rather encompasses various articulations and practices of radical political economy. This suggests the need for a closer look at its pedagogies in movement as a means of identifying both the limitations and the possibilities of their political practice for the emergence and consolidation of popular political subjectivities, social relationships, and ways of life.

The SE emerged as a defense of the working classes against neoliberal processes of accumulation by dispossession in the late 1980s and the early 1990s. Within this were a multiple of actors—investigators, university intellectuals, students, unionists, and religiously inspired activists among others. Each in their own way began to develop methodologies and experiences of cooperative microproduction generally with groups of the urban poor and unemployed (Munarim, 2007, pp. 19–21). By the mid-1990s a number of universities set up Incubadores de Cooperativas Populares (Incubators of Popular Cooperatives). These supported community groups to collectively develop economic activities. From there innumerable networks and organizations developed under the umbrella of the SE.

Numerous institutions have been created and statements have been made by the PT governments to support the SE and place it at the center of local, regional, and urban development (for further details, see Munarim, 2007, pp. 23–25). This includes the creation of the National Secretariat of the Solidarity Economy linked to the Ministry of Work in 2002. However, the realities are that government support is fragile with very low budgets and little commitment to the development of spaces of dialogue and strategic development (Munarim, 2007, pp. 30–41). Additionally, projects and institutional initiatives are dependent upon state bureaucrats and politicians' willingness to provide assistance (Tygel and Souza de Alvear, 2011, p. 4). The contours and confines of the support for the SE from the government have been one of co-optation and limitation of the more radical self-governing and antineoliberal energies of the movement (Neves de Sousa, 2008, pp. 55–57). Thus, there are tensions and struggles between sections identified with the SE and in their relationships with the PT government. Such tensions and struggles occur in relation to two tendencies in the movement that are as Arruda (2010, p. 4) describes "those that remain within the horizon of employment and wages (conservative tendency) and those that look to a deep transformation in the economy and social organisation with values embedded in the solidarity economy (transformatory tendency)."

Yet a transformatory tendency continues to consolidate its articulation and practice of the SE. It is thus through engagement with this "tendencia transformadora" that we can encounter the contours and experiences of pedagogical practices that are forging the unlearning of dominant subjectivities, social relationships, and ways of life and learning of new ones.

For those associated with the transformatory articulation, the SE is about the reproduction of social life in ways that are holistic, sustainable, and humane. Reflexive of this tendency is the critical scholarly practice of Marcus Arruda, one of the coorganizers of Instituto Políticas Alternativas para o Cone Sul (PACS) in Rio de Janeiro. As he (1998, p. 5) describes in relation to the emancipatory visions of SE,

> All social relations can be transformed into loving relationships. These relationships are not limited to acts of sale, occupation, penetration, control but also to giving, receiving and sharing…An economy of reciprocity, of gratitude, of sharing and of affection is not only an economy but a social economy or a human economy.

At the heart of this transformatory practice is a learning to create ourselves, our communities, and our earth in ways that are opposed to the dominant cosmology of colonial patriarchal capitalism. As was discussed in the introduction, subaltern and black feminists conceptualize patriarchal capitalism as built upon alienations and separations embedded within a worldview of individualism and materialism. This produces an instrumental and indifferent relationship to nature, the denial of other worldviews, the devaluing of the emotional and embodied, and its manifestation in relationships of power-over, hierarchy, and competition in the subjective and social realms (Anzaldúa, 2007; hooks, 2000). Such alienated subjectivities and social relationships are also gendered. Emotionality while feminized is also associated with the irrational, the unruly, and the shameful, something to be controlled to avoid disruption to the normal and rational social and physic order (Anzaldúa, 2007, pp. 38–40; Lorde, 2000, pp. 1–4).

Those of the transformatory tendency of SE would agree. For them the construction of a solidarity economy must be based on "a loving economy, and also an economy based on the feminine creator. She cannot accept a divorce from the social, the human, the affective, and the intuitive" (Arruda, 1998, pp. 6–7). It must involve our social relationships, ethics, bodies, minds, and spirits and through this re-create ways of reproducing and producing society. And like the postcolonial and decolonial Latin Americanist critique this must be based on a multiplicity of knowledges, subjects of knowledge production, and ways of producing knowledge (Arruda, 2010; Tiriba, 2004). Such epistemological counterhegemonies dethrone the imperial Western knowing subject from his epistemological privilege. They embrace and nurture "saber populares" enabling the emergence of subaltern political subjects historically denied intellectual and political power (from both elites and many leftist vanguardist articulations of transformation) (Arruda, 1998, p. 8; 2010, p. 2).

The pedagogical is conceptualized as an important way in which to foster, create, and nurture the conditions for a transformation and transgression of colonial patriarchal capitalism. As Bernardo (2006, p. 3, cited in Wirth, Fraga, and Novaes, 2011, pp. 10–11) argues, the transformatory capacity of autogestion lies in its pedagogical dimension in which

> generating micro-factories and society is something that one learns in one way: creating struggles to create these. Only like this workers can begin to emancipate themselves from all types of specialists and bureaucrats...however modest an experience seems, its participants, gradually habituate themselves to running their activities and learn through practice a solidarity and collectivism that opposes the capitalist. In the very experience of learning to create and running ad co-operative are pedagogical kernels that re-create the contours of everyday life and understandings of participants.

At the heart of this is, as in Freire, an ethical commitment to the oppressed and to a practice of reciprocity, openness, and love enacted by all educational agents. Such an ethical commitment is that which connects understanding of conditions of oppression with the desire to transform these conditions. It forges the grounds of recognition between self and other and enables the creation of spaces of trust, opening, and dialogue. As Arruda (2010, p. 3) explains,

> In the ethical plane, what is demanded is that each educational subject, the educator, the educatees, recognises and assume as a subject the ability to create knowledge and transform the world. They must also equally recognise everyone else as a subject and author, establishing a dialogical and collaborative relationship that aims to articulate and synergetically integrate knowledges, as opposed to a dogmatic and narrow closure of self-sufficiency.

Building on this ethical commitment is a political commitment to embrace multiple knowledges and the wisdom of others in a way that collectively constructs a radical classroom but whose process of unlearning dominant practices and subjectivities also transgresses these formal educational limits. This seeks to enact an educational practice that overcomes the dualisms between mind and body, self and other, and education and life that characterize colonial patriarchal capitalism. As Arruda continues (2010, p. 14),

> the demand to share power and knowledge, in a relation that is increasingly participative, which radiates from the class room to the family space up to the cultural and socio-economic frameworks of organising society.

Thus, the emancipatory horizons of the transformatory current of the SE embrace the embodied experiences of the oppressed as the epistemological privileged point of transformatory praxis. They thus conceptualize the subjects and practices of emancipation as multiple, becoming, and radically open to an ever-expanding affirmative power of self with the other and the planet.

As in traditions of popular education, therefore, the functionalist banking understanding of education in which to learn is separated from everyday life and the educator is the knower to deposit his knowledge in the educatee's empty head is critiqued and transgressed. An education of praxis concerns the formation of subjects—both individual and collective—so as to be able to develop and achieve the greatest autonomy in relation to the facilitator and all figures that are represented as hierarchically superior. The educational process is permanent in which all aspects of the lives of educatees, including the desires, body, mind, and spirit are included. As Arruda explains

(1998, p. 14), "The educator doesn't only teach a particular discipline, but at the same time, the art of living. And the educator of praxis knows that the only way of learning how to teach this is in the art of living it."

Such a conceptualization has impacted on the development of curriculum, workshops, and programs of the SE. Such pedagogical practices build a dialogue of knowledges including those of philosophy, theology, activism, and the knowledges of participants. As Lia Tiriba (2004, p. 10) explains, they thus of necessity "transcend the walls of the school" so that it is possible to "reclaim the popular in the economy and education." To do this it is necessary to recognize that it is from within the popular economy that alternative social relations of solidarity and reciprocity can be found. The transformatory current of the SE therefore engages with the complexities and contradictions within the popular. In Gramscian terms, this pedagogical practice engages with, builds upon, and nurtures the good sense fragments, conceptions, and cultural practices of subaltern everyday life and embodied experience.

Thus in workshops testimony and storytelling of participants lives are essential parts of the weaving together of an understanding of the SE, and of creating a cooperative through a critical and transformatory collective practice of construction. PACS supports the development of curriculum, training, and workshops including a program titled "Autodesenvolvimento: Práticas Autogestionárias e Solidárias" (Self-Development: Self-Governing and Autonomous Practices). This promotes spaces of dialogue and learning that foster the creation of socioeconomic initiatives embedded in a practice of integral development. This program, run for communities and individuals wishing to set up a cooperative, has two elements: the first titled "Práticas socioeconômicas de desenvolvimento integral" (Socioeconomic practices of integral development), which has two key axis of work: the strengthening of the organization of networks of the SE and the development of public policies through the organization of civil society.

The second element of the program explores the relationship between women and the economy. This has as its key axis of work the development of the solidarity economy embedded in an orientation that puts gendered exclusions and inequalities at the center of its practice (for further details, see www.pacs.org.br). Ana Margarida Esteves, in her participatory research with communities involved in the solidarity economy, demonstrates the pedagogical richness of this element of the program. She shows how a dialogue of knowledges is fostered between women's experiences of survival and organizing, radical political economy, activist knowledges from other movements involved in similar struggles, and material developed by the solidarity economy though reflection on its own practices.[1] As she describes (2013) in relation to a workshop called women and the economy,

> The topics of discussion...led to the sharing of personal stories of workplace discrimination, sexual harassment and intimate violence, as well as beliefs and assumptions resulting from internalized oppression...the coordinators promoted discussions, supported by audiovisual material, that show the connections between class, gender- and race-based oppression and the structural mechanisms of capitalism. It also connected racial stereotypes and everyday experiences of racism and classism to the legacy of colonialism and slavery in Brazilian society. The promotion of sustainable non-capitalist production units, as well as relationships of mutual support among participants, was presented and discussed as the key strategy of emancipation from such circumstances. A significant part of each workshop session was spent discussing possible options for dealing with specific circumstances of discrimination and violence.

Here, we see the influence of popular education methodology, which begins from experience/practice, moves to critical reflection and discussion, and returns to action. This methodology has enabled a politicization of the private, which is a central element in the creation of integral development. Thus, gendered divisions of labor, caring responsibilities, and violences experienced by women in the space of home and community are politicized. The creation of a politics of care and an ethics of everyday practice underlies therefore the successful creation of cooperatives as ways of life. Such pedagogies have enabled the emergence of the voices and building of the steps of self-liberation of favela women often facing multiple oppressions.

However, there are, of course, tensions and contradictions in the development of the transformatory current of the SE. This articulation develops multiple conceptualizations of power that focus on the separations, alienations, and hierarchies of colonial patriarchal capitalism and includes as political the private, the cosmological, the affective, the embodied, and the epistemological. They therefore develop a complex pedagogical understanding of the elements involved in producing ourselves and our communities differently. However, as Arruda (2010) comments, one of the most difficult and tension ridden elements of this process is an understanding of the importance of developing pedagogical processes dedicated to producing new subjectivities. Often this is some of the most discomforting work as it involves reflection upon the internalized relationships of power-over in ourselves and our relationships. Additionally there is still a focus on the textual and the spoken word as key pedagogies and knowledges of transformation with a neglect of art, ritual, and theater, for example. Thus, the development of multiple knowledges and ways of learning is still in an infant stage. Arguably it is through practices of border-thinking methodologies in which communities in struggle share their knowledges, experiences, and pedagogies as a means of mutual learning and reflection that ideas and suggestions for how to overcome and engage with these tensions and limitations might develop (for further development of this idea, see Motta, 2013c). This involves developing pedagogical connections across spatialities through which to foster the sustainability and flourishing of experiences of transformatory SE.

MST: Counterhegemonic Pedagogies of Insubordination and Emancipation

Brazil's MST is a social movement, born through the actions of families occupying *latifundios* (large-landed estates) in the early 1980s in light of the intensification of dispossession of peasants through processes of commodification of land. Through their organizing, communities push for schools, credit for agricultural production and cooperatives, which are then organized by building on community traditions, histories, and moral economies with an orientation to sustainability and providing for community need (Diniz and Gilbert, 2013). Currently, there are approximately 900 MST legally recognized communities holding 150,000 landless families in Brazil. The MST believes that education of rural communities—in rural communities—involves taking ownership of their history and becoming agents of change able to transform their reality (Caldert, Periera, Alentejano, and Frigotto, 2012). Accordingly, they develop forms of popular education premised upon a dialogue between knowledges, including "traditional" academic knowledge, oral histories, spiritual traditions, affective knowledges, and popular histories and culture.

Processes of informal learning have been key in the (re)construction of sociabilities, political subjectivities, and collectivities, so in the very creation of the MST as a movement that is deeply embedded in place-based communities of struggles and yet connected across multiple spatialities. The pedagogical is here not merely understood as practices and methodologies that enable the creation of collective readings of the world that can shape political strategy and analysis. Rather the pedagogical becomes an essential part in the coming into being of popular political subjectivities and organizations, of creating the openings, possibilities, and relationships to enable communities often silenced and violently invisibilized to appear as embodied political subjects. Here pedagogies of reoccupying and re-creating space as well as affective pedagogical processes that create solidarity, care, and friendship become central.

We can thus fruitfully conceptualize processes of mobilization, occupation of land, and the initial organization of occupations as pedagogical processes. Through these experiences rural communities and families unlearn dominant subjectivities and internalized logics of oppression. Through this are fostered the conditions of possibility for the emergence of a new popular political subject enacting a multidimensional politics of emancipation.

The government represents the families and militants of the MST who live on MST settlements as "beneficiaries" of land-reform policies. However, this hides the role of struggle that proceeds and enables the transformation of occupied land into legally recognized MST settlements. It also hides the ontological shifts in ways of life and practices of self that the occupation enables and is enabled by. Such shifts and transformations can be understood as "reoccupations of self" in which rural communities that have experienced expulsion from the land and reduction of their humanity into a commodity unlearn such dehumanizing conditions of existence. As Sandra Carvalho (2006, p. 66) describes,

> The arrival [of families] to the settlement is represented [by the community] as liberation from this subjectification, as a reintegration of the subjectivity that is desired. In other words, the process of constructing a settlement involves the reconstruction of sociability.

Such reoccupations of the self are enriched by the plurality of knowledges of participants. For example, in the case of the settlement of Santa Barbara,[2] Ceará, 130 families occupied the land in October 1996. As Feitosa (2002) has documented, some came from Paraipaba with experience of cultivating papaya, watermelon, pumpkin, coconut, and irrigated tomato. Others had been mobilized by the MST in the Municipality of Amontada, where they had worked on leased land in grain cultivation. Many came from the Caucaia municipality where they had worked in subsistence agriculture or lived in the shantytowns working in informal labor or were unemployed. As Feitosa (2002, p. 75) explains, "These differentiated experiences enabled a rich exchange of knowledges." Yet this was not an immediate and spontaneous process but rather as he continues, "It was necessary to create ways which could facilitate such a meeting of mutual enrichment."

Many challenges were faced in creating the conditions for a meeting of mutual enrichment, or dialogue of knowledges. As Maria Ocília Barros Monteiro (cited in Carvalho, 2006, p. 63) relates,

> In the beginning it was very difficult, there were nine families in the same house, with a small space for each of no more than a metre. It was difficult…you don't know anyone, you are without family, without water and light in the house.

Navigating these challenges is also a pedagogical process in which individuals and families learn new forms of relating premised on, as Sandra recounts, "dialogue, respect of others and recognition of difference." In this process, rural communities and families learn to live with different experiences and conceptualizations of the world, to negotiate with the state and its institutions, and to collectively organize production and social reproduction. As Neves conceptualizes (1997, p. 21), this produces a "process of unrooting and rerooting as part of the reelaboration and reorganisation of the social conditions of life."

Here individuals with previous experience in social movements and community organizing become pivotal, often taking on the role of a facilitator in initial community organizing. In the case of Santa Barbara settlement, this involved as Sandra Carvalho explains (2006, p. 66),

> [that] they proposed that the structure of the organisation of the settlement should incorporate a coordinating body which would be submitted to a general assembly in which representatives of different committees that organised the activities of the settlement would participate.

In this process of settlement organization, the community learns to administer productive activities and to construct pathways that foster the possibility for new forms of sociability. The successes, challenges, and errors promote reflections, attitudes, and actions that result in continual collective evaluation. In the case of Santa Barbara, the community was able to come to a collective decision about the type of production that most suited its histories, needs, and desires.

Like most of Ceará, they chose a form of mixed production (with both individual and collective land use) (Barreira e De Paula, 1998, p. 209).

But of course, pedagogies of learning sociability and collaborative living are full of contradictions in which there are advances and set backs, conflicts and logics of inclusion and exclusion. As Dezim (cited in Carvalho, 2006, p. 71) explains,

> Participation declined recently. Before there were two full days of collective work, no there is only one, and there are less people participating. Despite there being less people those who do participate do so consciously, and don't stay silent.

The processes of constant evaluation learnt by communities and the values and principles that orientate such collective construction, however, enable analysis and strategic reflection in relation to these problematics. This has resulted in a strong commitment to developing formal processes of learning as a means of visibilizing, reflecting on, and learning to overcome these tensions and contradictions. Thus, for example, there are multiple formal education projects organized in the settlement and it was the first MST community in Ceará to open its own secondary school with teachers trained in MST pedagogies.

Such informal pedagogical processes demonstrate the role of the cultural as a key linkage between the pedagogical and political. This bridging enables the creation of relationships of solidarity, care, and openings in the political horizons of previously excluded and disempowered communities (see Diniz and Gilbert, 2013; Gadelha de Carvalho and Mendes, 2011; Motta, 2011b, for further discussion of these processes).

Such informal learning processes weave together the threads that enable the emergence of new popular political actors, relationships, and institutions. They suggest that affective pedagogical processes, and reoccupations and re-creations of space and other temporalities, which overcome the dualism between the public and private and between friendship and politics, foster the conditions of possibility for the emergence of new forms of political subjectivities and social relationships. Or as Ceceña argues (2012, p. 212), "It is these spaces of everyday encounter that [are] of particular importance for us because it is in this space of conflict and intersubjective interaction...that subjects come together to say 'Enough is enough' ('ya basta'). This space is changed, a place of transgression and profanation. It is also a space for the playful creation of new subjectivities and relationships."

However, the pedagogical also comes to the heart of the MST's political practice of democratizing development in Brazil and beyond in the construction of MST communities who have been granted the right to remain on occupied lands.

The MST and Countryside Education

> They defend (those that fight for educação do campo)...a different education; an education of the subject people of the countryside; an education associated with emotions, symbols, ways of life, struggle, resistance, dreams, an education associated with an impossible dignified life within the contours of a capitalist society. (Pingas, 2007, p. 41, cited in De Almeida, Pingas, Pinto, and Knijnik, 2008, p. 103)

The understanding of agrarian reform developed over three decades by the MST, involves much more than a legal redistribution of land and legalization of occupations of unused privately owned land. The MST seeks the democratization of Brazilian society at the political, economic, and cultural levels through the self-organization of the popular classes. As Conte (2006, p. 43) describes,

> We propose is something that doesn't exist, and because of this it is a utopia and thus we must work to create this at the micro-level. We propose a reappropriation of power, of the power that has been stolen from us. They don't only steal our homes, our land, they also steal our power. They steal our power from us when they convince us that we don't have power.

This means that the organization of MST communities is multidimensional, involving the development of agricultural production, which has community need and sustainability at their heart, the self-organization of communities to ensure their social reproduction, and the development and honoring of cultural and spiritual traditions. At the heart of ensuring the emergence and consolidation of these processes and practices are autonomous forms of education based around concepts such as pedagogia da terra (pedagogy of the land) and educação do campo. Like Gramsci's conceptualization of hegemony and counterhegemony, the MST view these practices as deeply embedded in the everyday realities and experiences of subaltern communities. They are forms of producing dominated subjectivities or liberated subjectivities that in both cases are deeply pedagogical. As the MST describe,

> Through our work we produce knowledges, we develop capabilities and forms of consciousness. In itself work has a pedagogical potential, and the school can develop this potentiality, as it supports people to become aware of its connections with other dimensions of human life; its culture, values, political positions. Because of this our schools need to be connected with the world of work and with work. (Caderno do MST, 1999, pp. 8–9)

Such multidimensional emancipatory processes and subjectivities develop due to the organization of communities, their relationship with NGOs, critical educators and favorable government representatives, and institutional conjunctures. Thus, there has been a contradictory terrain opened up by the fragmentation and diversity inside of the PT government and the histories of struggle and levels of organization in different regions and municipalities. To gain a deeper understanding of these contradictions and conflictual processes it is important to focus in concrete places and pedagogical experiences. Taking education as a specific focus, we find numerous instances where the interface between movements, universities, and government has enabled the creation of educational projects that foster the emergence and consolidation of popular political subjectivities and processes of transformation that are multidimensional including the linguistic, conceptual, cultural, and affective.

The education of adults and young people is an important element in the emancipatory project of the MST. Through their continuous political struggle and mobilization, the MST has achieved the recognition of this strategy of transformatory education at the state level. First, during the Cardoso presidency, in relation to increasing national and international pressure in the aftermath of the 1998 massacres of MST families by state security forces, PRONERA (Programa Nacional de Educação na Reforma Agrária) was created. This aims to "strengthen education for agrarian reform in the MST communities, utilising methodologies that are specific to the countryside that will contribute to sustainable rural development in Brazil" (Pontes Furtado, 2003, p. 200). However, during the Cardoso administration this commitment was more formal than real. Institutional support and funding for the development of projects coconstructed between universities and the MST only developed in the first Lula government as a new secretariat in the ministry of education was created.

This legalized the granting of funds to four areas of educational work in formal primary and secondary school education and to teacher training in the Programa Residencia Agraia, which is a program for graduates to stay in MST communities and specialize in an area that interfaces with the development projects of these communities and their educational processes. Thus, despite continuity in the political economy of the PT governments, social policy, particularly education, is a site of some of the most interesting and productive contradictions. These contradictions are themselves a result of the continued struggle and organization of movements, such as the MST, without which policies would remain ameliorative and compatible with the broader neoliberal turn of the party as government and institution.

The educational philosophy and theory upon which PRONERA projects are embedded is educação do campo based in a methodology called pedagogia da terra, developed by the MST. Educação do campo is based on a critique of traditional rural education in which rural communities are presented as ignorant, underdeveloped, and conservative and in which curriculum are developed in abstract with no relationship to their everyday needs, struggles, and concerns. As Josê de Souza et al. describe (2008, p. 47),

> The rural school, overtime, was based on an idea of the social backwardness and precarity of those of the countryside. Education for this population was never in the national debate and much less in public policy. The historical representation of those in the countryside was that "to work with the land letter are not really necessary." According to Arroyo the rural school is considered "a choice where the teachers hardly knows how to teach and in some cases doesn't know how to read."

Here like the SE, there is a critique of the imperial knowing subject of colonial capitalism and an embrace of the placed knowledges of communities in struggle. Thus, for the MST educação do campo is a means of developing a rural education *in* and *for* the rural population. It is therefore connected to the everyday realities of communities and valorizes their knowledges and contributions to Brazilian society and history. Through the politicization and systematization of their good sense cultural, spiritual, and experiential ways of knowing it aims to foster the development of the capacities and potentials of individuals and communities so that they can produce themselves and their communities differently. This pedagogical practice is embedded in a self-liberatory practice that links education with life, politicizes pedagogy, and is embedded in an ethics of care and commitment to the oppressed (for detailed analysis of educação do campo, see among others, Gonçalves-Fernandes et al., 2008, p. 47).

Educação do campo is thus a manifestation of an emancipatory educational project that cannot be realized within the confines of capitalist agriculture and schooling (Caldart, 2000, p. 19). It escapes those confines and contours and instead necessitates the development of "other" schools and "other" teachers that work against and beyond the traditional and now neoliberalized schooling system. Thus, the MST has developed their own schooling network and teacher training programs autonomous from the dominant formal education system. Educação do campo is therefore a central site of struggle over societal projects and the possibilities of self-organized and deeply democratic socialist political and social transformation.

More specifically, if we look to the case of Ceará, for example, the growth of MST settlements, the consolidation of groups of popular educators, and the granting of funds for education projects by the government has enabled the development of multiple extension projects in adult and youth education, teacher training, and the building and equipping of primary and secondary schools in MST communities. However, such conjunctures did not ensure the realization of accepted projects; rather, continued struggle enabled their realization. In 2008, for example, funding for a number of PRONERA projects were suspended due to investigation into alleged corruption in the administration of one project in Mato Grosso. From this period, due to legislative intervention by forces opposed to these forms of popular, critical education, payment of teachers coordinating and teaching on the projects was also suspended. This was justified by the fact that there wasn't a law that allowed public teachers to be employed in external projects of an educational nature (formally called extension projects).

Thus, the MST, project coordinators, critical educators, and supportive deputies (federal and national)—particularly from PSOL (Partido Socialismo e Liberdade [Socialism and Freedom Party])—mobilized to pressurize the government into developing such a law. After numerous mobilizations and a number of public audiences in 2010, a law allowing new PRONERA projects was passed and payment for public educators allowed. However, two years of suspension of new projects and of funding and payment resulted in the noncompletion of many projects that had begun in the 2008–2009 period. Thus, the process of ensuring the continuation of these radical education projects is premised upon the politicization of pedagogy through political struggle to ensure that they are maintained and funded and that adequate infrastructure such as schools, courses, libraries, and materials are provided and developed (de Souza, Ferreira de Andrade, Mendes de Lima, and Bezerra Machado, 2008, pp. 52–54; Carvalho, 2003, pp. 220–221).

The critical educator thus creates solidarities and alliances with social movements and actors on the margins of formal institutional and state power to defend their labor from precaritization and defend their role as organic intellectuals committed to a pedagogical-political practice of social emancipation. Through these processes and experiences of struggle, educators learn immanently to produce themselves differently. They become critical intellectuals committed to processes of coproduction of knowledes, curriculum, and pedagogies for social change. They also become committed to, and practiced in, fostering mass intellectuality, which disrupts their epistemic privilege by breaking down the epistemological hierarchies of capitalist coloniality in which the knower enacts power-over those that are known.

It is important to look in more depth at the nature of the education projects developed as this gives us an idea of their importance in the creation of the conditions for the democratization of Brazilian society and a holistic agrarian reform organized by and for the popular classes. It also enables a deeper understanding of their limitations, particularly in respect to the contradictions fostered by the PT governments.

Two projects in Ceará, one of primary-level adult education and the other a teacher-training course to train individuals educated themselves through educação do campo on how to become movement educators, were developed through collaborative and democratizing methodologies of curriculum design (for details of these projects see PRONERA, 2007, 2007b, and 2008). This involved a participatory process of curriculum development, which included movement representatives and educators dialoguing with a group of popular educators and coordinators from the State University of Ceará. The projects were developed with a number of guiding principles underpinned by the social and ethical commitments to an emancipatory education. These included valorization of a multiplicity of knowledges, including those of rural communities; the development of methods that enable a dialogue of these knowledges, responsibility, and commitment to life, social, and human ethics; the recovering of the cultures and identities of social movements in the countryside; and collective construction of knowledge for transformation of situations of oppression (de Souza et al., 2008, p. 49). As Sandra Gadelha, one of the coordinators of the teacher-training course, explained to me in April 2010, the group of educators and MST representatives met for days to discuss the basic contours of the curriculum. This included the conceptual underpinnings that would orientate different segments of the course.

The projects demonstrate a commitment to building of emancipatory pedagogical practices in the everyday realities of communities that build upon their goodsense elements of consciousness, understanding, culture, and history. There is therefore a valorization of the wisdom of peasant communities that directly contests the politics of knowledge of colonial capitalism in which landless peasant are presented as conservative, ignorant, traditional, and uneducated. There is an active commitment to the production of mass intellectuality and organic intellectuality from and for the popular classes. Thus, there is a counterpolitics of knowledge that seeks to decolonize the practices and relationships of rural communities in struggle (Pontes Furtado, 2003).

An example of this can be found in the segment of the curriculum organized around the sociology of education. Here the elements of this part of the training concerned the empirical and theoretical aspects of the sociology of education; the relationship between education and society; the role of education in social development and transformation; a sociological analysis of schooling; the relationship between education and the state; the social relationships between the countryside and the city; the social and political organization of MST communities; and the role of education in agrarian reform. The contents of the course combined classical texts in critical sociology of education, Brazilian subaltern thinkers' conceptualization of the sociology of education, MST texts and reflections, and the participants' experiences in relation to the themes discussed.[3] The methodology of the course combined theory and practice.

In table 5.1 one can see the multiple knowledges that are involved and the attempt to create a dialogical learning space in which there is commitment to listening to the other and embracing multiple knowledges, including self/collective knowledges of participants. Affective pedagogies embedded in imagination and solidarity brings dignity to the lives and histories of struggles of participants and the communities to which they belong, develops their organizational capacities, and deepens their political commitments and connections between different MST communities and other communities in struggle. Such processes involve the resignification of subjects and the development of educators trained in the distinct pedagogical commitments of pedagogia da terra and educação do campo.

Table 5.1 Outline of activities in sociology of education for trainee educators in Educação do Campo[a]

First day

First moment: Morning

1. Initial contact with students, preliminary considerations in relation to the discipline of study, dynamics of the group, knowledge levels of the group
2. Study of the poem—A Ávore
3. Relate the poem to your life as teacher
4. In groups—identify common themes and points in the lives of the group of teachers (feedback)

Second moment: Afternoon

5. Interview people asking them what they understand by the concepts "land" and "work"
6. Share your experience of working as a teacher
7. Study of the text: Practices of training and teacher narratives
8. Identify common themes in the work of teachers (collective activity)

Second day

First moment: Morning

Text: A carta do Ciço (Ciço's Letter)

1. Discussion of the quote "We are not people if we cannot work"
2. Sharing of personal and professional life (looking at the narratives prewritten by some students)
3. Development of collective histories and stories (in groups and identifying common themes)

Second moment: Afternoon

4. Reading and discussion of the text "Teaching in MST Settlements: Teaching in the Context of the Struggle for Land"
5. Organize a schedule of investigation (research about the work of teachers in MST settlements)

Third moment: Evening

6. Development of personal projects of students "Memory of Educational Practices and Training"

Third day

First moment: Morning

1. Prepare a synthesis of the thematics and reflections of the two days (using theater, music, poems, satire, humor, etc.)
2. Presentation of synthesis and final reflections

Note: [a]Details of this project were obtained via personal email communications with Ernandi Mendes and Sandra Gadelha, April 2010.

The courses themselves create another temporality for educatees (who are also militants in the MST) from that of the constant demands of political organizing, social reproduction, and collective production. This helps foster spaces of reflection and processes of systematization in relation to everyday life and its relationships with broader social, economic, and political processes. The course also creates multiple learning spaces, as in the SE, which stretches the narrow definition of schooling beyond its association with classrooms separate from everyday life, reconnecting learning with practice and experiences. As Fonseca et al. (2008, p. 64) describe,

> The school that we seek organises educational processes through their reconciliation with everyday life. Thus, it is necessary to find other spaces, outside of the class room. As spaces of construction, reflection and learning...Social movements create other spaces, outside of the school, as spaces of potential learning; struggles, marches, occupations, experiences of cooperative production in the countryside and the city which foster relationships of solidarity.

Multiple pedagogies are developed that engage not only with the conceptual but with the spiritual, symbolic, and the embodied realities of communities' struggles and histories. Thus, there is a use of poetry, art, and theater, including the recovery of histories of struggles and dignity of communities. This involves practices such as mística, which is an artistic/cultural practice that opens and closes MST events, including workshops, meetings, occupations, and marches. As Lucíola Maia (2005, p. 165) describes, "Mística is an educational process which creates education with and as art, resistance and popular culture." Mística can take the form of poetry, a re-action of popular struggle and history, dance, song, and often ends with all participants touching each other by holding hands or through a collective embrace (for more details, see MST, 2001). Mística involves pedagogies of the body in which new intimacies and levels of trust are developed between participants in their embodied enactment of their histories of struggle and embrace of each other.

For the popular educators involved in the design, development, and implementation of the projects, this has involved a radicalization of university praxis through its embedding in the logics of subaltern struggle. Such practice has also involved a process of the politicization of education and the role of the educator. Educators have had to organize collectively to defend these institutional spaces of possibility and their relationships with the MST and other movements. This has been particularly fraught in a time of the increasing marketization of higher education (HE) and the development of external ranking and evaluation systems. Thus, for educators this work has often had to occur on top of their normal working day; the conditions of which have deteriorated in terms of hours of teaching, publication demands, and wages. University management has also tried to block the validation and implementation of projects. Here the educators have also had to mobilize and importantly with the support and solidarity of the MST have been involved in occupations of the rector's offices, for example, in the State University of Ceará.

These popular educators have become the border thinkers[4] who bridge the university and the movement creating practices that challenge the neoliberal contours of the former and help to foster the socialist contours of the latter. In their forging of spaces of possibility within the university environment, they are contesting the logics of competition, ranking, and deintellectualization of neoliberal education. These practices, however, demand extraordinary levels of commitment and energy, can result in burnout and exhaustion, and are often not met with accolades and rewards at the university level.

This places critical educators in a very vulnerable and risky situation with no certainty of success. They can result in moments of crisis and confrontation that are not of necessity destructive but which take collective praxis and education of fear so as to transform such experiences into collective pedagogies of courage. As Shor and Freire (1987, p. 57) describe, "the more you recognise your fear as a consequence of your attempt to practice your dream, the more you learn how to put into practice your dream." Pedagogies and critical educational praxis such as this are therefore risky and take courage to accept being, and desire to be always "other" in the dominant space of hegemonic educational practices and rationalities.

Thus, working collaboratively as critical educators is a transgressive act of becoming other, of liberating the educator-self from the confines of the individualized and commodified university worker. Helping to forge spaces of possibility with movements can be an inspiring experience that forges relationships that transcend the boundaries of the classroom and the university. It is a liberatory, surprising and inspirational experience and yet often unsettling and emotionally demanding. It involves, as Lillia Bartolome (1994, p. 184) argues, the development of "an anti-methods pedagogy which rejects the mechanization of intellectualism...[and] challenges teachers to work towards reappropriation of endangered dignity and toward reclaiming our humanity." The antimethods pedagogy adheres to the eloquence of Antonio Machado's poem "Caminante, no hay camino, se hace camino al andar" ("Traveler, there are no roads. The road is created as we walk it [together]") (Macedo, 1994, p. 8). Pedagogies of possibility such as these are conceptualized by many critical educators that I spoke with as acts of revolutionary love and commitment. As

Freire (2006, p. 29) argues, "As individuals or as peoples, by fighting for the restoration of [our] humanity [we] will be attempting the restoration of true generosity. And this fight, because of the purpose given it, will actually constitute an act of love."

As in the SE there are internal tensions within the movement and as regards the PT governments in relation to the development of this emancipatory pedagogical practice. As in other PRONERA programs the tensions with government agencies were often acute with delays in payments to facilitators that resulted in them being unable to continue with the project. This undermined the consolidation of the relationships necessary to form bonds of trust and openings to mutual transformation and ensure the completion of some of the programs. As Escobar de Almeida describes (Escobar de Almeida et al., 2008, p. 162),

> Educação do e no campo has confronted many difficulties in concretising its objectives in the relation between school, community and movements; particularly educator training, infrastructure, school transport, educational materials. The principal cause that permeates all of these difficulties is the State's omission.

Thus the PT's' overall deepening of the epistemological logics of neoliberal capitalist coloniality enable a contextualization of both the limits and possibilities of working in relation to "popular" governments of the Pink Tide. Particularly, those like the PT who have become caught up in ensuring the logics of governmentality as opposed to building the social autonomy and political power of the subaltern.

As in many cases of activist educators, many continue despite the lack of payment and recognition of their work. They thus dedicated time and energy to these projects on top of their formal paid work resulting in levels of exhaustion and burnout common to many activists. Recognition of these conditions of labor is a first step in the politicization of these faultlines and tensions. Additionally, the practicing of methodologies similar to those practiced with the MST that build solidarity, friendship, care, and the conditions of active listening could help develop solutions through the politicization of the "private" and the fostering of a politics of care between educators and educatees.

Internally, there are still many within the MST leadership that do not view radical education and pedagogical practice as central to their emancipatory project. Thus, there is uneven commitment to the training of MST educators that results in uneven patterns of mobilization and militant and community commitment. As Borges de Souza, Conceição Ferreira, and Gritti comment,

> Even though there is interest and concern in the Movement for the training of educators of adult education, there isn't consensus on the importance of this amongst the leadership. This impacts on the pedagogical process and also on the internal Movements politics in relation to educators. It can produce disinterest and demotivation in the student's commitment. (2008, pp. 119–120)

This ambiguous commitment to emancipatory education is compounded by the broader context of the government's ambiguous commitments to PRONERA, its continuing marriage to agribusiness, slowness in legalization of settlements, and resultant lack of redistribution of land. As Borges de Souza el al. continue (2008, p. 122),

> Slowness in processes of disappropriation and the lack of land conquest for community production also help to explain the wavering commitment of educators and educatees. This wavering is particularly acute in those that do not realise that these conquests are often not realised immediately; that this is a slow process...Such understandings make it difficult to advance a process of critical reflection embedded in praxis.

Thus, much of the political energies of the movement are taken up in these more obvious struggles and conflicts with transnational capital and local government. And unlike the pedagogical conceptualizations and practices of the SE, the private and gendered relationships of power have taken a secondary role in the development of educação do campo (see Conte, 2011, for a broader analysis of women and gender in Brazilian rural movements, including the MST). Thus, gendered divisions of labor within settlements with women taking on less leadership roles, identified with the domestic sphere and men with the public and work sphere are often reproduced. Often the more pernicious gendered oppressions and exclusions characteristic of the patriarchal colonial logics of capitalism in Brazil also remain unproblematized and depoliticized in pedagogy and practice.

As I have demonstrated the emergence, development, and consolidation of the emancipatory pedagogical project of the MST, educação do campo, can be viewed from both above and below. From above we can see how these programs are scattered and conditional and are not an attempt by the government to instate and institutionalize universal popular educational projects. They can be absorbed within the broader political economy of disarticulation of the developmentalist state and consolidation of neoliberal disciplinary state. This results in an uneven terrain of political-pedagogical development in which the pedagogies, practices, and projects remain fragmented in time and space. In many ways this mirrors the historic fragmentation of Brazilian popular classes. Yet a closer look from below at these practices suggests that those rural forces often excluded from the broader political economy are articulating their agency in the formation of an autonomous emancipatory education linked to the development of solidaristic and socialist ways of life and social reproduction. However, gendered divisions of labor and the private have remained a noted absence in this pedagogical work resulting in the reproduction of gendered power relationships within the movement. Nevertheless, spaces and practices have been consolidated in which autonomous relationships, visions, and practices, institutional processes of transformation and building the power of the rural popular classes have been developed. The MST with radical educators has appropriated the social policies associated with educação do campo, which has become a site of constant struggle. Struggles over curriculum, resources, and the provision of movement educational spaces and schools are struggles over societal projects. When the movement and its allies, the outsiders-within, manage to implement and consolidate this alternative politics of knowledge they foster the creation of popular political subjectivities able to resist and transform the epistemological hegemony of neoliberalism in Brazil through producing revolutionary subjects, social relationships, and ways of life.

Conclusion

Shifting conceptual and analytic focus to the emergence, development, and consolidation of counterhegemonic pedagogies from below disrupts the potentially pessimistic reading of the possibilities of counterhegemonic struggle in Brazil due the PT's absorption into the neoliberal historic bloc and its monological, disciplining, and depoliticizing epistemological politics. It demonstrates forcefully how contradictions in this project can be politicized and possibilities appropriated by subaltern agents in struggle. Counterhegemonic epistemological politics have built on the microprocesses of construction of the transformative current in the SE movement, the committment to a pedagogical-political project in the MST and the everyday construction of critical educators and educational practices in formal educational spaces. It is thus politically and pedagogically important to remember that these deeply democratic and innovative pedagogical-political practices outstretch the election to power of the PT and will continue after they leave national power.

These pedagogical-political practices and projects open the horizons of counterhegemonic epistemological possibility. They involve commitment to pedagogizing politics and politicizing the pedagogical through the creation of counterhegemonic educator subjectivities. As part of this, educators reclaim their intellectual and political capacities, are ethically committed to developing a liberatory pedagogy that is embedded in the concrete needs and knowledges of oppressed communities, and view their practice as an act of love for self and other.

For the university educators involved in such a reimagining, their commitments and struggles are risky and in the conditions of neoliberalized labor prove emotionally and physically draining. They thus take courage and daring and involve in practice the production of other-educator subjectivities to those of the commodified and disciplined neoliberal teacher. Such educators become border thinkers who transgress these logics through a practice that connects university with community and makes an epistemological commitment to privilege the margins as sites of the richest emancipatory potential.

Such pedagogical-political practices also involve commitment to the forging of "other" schools and educational spaces. These of necessity transgress the institutionalized conceptualization of the school as separate from life and instead embed educational practice in multiple spaces—the community, the occupation, the cooperative, the home, and the self. Curricula are coconstructed on the basis of multiple knowledges and embedded in the experiences and struggles of subaltern communities. The spaces created in, against, and beyond the classroom are dialogical and rupture the monological and authoritarian logics of commodified education. They shift relationships of competition, hierarchy, and instrumentalization into those of solidarity, care, and commitment. They thus open spaces for the production of our worlds, selves, and communities through practices that move us beyond the cosmology of capitalist coloniality and yet do not seek to reenclose these practices into an alternative monological practice of life.

As Stoler (cited in Agathangelou and Ling, 2004, p. 41) suggests to transform colonial (patriarchal) capitalism through a decolonizing practice requires recalling "other kinds of memories...and stories to tell." The pedagogies developed by the SE and MST in differing ways and with different intensities are decolonizing, in that they embrace multiple forms of knowledge and work through the affective, spiritual, embodied, cultural, oral, historical, and cognitive. These pedagogical practices enact the collective construction of multiple readings of the world in which oppressed communities speak in multiple tongues, rethinking and creating what it means to speak, to write, and to theorize. As Anzaldúa (2007, p. 81) describes in relation to her experience—and eminently applicable here—"I will no longer be made to feel ashamed of existing; I will have my voice... I will have my serpent's tongue—my woman's voice." These practices enact a decentering and unlearning of dominant literacies and embrace of different and multiple epistemological grounds of transgressing patriarchal capitalist coloniality and becoming other in multiple postcapitalist ways. In this transgression they reimagine and re-create the political, and the meaning and practice of twenty-first-century socialism.

Chapter 6

Decolonization in Praxis: Critical Educators, Student Movements, and Feminist Pedagogies in Colombia

Sara C. Motta

Colombia has a rich and often-overlooked tradition of decolonizing pedagogical practices. Crucially, this tradition transgresses the monologue of capitalist coloniality and the occupation of the embodied subject and social relationships by the logics of colonial patriarchal capitalism. Such practices, heritages, and philosophies of life have developed from the epistemological margins and from the lived experiences of those people experiencing the violences of the epistemological logics of militarized capitalist coloniality in Colombia, which seeks to silence all other knowledges, pedagogies, and subjectivities.

This chapter is divided into two sections. The first section explores the role of educators and students in formal education that are reimagining alternative educational logics, practices, and forms of democracy. The second section explores two social movements that form part of Pazíficas Women's Collective, a network that emerged in 2000 in Cali, Colombia, with the aim of developing nonviolent, feminist proposals and practices within Colombian society, in order to denounce and make visible the violences experienced by women: La Máscara feminist theater of the oppressed collective and La Escuela Política de Mujeres Pazíficas (Political School of Pacifist Women). Through this exploration I seek to visibilize and conceptualize the cornucopia of pedagogical and epistemological practices that reweave communities, subjects, and Colombia society in ways that transgress colonial patriarchal capitalism. This offers a rich well from which to draw insights and possibilities for a re-creation of ourselves, relationships, and societies in multiple postcapitalist ways.

Reinventing Democracy through Struggles over Education

Educators: *Otras Escuelas y Otros Maestros* (Other Schools and Other Teachers)

Educators are key actors not only in the hegemonic construction of patriarchal capitalist coloniality in Colombia (as shown in chap. 1) but also in the development of pedagogical and epistemological counterhegemonic alternatives. They are workers defending their well-being and rights, and public education through union organizing. Moreover, these educators are cocreators of educational alternatives through their critical praxis.

The heritages that have impacted upon the development of popular and critical education in Colombia are steeped in liberation theology, popular education (conceptualized in the Colombian context from the 1940s as Acción Cultural Popular [Popular Cultural Action]), and a critical positioning against all forms of authoritarianism. This is particularly acute in the experience of radical educators in the militarized Colombian context (Moreno and Jardilino, 2007, pp. 409–415). This has led to political traditions, which have actively distanced themselves theoretically and philosophically from the state and the dominant education system, thereby fostering alternative experiences that work in, against, and beyond the formal system of education at the level of primary and secondary schooling, higher education (HE), and in adult education (AE) (Cendales and Muñoz, 2013, pp. 33–37).

An institutional and political expression of the power of critical education in the growth of a radical teacher's movement and practice is the Movimento Pedagogico en Colombia (Colombian Pedagogical Movement [CPM]), formed in 1982 for teachers through the Federacion Colombiana de Educadores (Colombian Teachers Federation) and uniting over 200,000 teachers in public institutions of education. The conjuncture that facilitated the emergence of this movement combined the growth of social movements and the beginnings of the imposition of a "modernized" education system. The CPM actively critiqued such a restructuring of education which for them

> disarticulates conceptually pedagogy, reducing it to a simple method of design and programming that all teachers should implement...the teacher becomes unrecognised as a cultural worker and removed from his political role whilst the child is reduced to a subject to be moulded to the dictates of "development." (Cited in Tamayo Valencia, 2006, p. 102)

Instead, the CPM had an alternative vision of the educator as worker in which the union should not be reduced to a mere defense of particular rights. Rather the union should foster the development of a political-pedagogical project with "a national and democratic content at the service of the liberation of the country and social revolution" and create a political and theoretical dialogue between Left unionism and intellectuals and researchers of pedagogy (Tamayo Valencia, 2006, p. 102). At the heart of their praxis was an alternative understanding of the role of the educator and of the school, linked concretely to cultural and political work to create the conditions for the liberation and democratization of Colombia.

Here the teacher's role was conceptualized as fostering critical thinking and practice that built from the concrete experiences and needs of the communities in which a school was based. Teaching was not separated from research but rather, integrated through the creation of a dialogue of knowledges facilitated by educators between students, families, researchers, and other actors so that education could be meaningful for oppressed communities. As the CPM stated in their document *Fundamentos y Propositos del Movimento Pedagogico* (1984), "Educators, can become part of cultural forces that are relatively independent from the power of capital and the state...there is much that can and should be done in the field of political cultural work" (cited in Tamayo Valencia, 2006, pp. 102–103).

Culture was the linkage between pedagogy and politics that was based on an understanding of subaltern consciousness similar to that suggested by a Gramscian analysis. Here everyday subjectivities and experiences are conceptualized as contradictory, weaving together elements of common and good sense. The fragments of good sense are the pedagogical basis from which the conditions for collective and critical reflection on practice can emerge. At the heart of this was an expanded conceptualization of knowledge to include oral history, music, art, language, literature, and dance. Pedagogy in this context is understood not as an exterior, transcendent, and singular method but rather, as knowledge in construction—necessarily multiple, deeply embedded in the experiences of concrete communities in struggle and therefore immanent to practice (Boom, 2010, p. 4).

Importantly this political-pedagogical project treated educators as intellectuals recognizing their knowledge and wisdom. This acted to recuperate their political and professional identity and to support their conquest of the right to be subjects of educational policy and key agents in educational reforms. As Boom (2010) explains, educators were revitalized, facilitating the emergence and development of teachers' dignity and voice. CPM supported the creation of pedagogical practices through which to foster autonomous and critical understandings of education, pedagogy, and schooling. This enabled teachers to become a central actor in educational politics and transformation and develop their own understandings of education, learning, and the role of schools. Here the critical educator was conceptualized as an organic intellectual of the subaltern, able to foster the conditions for mass intellectuality. Importantly the movement respected the right to difference and plurality in the practice of this pedagogical-political project. This shaped a cultural, political, and epistemological heritage and ethics around principles and practices of multiplicity and dialogue out of which counterhegemonic educational struggles of the twenty-first century would emerge.

The CPM fostered national and local meetings, and supported local and regional research projects dedicated to the development of political-pedagogical project of liberation. One example was the research collective *Historia de la Practica Pedagogica en Colombia* (History of Pedagogical Practices in Colombia), coordinated by Dr. Olga Lucia Zuluaga in the University of Antioquia. This involved researchers from the National University in Bogota and Universidad del Valle in Cali, the creation of numerous publications including the journal *Education and Culture*, and the creation of Centros de Estudios e Investigaciones Docentes (Centers of Teacher Learning and Investigation [CEID]). These institutional, intellectual, and collective spaces of political-pedagogical possibility fostered processes of collective reflection by educators and other community actors in relation to the identity and cultural role of the educator, as well as their relationships with the community and context in which they found themselves. They also developed the conditions of possibility for the elaboration of a political platform of and by educators, overcoming isolation and fragmentation, which has supported the consolidation of one of the most powerful teaching unions in the continent (Dorado Cardona, 2008).

The CPM was at its strongest during the 1980s and the early 1990s. However, there were splits and co-optation of sections of the movement as a result of their participation in the development of the 1991 constitution and in particular the Ley General de Educación (General Law of Education). Despite the resultant decline of the formal and visible presence and power of the movement, it planted important pedagogical, epistemological, political, and ethical seeds that enabled the continued development of multiple micropolitical-pedagogical projects across Colombia throughout the 1990s and 2000s. As Tamayo Valencia argues (2006, pp. 111–112),

> The pedagogical movement has continued to flourish in the actions and reflections of many educators who constitute, despite Fecode, multiple networks of pedagogical innovation and reflection...what we have lived in this period then, is the exhaustion of a particular process and form of the pedagogical movement that was centralised in a union organisation, and the opening to multiple pedagogical movements that develop multiple ways of developing the political-pedagogical for our reality.

An important example of the seeds that were planted by the pedagogical movement are the development of Redes Pedagogicas (Pedagogical Networks) in which critical teachers meet to share experiences of teaching, curriculum, school projects, adult education, and projects that span the university, NGOs, and school educators. As Bohorquez (2013, p. 1) explains, these networks

> are orientated to the reconstruction of a broken social fabric, to create links to solidarity that enable the overcoming of fear to communicate with others in trust...the pedagogical networks strengthen exchange between pedagogical knowledges, experiences and projects between equals.

Through these, pedagogical knowledges and experiences have been mapped, analyzed, and systematized, realizing a key principle of the pedagogical movement, which is the constant critical reflection of the educator in relation to their practice as a means of developing political-pedagogical projects immanent to the concrete experiences of communities.

From these networks has emerged the Red de Investigacion Educativa (Network of Educational Research, ieRed) in the University of Cauca. As part of this, educator seminars are organized that aim to create a space of self-reflection, which enables the possibility to think collectively about both the barriers and the possibilities of critical educational practice. Out of these discussions, study groups are formed as a means to think through ways to overcome barriers and strengthen critical pedagogical work. As Bohorquez (2013, p. 4) continues, this is "a permanent process of deconstruction at both the individual and collective level" that enables the development of communities of pedagogical knowledge that produce processes of systematization, investigation, and collective construction of projects and experiences (Mejía, 2002).

Additionally various educator collectives have networked through the Red de Cualificación de Educadores en Ejercicio (Network of Educator Qualification through Practice, RED CEE) located in the Universidad Pedagogica Nacional (National Pedagogical University). This offers an alternative to traditional teacher training that is committed to a practice that changes the reality of the classroom and the community. The principle lines of investigation and study are teacher training and pedagogical innovation organized around action research in which teachers reflect on practice and become researchers and intellectuals of the development of this practice. As Bohorquez describes (2013, p. 4), "All of these networks and projects put the educator in a key role, distinct from that of a simple consumer of elaborations produced by other researchers."

Linked to this is the national pedagogical expedition, which brings together the National Pedagogical University, NGOs, and other research collectives as a means of systematizing the experiences of teachers and fostering the development of "other" schools and "other" teachers. As Bernal et al. (2003, p. 97) describe, this experience fosters "alternative ways of creating schools and educators, a rainbow of experiences which speak for themselves and attempt to co-ordinate amongst themselves in order to remove the innovative educator from her isolation."

Out of these experiences developed numerous archives, resources, and systematization of experiences that form an alternative epistemological basis for education in Colombia, which is explicitly opposed to the hierarchical and monological epistemological politics of militarized neoliberal education and development (Bernal, Orozco Cruz, and Cespedes, 2001, pp. 1–5).

Such a dialogue of knowledges enacts a critique in practice of authoritarianism in politics, pedagogy, and knowledge creation, and instead fosters the creation and re-creation of horizontal and democratic educator subjectivities, social relationships, and pedagogical-political projects. The subjects of knowledge, forms of knowledge, and ways of producing knowledge rupture the politics of patriarchal capitalist coloniality by embracing multiplicity and creating the conditions for radical difference and "otherness." These heritages, practices, knowledges, and traditions of critical pedagogy and the critical educator are a hidden history that helps us to understand the emergence, creativity, and consolidation of the Colombian Student Movement in the twenty-first century (Bolaños and Tattay, 2013).

Student Movement: Pedagogies of Re-creating Democratic Life

The Colombian Student Movement, Mesa Amplia Nacional Estudiantil (MANE), ruptured politics as normal in Colombia by appearing on the national political stage in March 2011 in protest against the proposed reform of Ley 30 related to the financing of HE institutions. Ley 30 proposed the creation of profit-making HE institutions and institutions *mixtas* (mixed institutions), which would augment the role of the private sector in HE and continue the erosion of state support for public HE through its definancing. MANE appeared in the cracks of contradiction of how education had been articulated as the nexus of possibility of progress, development, and dignity in the age of globalization. The continued exclusion of large sections of Colombian society from access to HE, the increasing indebtedness of the poorest in their attempt to access HE, and the augmenting divisions in quality of education (see chap. 1 for further details) particularly impacted on students from poorer socioeconomic backgrounds, creating a fissure between government rhetoric and reality (Cabezas, Casas, and Valencia, 2011, pp. 2–3).

MANE articulated their struggle against the reform in the language of democracy in which education was represented as a public good to which all Colombians should have a right to access without payment. This cleverly played on Santos's own rhetoric of popular participation in the educational reform process. Thus the power of the dominant discourse of education in the subjectivities and desires of Colombians created an ambiguous context in which this acted not only as a hegemonic mechanism of depoliticization and disarticulation but also as the basis of a goodsense counterhegemonic moral economy of rights, dignity, and desire.

Thus, MANE was able to bring together large sections of society including students from across the HE sector, secondary school students, their families, unions, NGOs, educators, and the political party el Polo Democrático (Democratic Pole). Despite government Santos's attempts to misname, delegitimize, and criminalize the mass mobilizations when they were at their height between March and November 2011, the movement continued to attract widespread public support (Rodriguez, 2013, pp. 1–3). MANE's Programa Minima (Minimum Programme) (agreed at their August 2011 National Meeting) made six key demands in relation to: finance; democracy and autonomy; well-being; academic quality; democratic freedoms; and the relationship between university and society. In finance they opposed the increasing private financing of HE proposed by Ley 30, articulating education as a right to enable national and democratic development that should be provided free by the government. As part of this they called for public participation in natural resource development and rejected all privatization of public services. In autonomy and democracy their focus was the strengthening of the autonomy of universities by ensuring the right to elect their management, decide their curriculum and research orientations, and determine collectively their own standards of quality, thus rejecting the external evaluative and ranking systems implemented as part of the "educational revolution." The demands of well-being included that all outsourcing of educational services, including health, housing, and sport, should be reversed and returned to the university to ensure the well-being of students. Additionally, they supported the rights of university workers through the guarantee of permanent contracts and their employment by the university, and not private companies.

At the heart of academic quality was supporting the autonomy of the academic community and their well-being. In democratic freedom, the student movement demanded respect of human rights and democratic participation on campuses and rejected the militarization and presence of security forces on campus. Finally, in the relation between university and community they demanded that the university's mission and practice be linked to the needs of Colombian society. As they argued, "This implies that the public university should discuss and adopt a new pedagogical model that discusses and generates alternatives in relation to the social economic and environmental problems that Colombia faces...We understand that university extension projects are an integral part of this to ensure that it can respond to the priorities and needs of the Colombian people" (MANE, 2011a).

Through their mobilizations and broader strategy they were able to force the government to withdraw the reform proposal and commit to its revision. They also won the social and political legitimacy to develop an alternative educational reform that opened the space for an unprecedented national pedagogical-political practice that continues to the present time (Rodriguez, 2013). As Garcia (2012, p. 449) describes, "The students declared that they would dedicate themselves to realising what they had promised; to elaborate, with teachers, workers, parents and rectors an alternative project of reform."

Pedagogies of Emergence of the Student Movement

The pedagogies of possibility for the visible emergence of the student movement in 2011 are a nexus of the pedagogical practices and heritages of the CPM and its successor—microprojects of critical education—which transverses the formal and informal educational sectors and the processes of student organization in public and private universities. The latter explicitly emerge in protest to the "education revolution" begun under Uribe. Here affective pedagogies of building trust, solidarity, and communities of resistance against the militarized populist epistemological logics of educational reform were enacted. These were fostered by processes of learning to create other times and spaces from that of commodified, homogenized, and marketized education and developing methodologies with which to coconstruct critical understanding and strategies of counterhegemony.

In the early 2000s, students began organizing in private and public universities, including workshops and assemblies to discuss and reflect upon educational reforms and their impact on access, quality, and opportunity. Issues of corruption in university management were addressed. Also discussed was the increasing encroachment of security forces, including intimidation of critical educators, the introduction of CCTV cameras and the presence of Escuadron Movil Antidisturbios (Esmad) police on campuses throughout the country, supposedly in the name of democratic security (Garcia, 2012, p. 451). These spaces were pedagogical as they created the possibility of "other" logics, practices, and relationships, in contrast to that of the consumer, competitive, and individualized student with an instrumental relationship to education and the university community.

Here stories and experiences were shared and reflected on to cocreate other readings and practices of student subjectivity and the meaning of education, pedagogy, and democracy (Rodriguez, 2013, pp. 5–6). These experiences began to overcome the isolation, separation, and fear of militarized neoliberalism and foster relationships of trust, solidarity, and commitment. While uniting a plurality of groups and individuals they emphasized overcoming sectarianism and creating a space of unity through difference. This clearly built upon the heritages of pedagogical-political projects that emerged in the 1980s, motivated to move beyond militarized and authoritarian politics of knowledge and toward a culture and pedagogical practices of dialogue, multiplicity, and difference.

During 2003–2006 these processes of local organization were articulated at the regional and national level through the Coordinadora Nacional de Estudiantes Universitarios (CNEU). From 2007 national meetings were organized to coordinate a series of mobilizations that would articulate from the local to the regional and national simultaneously. From these emerged MANE, which brought together more than three hundred organizational processes and groupings at the national, regional, and local level, structured with a commitment to democracy and participation through plenaries, operative committees, and various working groups. This aimed to democratize the creation of movement strategy, distribution of information, and movement organization (Rodriguez, 2013, 7). The movement was committed to the development of communication, dialogue, and conversation as the basis from which students, with other actors could become part of the formation of a democratic public education and the development of Colombia society, people, and culture (Rodas, 2007, pp. 14–15). As MANE declared at the beginning of the 2011 mobilizations,

> We are a broad, democratic and pluralist space that brings together organisation and students from institutions of higher education and technical and technological education…in its politics of unity with our country's social and popular movements we aim to articulate with other sectors and processes in order to advance the defence of the fundamental right to education and other social rights. (MANE, 2011b)

MANE's Programa Minimo, released at this time, was thus an expression of the deep pedagogical-political processes of organizational and intellectual construction that had enabled their emergence as a powerful political force. Their inclusion of democracy, autonomy, workers' rights, and access to quality education demonstrated engagement with traditions and heritages of critical education in Colombia. This enabled the creation of collective processes of learning from which emerged alternative counterhegemonic readings, practices, and subjectivities of education and democracy.

Pedagogies of Resistance and Consolidation of Counterhegemonic Epistemological Horizons

These pedagogies of construction were the basis from which plural and creative repertoires of resistance were created, developed, and enacted by MANE throughout 2011. Such repertoires of resistance included occupations of public space (physical and virtual) and their construction—albeit temporally—of alternative spatialities in terms of relationships, meanings, and practices. The experience of mobilizing, of confronting police, media, and government, and of finding ways to engage other social and political sectors and the general public, enabled a qualitative leap in the production of alternative horizons of education as part of a popular, national (and international) project of democratization and development. Thus, throughout the protests there was a wide repertoire of collective actions, both institutional and noninstitutional: workshops, debates, teach-ins, carnavalesque action including hug-ins at university campuses, chains of affection for life and democracy, direct action with nude bodies, kiss-ins, occupations of educational establishments, road blockages, creation of videos, YouTube clips, music, Twitter, and Facebook (Garcia, 2012, p. 453). Such a plurality of forms of protest demonstrates the depth, creativity, and radical openness of the student movement and the immanent construction of its strategy and political practice. Through reoccupations of public space and their creation in other ways, students began to deepen processes of creating themselves and their relationships with others and Colombian society differently and of developing their political, intellectual, and creative capacities. The process and the ends of educational struggle were inseparable from democratic participation which fostered and nurtured multiplicity. This deepened a political-pedagogical project around the reconstruction of the idea of the right to education. It demonstrated elements of this educational project in practice— through practices of protest that encompassed the cultural, intellectual, and embodied. Protest was not merely oppositional but also constructive through an immanent practice of producing alternative forms of democratic life and relationships.

De la protesta a la propuesta
(From Protest to Proposal)

Once the students had been victorious in their initial objective of forcing the Santos government to withdraw their reform proposal, they declared that they would dedicate themselves to realizing what they had promised. This was the elaboration with teachers, workers, parents, rectors, and others sectors of society of an alternative project of reform for public education. Throughout 2012 and into 2013, MANE enacted unprecedented processes of participatory creation of this alternative reform proposal. The pedagogies of these processes enabled the politicization of educational practice and pedagogization of the political at multiple spatialities, fostering the unlearning of hegemonic conceptions of self, social relationships, and society and the immanent construction of new ones.

Again foregrounded in their pedagogical practice is an epistemological commitment to multiplicity and coconstruction of education as a project of life and democracy. As MANE declared in early 2012, they sought to

> consolidate university education as a fundamental and inalienable right and as a societal common good, and to advance the construction of a system of higher education whose nuclei is a state and public HE, as a popular, democratic, critical, international cultural, pluriethnic, antipatriarchal and scientific education that guarantees the technological, scientific and cultural independence of Colombian society. (Cited in Garcia, 2012, p. 449)

A participatory methodology of coconstruction at multiple scales was developed through *mesas amplias locales* (local participatory working groups [MALES]). Here particular groupings and university organizations were given autonomy in the methodology chosen to create the generative principles and problematics around which the new reform proposal would be developed. As they described (MANE, 2011c),

> In agreement with the original principles of MANE, the autonomy of each university is respected in relation to deciding the best methodology to create proposals. With the objective of elaborating an alternative education left in this first moment, local assemblies will form to develop critique of and alternative proposals to that of the ley 30 of the government.

The next stage involved the organization of a national student meeting in which the different proposals and problematics of the local assemblies were debated to agree, by consensus a general set of principles from which to deepen the development of the alternative proposal. This was then followed by a meeting to which other social and political actors, including teachers and university workers were invited to participate in the proposals' discussion and initial development (MANE, 2011c). At the end of 2011, the national committee organized another national meeting at which was developed the methodology that would shape the systematization and deepening stages of the construction of the alternative proposal (see Annexure 1 for details). At this meeting, as a member described (MANE, 2011d),

> the fourth national meeting reflected the intense desire for change, of ideas for the construction of the country, of collective, critical, thoughtful, romantic consciousness...it is romanticism that makes

possible the existence of dreams, desires and utopias. Dreams such as these of a space where all students, university, technical, technological, secondary, can come together flow and create.

Here affective pedagogies were created that brought together the creative capacities, critical realities, and emotional desires and imagination of students and multiple other participants in education. The process of coconstruction built on the heritages, experiences, and knowledges of movement members, developed these capabilities and was transformatory. Hegemonic subjectivities of the educator as isolated, deprofessionalized, and deintellectualized were transgressed into counterhegemonic subjectivities of critical facilitators in the development of a pedagogical-political project for society. Here, hegemonic subjectivities of the student as commodified, competitive, and docile were transgressed into counterhegemonic subjectivities at the heart of the formation of communities of resistance, cultures of solidarity, and practices of coconstruction of knowledge for transformation.

All materials developed, methodologies chosen, and decisions made were made public, not only to the movement, but also to Colombian society who were included as key agents in the coconstruction of this pedagogical-political project. The launch of the alternative project containing 65 statutes happened in January 2013 but the process of debate, discussion, mobilization, and development of local critical education projects continues. The Santos government has not responded to this proposal and has instead constructed its own proposal inviting those actors it considered to be representative and important in the development of a modern HE sector. Despite the government's monologue of silence and deepening of the epistemological logics of militarized neoliberal capitalist coloniality, an alternative democratic project embedded in plurality that seeks to transform subjectivities, social relationships, and everyday life at multiple spatial scales is in the process of construction.

Social Movement Decolonial Feminist Pedagogies of Unlearning of Hegemonic Practices of Self, Other, and Society

La Máscara: "se abre el techo para que tambien entre el infinito" (Open the Roof So That the Infinite Can Also Enter)

La Máscara Theatre Company is a unique feminist theater group in Colombia that works with *theater of the oppressed* pedagogies and methodologies. They formed in the 1972 out of the heritage and practices of New Theatre in Colombia, which sought to develop a popular Owner theater that combined cultural, pedagogical, and political work and often emerged from the interface between critical intellectuals and student activists. In the early 1970s a key document, "Apuntes para un Metodo de Creacion Colectiva" (Notes toward a Method of Creative Construction), which systematized the methodology that characterizes New Theatre in Colombia, was produced by Enrique Buenaventura and Jacqueline Vidal. Here the collective coconstruction of popular theater that linked pedagogies with radical politics was articulated. As Buenaventura describes (cited in Restrepo, 1998, p. 74),

> An apolitical artist is an artist that is supporter of a culture without a face, of a subjugated culture and their work will be marked by this fact. An apolitical artist is then, actually political and creates art at the service of the conservation of that which is unsustainable.

As groups of Colombian New Theatre consolidated, the methodology of creative construction was developed and refined. Theater groups were collectively organized and theatrical productions collectively created in which all were involved in the investigation and transformation of open performances. These performances aimed to stimulate public debate to modify the production and deepen critical reflection about social and political reality.

The Máscara Feminist Theatre collective emerged from this historical and intellectual context and is therefore committed to this pedagogical-cultural practice of coconstruction. Through experimentation with the methodology of collective creation and other traditions such as theater of the oppressed and forum theater, the participants in the collective have produced themselves as integral actors, articulating individual and collective voices of liberation and empowerment linked to key problematics facing women. They have achieved this through developing multiple pedagogies, which are embodied, affective, spiritual, intellectual, imaginative, and include dance, poetry, voice, music, bodywork, and methods of theatrical expression (Restrepo, 1998, pp. 79–81). Importantly in their reweaving of themselves and their world, they do not privilege any form of pedagogy or a form of knowledge. They thus enact in their practice a dialogue of knowledges that decenter the imperial subject of knowing and the written word produced through abstract conceptualization as the pinnacle of knowledge and development.

Through processes of self-reflection on their cultural practice and its relationship to the concrete political conjuncture of Colombia, and Cali more specifically, the collective decided in 1985 to orientate their work to a feminist praxis and explore the dynamics of gendered articulations of power. For the Collective their conceptualization of feminism involves the creation of alternative epistemological, political, cultural, and embodied relationships and practices to that of capitalist patriarchy (Restrepo, 1998, p. 120). They are committed to an ethical practice of dialogue and listening but also, as Lucy Boloña (interview December 2010) explains, "the need for the oppressed to at times enact monologues, not to silence, but to create the spaces necessary for those who have been without voice and visibility to be heard and seen."

The Collective presents within a theater setting, as well as street performances, and actively seeks to create ruptures in the hegemonic representations of gendered relationships of power as they interpolate the personal, collective, and political. By creating narratives, images, sensations, and representations that enact a discontinuity in the hegemonic narrative of social life, they seek to open up possibilities of critical reflection and practice. They engage with problematics of gendered violence, motherhood, sex work, infanticide, the family, sexuality, and desire through reinterpretations of works, which are often not theatrical works but poems or novels by Brecht or Colombian writers such as Carolina Vivas or Marybel Acevedo (Restrepo, 1998, pp. 148–150). They enact multiple interplays between bodies, spaces, lightening, silence, and sound, developing pedagogies of the sensations and emotions, which create the condition of imaginative and conceptual openings to otherness. As Pilar Restrepo describes,

> We need to produce works that develop through humour, irony, the dancing body (and) circus techniques, break the silence, provoke reflection and questions...We open dialogues, inviting others to think, open and transform themselves.

These experiences have also radically transformed the actresses of the Máscara, allowing them to cocreate multiple readings of the world and ways of weaving themselves, their relationships, bodies, sexualities, desires, and broader communities of which they form a part. For Pilar this was an intensely uncomfortable and challenging experience despite its leading to joy, creativity, and self-valorization. As she explains, "We were used to the men deciding everything, directing, writing the script, managing theatre groups." These women have embraced the discomfort that accompanies processes of unlearning the subjectivities and relationships of patriarchal colonial capitalism. Such intensely embodied experiences of transformation enable, as Pilar Restrepo continues, "ways to re-think resentment, anger and bitterness that arise out of multiple experiences of oppression and violence...ways to convert pain into creation."

Their cultural pedagogical praxis in the context of militarized colonial patriarchal capitalism has opened them to coercive and violent attempts at exclusion, delegitimization, and disappearance. Mainstream media and corporations have rejected and derided their work. Traditional Left parties and organizations have also derided and devalued their political-cultural praxis. La Máscara Feminist Theatre has been subject to aggressions, threats, and intimidations by the parastate. As Pilar Restrepo explained to me, "In 1988 some of us were forced into exile in central America after repeated death threats by paramilitaries/death squadrons." Despite these conditions of militarized patriarchal capitalism they continue to reinvent the political through pedagogical-cultural work that revolutionizes the practices and processes of social emancipation.

The Máscara also develops participatory theater with excluded and oppressed communities in which members become critical community facilitators that foster the voice, dignity, and agency of oppressed women. Isabella and Elizabeth two displaced Afro-Colombian women are participants in Aves de Paraíso (Birds of Paradise) community theater groups facilitated by La Máscara. After being displaced in 2001 from Nariño and Chocó states on the Pacific coast of Colombia, they left the violence of state-sponsored paramilitary groups and guerrilla groups to arrive into the neoliberal violence of urban poverty and exclusion. Elizabeth is a grandmother, tall and proud with lines of sorrow around her eyes. Isabella is a single mother of five children, a deep voice and laugh, yet with a well of sadness in her eyes. Ageless and yet with the weight of much suffering on their shoulders, they have participated in the theater group for four years. It is, as Isabella told me (Motta, 2010), "a space of peace, of escape, of warmth and humanity." It is a place of laughter and creativity where for a moment the realities of physical, cultural, economic, and political violence are overcome.

As both explained, in their *tierra* (land) no one went hungry. There was always food as they lived in the countryside where there was abundance. Neighbors shared and supported each other. The region where Elizabeth is from has been taken over by multinationals, supported by the Colombian government. Egyptian palms are grown for export, which destroys the surrounding land, further undermining *campesino* (peasant) ways of life. There is obviously a lot more to displacement than conflict between paramilitaries and guerrillas. To be violently displaced in this way from your land, way of life, and community, and then arrive to more violence and displacement, is a form of long-term trauma. The violence in their lives is multidimensional; the way that the power of the United States, the Colombian state, and neoliberal capitalism has scarred and traumatized their lives cannot be understood or transformed from the outside or by a model developed in another place and another context. Such violence is intensely placed, subjective, affective, intellectual, and psychological.

It is this multidimensionality of power, its effects, and how one transforms these conditions into liberation and social justice, which is one of the major problematics of La Máscara Theatre. The theater of the oppressed methodology with excluded communities seeks to facilitate processes of collective understanding, representation, and transformation through the development of theater. Its objective—like popular education—is self-liberation from oppression, facilitating the self-liberation of people from the passive state of spectator to actors that self-determine the theater but also their everyday lives. As theater is multidimensional—affective, cultural, psychological, embodied, physical, and intellectual—it has the potential to transform the multidimensional nature of oppression.

For La Máscara the key elements of their work are that it is dialogical and integral in the types of collective and individual experiences developed and facilitates free play that accepts and values people's life experience, diversity, and expressions. Importantly, this facilitates experimental space in which communities have the time and space to reflect upon their realities and experiment with their transformation. This aims to encourage rebellious thought, promoting ideas, perspectives, and actions that are nonconventional and which generate a plurality of options and alternatives (Restrepo, 1998).

La Máscara develops multiple affective pedagogies, for example, using the power of laughter in a way that relativizes the power of order and control through the counterpower of uncontrollable laughter. It opposes desperation and bitterness with the power of liberatory laughter. As Elizabeth expressed, "It would be so easy to be full of bitterness, to become cold hearted. Here we prevent this and keep it at bay. This doesn't mean we don't continue to suffer but it does mean that it doesn't destroy us."

Finally, it is dedicated to public work, making visible to the public the self-liberation and determination of otherwise excluded and demonized communities. As Isabella explained, "We have shown our work in Cali. It creates a bridge between displaced communities and Caleños. Our work really needs to be presented in every barrio (community)." Theater of the oppressed brings the creative, affective, and intellectual capacities of communities and individuals to the center of the praxis of social transformation.

As Pilar Restrepo Mejía participant in La Máscara explains, "Amongst the arts, theatre possesses the privilege of being a live art, which allows us to see the complexity of social relations and interpret reality in an inventive way, which develops an experience of reflection. Theatre becomes an extraordinary instrument for people and community development." In particular La Máscara aims to make visible women's struggles, suffering, and the violence they confront and through this process manifest the dignity, strength, knowledge, and creativity of women who are otherwise represented as either merely victims or dangerous delinquents. In this way La Máscara facilitates collective storytelling through embodied, creative, and affective pedagogies that enable the women participants to weave themselves and their communities anew.

Working with women like Isabella and Elizabeth, La Máscara supports the development of theater groups in marginalized communities. In the case of the group in which Isabella and Elizabeth participate, La Máscara had worked with la Hermana (sister) Alba Stella Barreto, founder and director of Fundación Paz y Bien in Comuna 14, Aguablancas. The foundation provided training and offered a meeting space to discuss the problems being faced by displaced and impoverished communities in the area. La Máscara organized a two-day series of workshops that opened up space to discuss the key themes of human rights, reproductive rights, and sexual rights. The workshops used play, image, film, text, and dramatological methods to develop a collective understanding of these key themes and their relation to participants' lives. An example of the methods used in one of the human rights workshops is an activity called "the violence in my life." The objectives of the exercise are to explore and identify how one can be both an object of violence and also exercise violence against others; strengthen the development of ways of dealing with violence and develop values such as solidarity and responsibility for each other and oneself (Medina and La Máscara, 2010).

The facilitator begins by explaining to the participant that this exercise is an opportunity to share ideas, feelings, and experiences in relation to not only violence exercised against participants but also violence exercised by participants. Ground rules are set such as respect for each other, maintaining the privacy of what is said in the workshop, and that none need feel inhibited to say something that they think might make others uncomfortable. The participants are then divided into groups and asked to brainstorm about types of violence that they know or think of when they hear the word "violence." They make a list of these and then are asked to add examples of how these violences are exercised. Next there is five minutes for all to reflect about their personal experiences of violence in which either they have had violence used against them, used violence against another or themselves, or seen violent action and not intervened.

There is then an open discussion led by the facilitator in which the participants are asked if they found it difficult or not to think about themselves in relation to violence. Assembled in groups, they explore what they think are the causes and effects of the situations of violence in their lives. Each group is then asked to choose one volunteer who will talk about their experience to support the general debate. The debate is geared around general questions such as why did this violent situation occur; why did the person act like this; how would other members of the group have acted; and are there suggestions of how one might act differently in a similar situation?

After the discussion the groups are asked to develop one or two improvisations in relation to the experiences discussed. These are presented as forum theater in which the audience have the right to interrupt the performance to ask the audience their opinion about something, to suggest a different next step of the performance, and to become actors that change what is happening and to suggest solutions to the violence or conflict. This attempts to undo the traditional audience/actor partition and bring audience members into the performance by having input into the dramatic action they are watching. Through this process, the participant is also able to realize and experience the challenges of achieving the improvements suggested.

These processes are highly emotional and potentially explosive. Thus, the role of facilitator in supporting participants through the workshop and encouraging participants to listen and learn from each other is central to the realization of the workshop's objectives. This is particularly important as participants will make judgments about each other's situation without necessarily knowing the context, conditions, or life story of the other. However, La Máscara facilitators continue to stress that without understanding the causes of violence it is impossible to change and overcome violence, however difficult that process of understanding is.

After a series of workshops, the next step is to build a theater group with the participants in their community. The group in Comuna 14—one of eight groups formed—comprised women and children, all displaced Afro-Colombians from the Pacific coast regions of Cauca, Chocó, and Nariño. They built on the rich traditions of song, dance, storytelling, and poetry of their communities. Elizabeth is a poet and Isabella a storyteller. Yet their everyday traumas of hunger, homelessness and humiliation left little space and time for reading, writing, or storytelling. Their participation in the theater group helps, at least in the time they are in the space, to develop these skills and talents channeling them into thematics of displacement chosen and developed by the participants. Their last work—Tierra en Guerra (Land at War)—was a shout of dignity in the face of discrimination and demonization. It captured their lives as they had been in their *tierra*, encapsulating the richness, knowledge, and histories of their communities, as well the experiences and causes of their displacement. Using body, mind, and spirit it was a means of representing their reality and humanity to each other and the world, and of turning upside down the stereotypes and representations of Caleña media, politics, and culture.

The process of collective construction itself was a process of self-determination, discovery, and strengthening of voice. As Elizabeth articulated, "When I arrived in Cali I couldn't express myself. I was panicked and shaking all the time. In the group I have built the confidence in, myself and my abilities." Or as Isabella described,

> They say we are ignorant and we can't talk Spanish properly. I knew what I wanted to say but my tongue wouldn't work. My self-esteem had been destroyed. The projects, Lucy and others with their love and warmth and sincerity have helped me feel I have knowledge, understanding and rights. I still shake, I still suffer but there are lights of hope, places of breathing.

Facilitators are trained in a number of elements to enable them to bring to fruition the development of plays and help build and sustain the group. These are corporal expression, vocal and instrumental techniques, introduction to theater conventions, stimulation of dramatic creation of narratives, nonverbal language, acting and concepts of improvisation, and dramatic organization. An example of an exercise used to develop dramatic creation of narratives is through written texts. As it is possible to develop a work of theater through a poem, a song, or a written text by one or more participants, the exercise begins by asking the participants to write a text to poem in relation to a chosen theme. In groups, improvisations are developed to explore how one might use such a text to develop the theater piece. Oral elements are also introduced in the improvisation such as oral stories, dreams, anecdotes, and life stories.

Facilitators need to be able to recognize that which is most needed in the group, and therefore, how to orientate the work and process of collective construction. The facilitator of Aves de Paraíso uses yoga as a way of helping the affective psychological healing from the long-term, ongoing traumas experienced by participants. The weekly meetings, which are usually four hours duration, begin with yoga work. She also encourages participants to build on cultural traditions of storytelling, enabling a retelling of stories of trauma as a means to transform these stories creatively with a pedagogy that facilitates a distancing from the most painful experiences. Collective processes of storytelling and improvisation create links of solidarity and enable an overcoming of the monologue of isolation into dialogues of understanding, voice, and pleasure. As Pilar continues, "telling stories is a way of reconstructing reality, and sometimes, it also enables the healing of deep wounds."

Aves de Paraíso's next work moves away from a focus on displacement and violence, which as Isabella and Elizabeth explained, they feel they have exhausted, and are exhausted by. This second process develops a utopia of how the world would be if all women joined together to overcome violence, to encourage men to move away from violence against each other, and over money, power, resources, and pride. It is an act of envisaging a different world. While a representation, the cultural-pedagogical work of La Máscara fuels their everyday struggles against violence and attempts to construct moments of paradise on earth.

La Escuela

The Escuela Política de Mujeres Pazíficas, coordinated by the Pazíficas Women's Collective, is a network that emerged in 2000 in Cali, Colombia. Its aim is the development of nonviolent, feminist proposals and practices within Colombian society, in order to denounce and make visible the violences experienced by women. Through a series of monthly reflexive workshops over 18 months, the collective concluded that women have multiple and rich experiences of agency and resistance, yet often lack the reflexive processes and systematization that could facilitate the individual and collective learning, enabling transformation of their realities through these knowledges. As Norma Bermúdez (2013, pp. 4–5) recounts, "From the beginning we knew that the debate and dialogue we had opened would have major consequences for us and for moving beyond the old formulas of politics. We were facing something deeper; to question the meaning of politics, its objective and its means; to question the sense of power that power is enacted not only in parliaments and battlefields, but also in social relations, on the streets, in the square, at home and in the bedroom."

Thus, emerged the Pazíficas Women's Political School, which works through traditions of nonviolence, feminism, and popular education to create learning spaces in which the knowledges of all women are valued. The program runs typically for four months and involves four stages of reflection and systematization. From these experiences have emerged multiple themes to orientate practices of transformation: celebrations of diversity; poetic politics; humor as a vehicle to show that other gender relations are possible; and incarnated memory. Out of these have flourished multiple and diverse practices of individual and collective transformation (www.infogenero.net/sitio/; www.aul lemosmujeres.blogspot.com).

Processes of informal learning have been key in the (re)construction of sociabilities, political subjectivities, and collectivities. Indeed, phoenixlike, the movements have risen, out of the ashes caused by the destructive processes of neoliberal capitalism in communities' lives. The pedagogical is here not merely understood as practices and methodologies that enable the creation of collective readings of the world that can shape political strategy and analysis. Rather, the pedagogical becomes an essential part in the coming into being of popular political subjectivities and organizations by creating the openings, possibilities, and relationships to enable communities—often silenced and violently invisibilized—to appear as embodied political subjects. Central are pedagogies and processes of reoccupying and re-creating space and the body.

In the Colectivo de Mujeres Pazíficas the pedagogies of possibility for the emergence of a feminist school began as a reaction to exclusion and silencing of the needs, demands, desires, and dreams of women within mainstream culture and politics. As Norma Bermúdez explained to me in relation to the history of emergence of the idea for the Escuela,

> In the early 2000s peace talks were occurring between the government and armed guerrillas in which women and their voices and

experiences were excluded. There was no space to talk of the politics of motherhood, relationships and loss, love and desire within the experiences of female combatants. There was no place for a humanising of combatants. So we decided to write a letter to the women guerrillas in which we asked to hear their stories of motherhood, of loving and loss within conditions of war and conflict. We sought to open a dialogue that could break the logics of patriarchal capitalism of politics in Colombia in which politics is an extension of war and war and extension of politics.

This experience of appearing in public as political subjects with distinct voices, histories, and experiences acted as a moment of rupture, which disrupted politics as normal in Colombian society and for the women who would come to form the Escuela. Women who were used to men deciding everything, writing and directing the scripts of politics and power began to realize that they could be active agents in Colombia's future. As in the case of La Máscara, this involved a process of unlearning subjectivities in which women were objects of other's discourses and represented as passive victims of the violent logics of Colombian politics. It involved creating new forms of sociability as women came together to support each other's acts of speaking. This experience began a process of rerooting of subjects within their own agency and dignity. As Norma continues,

> Out of this processes of facilitating dialogues of understanding and of sharing our stories it became clear that women are at the centre of community life. They ensure the survival of their families and are at the centre of the conflict. Yet their experiences and practices are often denied and silenced. We realised that it was necessary to create a space in which we could systematise and develop the knowledges and wisdoms of women that emerge from their everyday struggles.

From this emerged the call for a series of seminars which discussed the question of what kind of learning space would need to be created to enable this process of unlearning and learning to produce new ways of life and social relationships. After 18 months of discussion and reflection it was agreed to organize a school of feminist political education.

This experience of informal learning for the participants who came to form the Escuela demonstrates the importance of solidarities and friendship in building relationships of trust, mutuality, and openness, which build the groundwork for the emergence of feminist spaces of emancipation. It is in the social spaces and moments of struggle in which friendships, connections, histories, and relationships are forged that enact affective noninstrumental pedagogical processes. In these safe spaces, women who have often felt without voice can create the tender conditions of articulating their voices and needs and encounter other women who are open to actively listening (Bermúdez, 2013). The blurring of boundaries between the political (public) and social (private) creates the conditions of possibility for the overcoming of internalized forms of oppression. It also creates fertile terrain to overcome informal raced, classed, and gendered hierarchies, thereby creating horizontal relationships and individual and collective voices in public politics and learning spaces.

These informal learning processes foreground the importance of embodied and affective pedagogies in processes of social change. They suggest that critical educators need to pay attention not only to visible forms of power but also to those invisibilized dynamics of power which structure who talks and who is silent in both intimate and public spaces. It also points to the power of pedagogies of silence in the process of coming to individual and collective voice. As in the practice of La Máscara, creating the conditions for a dialogue of knowledges often involves those silenced speaking in monologues about their silencing. This speaking is, importantly, not merely verbal but can be bodily, emotional and spiritual. Thus the pedagogical conditions of the coming into being of new emancipatory subjects involve a delicate interplay between silence, speaking and listening. This, as the practice of the Escuela demonstrates, is embedded in a commitment to epistemologically privilege the wisdom and knowledges of women's bodies and the body of the land.

"Changing Not Only the Content of the Conversation but the Terms of the Conversation": Collective Knowledge Processes and Multiple Knowledges

Walter Mignolo articulates (2009, p. 9) that developing alternatives to colonial capitalism involves not only changing the content of the conversation, or producing new emancipatory knowledges, but also changing the terms of the conversation, so transforming the way we produce such emancipatory knowledges. This involves shifting our focus to the subjects of knowledge construction and reconceptualizing the nature of intellectual production in a way that overcomes the epistemological politics of capitalist coloniality. This pernicious process of capitalist coloniality allows the letter and word to become the anchor of knowledge, resulting in a divorcing of the word from the world and construction of hierarchies between those who know and those who are known.

By building on the lived knowledges and experiences of participants, the Escuela enacts a changing of the terms of the conversation. They nurture new pedagogical practices that enable the development of a collective and critical reading of the world and women's experiences of oppression, violence, and displacement. Here the pedagogical process is organized in a four-month diploma course. The course is divided into one-month parts. The first, which begins the dialogue of knowledges, is a time of the sharing of experiences and knowledge of participants by grounding each other in the histories and paths of their lives. As Norma Bermúdez (author interview, April 10, 2012) explains,

> So for example if a woman has learned to make recipes with which she had fed her family well and cheaply, the group makes it, tastes it, shares similar experiences. We then link this experience of making the receipt and the conditions of her life and learning to reflect on questions such as food sovereignty. We read texts, watch videos about food sovereignty movements in Colombia and other places. We also talk about the neoliberal crisis and how this increases the weight of labour on the shoulders of women. We explore alternative forms of economy such as the feminist economy.

From this thematics or generative questions are built for the group to explore in future workshops. The second month moves into a structured exploration of key thematics led by activists, scholars, and popular educators. The themes explored include the history of women's human rights, the nonviolence movement, and concepts such as gender, sexuality, diversity, and ethnicity. The third month is spent focusing and exploring key thematics and questions that the group develops by reflection about the first two months. The deepening of the dialogue of knowledges creates the groundwork for the final month in which the group asks themselves—now with the insights of the learning, relationships, and emotions aroused by the experience— how to translate these learnings and experiences to the public sphere? With what aesthetics, which message, and which practices do we want to share with our communities and broader society? (see Bermúdez, 2013, for further details.)

From the Escuela's practice has emerged an ethical commitment to fostering collective knowledge processes that break down the division between thinkers and doers, crucially validating the histories, experiences, cultures, and knowledges of subaltern communities. These pedagogics break the epistemological and representational logics of domination in communities' lives, nurturing the conditions for the consolidation of emancipatory subjectivities and social relationships.

Pedagogies of Everyday Life: Politica Afectiva and the Body

In the pedagogical work of the Escuela with women, some of the most complex pedagogies of crossing between self/other and cosmos are developed. These work through the erotic, which as Audre Lorde (2000) describes, "lies in a deeply female and spiritual plane, firmly rooted in the power of our unexpressed or unrecognized feeling." It is a deep knowing or joy that we feel when we authentically express our creativity and desire, which once experienced, cannot be forgotten and reburied. Their development of pedagogies that include ritual, the senses, dreaming, dancing, storytelling, singing, and massage, combined with more traditional textual forms of knowledge, builds the conditions for participants' reoccupation of the world and ability to challenge and transform conditions of multiple oppression (Bermúdez, 2013). However, they also open the possibility of a reoccupation of their bodies and selves. The internalization of the oppressor's gendered, classed, and raced embodied beliefs and practices are subverted. In its place flourish transgressive relationships with the self, others, and the world. As Gutiérrez (2012, p. 61) describes in relation to Bolivian practices of creating an "other" politics "[that] means as Aymara feminine wisdom says, that 'we understand' the size and strength of our own ability and that we should not surrender that ability to anyone."

This cornucopia of pedagogies and methodologies based in popular education do not therefore merely engage with intellectual and theoretical production, as if these were disembodied and objective processes. There is a questioning of the alienation of human experience through which capitalist social relations are reproduced and an attempt (sometimes explicit sometimes implicit) to unite and dealienate our capacities and creativity. These processes of collective knowledge construction seek to overcome the dualisms between intellect and emotion, mind and body, and thought and action, so characteristic of the "neo-liberal capitalist one-dimensional *man*." They create as Porto Gonçalves (cited in Ceceña, 2012, p. 11) argues, "Material knowledge is a knowledge of touch, of contact, of tastes and knowledges, a knowledge with (the knowledge of domination is a knowledge over) it is inscribed knowledge (ins-crito) and not necessarily written [es-crito]."

Conclusion

From the position of exteriority from the militarized logics of neoliberalism in Colombia have emerged subjects, projects, and practices of revolutionary epistemological decolonization. Not as victims but as survivors do these subjects emerge to contest and transgress the violences of the epistemological logics and politics of patriarchal capitalist coloniality. The pedagogical-political projects and practices that are flourishing are a contest over societal projects understood as a struggle over the heart and soul of a people and their rights to self-determination and self-government. Central to these practices is recognition of the pedagogical nature of hegemony and embrace of alternative pedagogies through which to decolonize mind, body, heart, soul, and produce social relationships in multiple anticapitalist ways.

As in the Brazilian and Venezuelan cases this includes commitment to producing "other" educators and "other" schools in which the separations and alienations of capitalism are transgressed, including that between knowing and known, mind and body, education and life, and theory and practice. In the Colombian case these struggles have been marked by autonomy and mistrust of the state and transgressive practices that bridge radical educators and schools/universities with communities and movements in struggle.

This reinvention of counterhegemonic pedagogical-political projects involves transgressions of the epistemological politics of monologue, authoritarianism, and closure of capitalist coloniality and instead an embrace of multiple forms of knowledge, multiple subjects of knowledge production, and multiple collective ways of producing knowledge for social transformation. It aims to produce mass intellectuality and thus presents a challenge to the political and epistemological logics of representation characteristic of dominant articulations of twentieth-century socialism.

Out of these experiences emerged one of the most powerful student movements in the world that enacted a prefigurative politics of everyday life in which pedagogies of possibility opened the horizons of new forms of democratic life. Reoccupations of space and reorderings of social relationships were fostered through affective, embodied, and conceptual pedagogies that embraced multiple forms of knowledge. Methodologies of collective construction of knowledges for transformation were systematized and socialized at multiple spatial scales. This movement arguably lay down the foundations of a rearticulated popular and democratic political project that explicitly seeks to disrupt the epistemological politics of capitalist coloniality in Colombia and beyond. The future possibilities of its consolidation in many ways depend on the ability to create relationships and connections with other social struggles articulated by social movements within Colombia and beyond its geographic borders.

The pernicious and perverse patriarchal logics of capitalist coloniality in the Colombian context through the militarization of politics and politics of militarization have been responded to by the development of feminist popular education projects and movements. La Máscara and La Escuela pedagogize the political in complex and deeply transformative way, taking our analysis of the production of capitalism to the level of the deep internal wounds that capitalism produces in oppressed communities, particularly subaltern women. This pedagogical practice enacts a stepping inward to bring to awareness to how systems of oppression work to remove us from our capacity to enact relationships other than those of alienation and power-over and to embed in our hearts, minds, and body separation and fragmentation. At the heart of this practice is thus an exploration and conceptualization of how the wounds of oppressed peoples become embedded in their (our) bodies, distort their (our) emotions, separate them (us) from our souls, and limit their (our) creative capacities.

As I have demonstrated, the decolonial feminist popular educator does not reenact and mirror the dualisms and affective hierarchies of colonial patriarchal capitalism. Rather she embraces a full and multiple emotional palette. She is able to share and make visible her vulnerabilities as the epitome of strength and solidarity and enters in her integrity and wholeness in this process of epistemological reinvention. She does not enter as an external liberated knower to educate and speak for the unfree masses. She does not reproduce a victim representation of the oppressed in her practice but rather begins from a commitment to weaving together subjects, practices, and stories of agency, dignity, and survival. She is thus committed to coconstructing spaces of communion through nurturing safety and recognition.

The affective attributes of enabling such a practice of love cannot involve practices of shaming, which is one of the central ways of creating the distorted masculinities of colonial patriarchal capitalism. Rather it is enacted through critical practices of affirmation and emotional opening. These do not deny the importance of pain, grief, or anger in the coming to voice and agency but rather suggests the development of practices of emotional alchemy that are "difficult...painful" but which enable their transformation into joy, courage, and love, "without which there can be no wholeness" (hooks, 2004, p. 156).

Here song, dance, and ritual in which bodies, hearts, minds, and souls meet are the epitomes of this decolonial feminist pedagogical practice in which through each thread of weaving communities and individuals remember and honor their histories and rework novel structures, conceptions of self, and social relationships. Such transformation and encounters enable a reconnection of women with themselves as people, with each other, and with their erotic power. Once connected with such deep emotional knowing they can develop the capacity for joy—to "know" what joy and affirmation feels like and conversely to know what separation, estrangement, disassociation, and lack of meaning feel like.

Thus, oppressed communities learn to "see" the processes, situations, relationships, and ways of being to which they must say no as well as those to which they can surrender. As hooks describes such pedagogies "expressed in writing, teaching and habits of being [are] fundamentally linked to a concern with creating strategies that will enable colonised folks to decolonise their minds and actions, thereby promoting the insurrection of subjugated knowledges" (1990, p. 8). Those of us committed to developing decolonizing pedagogies of transformation that foreground twenty-first century socialism(s) have much to learn from these rich and complex pedagogical practices and epistemological politics in their reimagining of social transformation and political change.

Part III

Constructing Twenty-First Century Socialism in Latin America and Beyond

Chapter 7

Constructing Twenty-First Century Socialism: The Role of Radical Education

Sara C. Motta

On the Violences of Marketized Education in Latin American and Beyond

Neoliberal patriarchal colonial capitalism attempts to eradicate spaces and times of possibility and, with this, criminalize and erase forms of being, acting, and thinking outside of commodified logics. Such violences are also being enacted throughout the education sector, particularly as education is at the heart of the hegemonic articulation of global neoliberalism. It is articulated as representation, practice, and subjectivities and attempts to construct a monological epistemological logic of being, relationships, and society. Ultimately, the prophets of the end of history and politics seek through such an epistemological politics to produce individualized, commodified, and exclusionary subjects, social relationships, and ways of life.

In the Latin American context as our case studies have demonstrated, particularly for Brazil and Colombia, this is articulated through a discourse in which it is claimed that progress, development, and dignity are individually attainable through making the "right" educational choices. Marketized education as it is drawn into the orbit of global capitalism seeks to mobilize, as de Angelis and Harvie describe (2009, p. 8),

> even more effectively the imagination, creativity, skills and talents of all our people. This instrumental understanding of education in turn depends on using that knowledge and understanding to build economic strength and social harmony.

Education is thus conceptualized as a consumable commodity that enables individuals to become ideal liberal democratic citizens and provides them with the necessary skills to enable entrance into the globalized market, both as worker and consumer. Embedded, therefore, in the praxis of neoliberal global education is an epistemological-political project that aims to bring to truth the claims of the end of history made by the prophets of the neoliberal historic bloc.

External standards of regulation and ranking are introduced throughout the educational system through which schools, teachers, and institutions of higher education (HE) are ranked, judged, and disciplined into performing these commodified epistemological logics. Educational autonomy—from the smallest primary school to the largest institution of HE—is eroded. These practices seek to produce knowledge as a codifiable and easily transmittable object of consumption that is separated from the processes and subjects that have produced it. As Beck (1999, p. 225) describes paraphrasing Bernstein, we are "witnessing a fundamental rupture in the structuring of the relationships governing educational transmissions—a rupture which decisively (and in new ways) subordinates academic communities and priorities to purposes determined elsewhere—notably through the operation of neoliberal modes of governmentality." In the name of apparent neutrality there occurs a separation between social critique and educational endeavor (Yogev and Michaeli, 2011, p. 313). Such a separation attempts to silence indigenous knowledges, educational heritages, and pedagogical practices and instead creates logics of division, separation, and fear within educators that disarticulate pedagogical-political alternatives.

Such logics are constituted through multiple micropractices of bureaucratization and professionalization yet empower transnational economic and political actors, dedemocratizing the power of educational, pedagogical, and epistemological decision and instead placing it into the hands of the unelected elite representatives of the neoliberal historic bloc. As Beck (1999, p. 227) argues the constitution of global ranking industry contributes to the consolidation of a "regime of institutional control" that has "the capacity not only to impose the new dominant principles of market relevance, but also to ensure that these principles extend into every corner of every sector of education."

The global ranking system perniciously manifests the neoliberal logics of capitalist coloniality in which the elite institutions (representing 1%–2% of the world's universities) are overwhelmingly found in the North, who are represented as the producers of knowledge and research. Meanwhile, the global South is represented and reproduced as the passive receiver of this knowledge. Quality knowledge is represented as measurable knowledge, pedagogy as a set of techniques, and education as providing access to skills to enable entry to the globalized labor market. This reproduces an epistemological politics in the name of an objective truth that separates the word from the world and education from social transformation and political change. In the process indigenous knowledges, ways of creating knowledge and forms of knowing are disarticulated.

Of course, this also solidifies the international division of labor in which Latin America and the global South produce subjects who are competitive workers—indeed, flexible, precarious, and ultimately disposable—for transnational capital investment. These workers themselves become the massified, consumer market of transnationalized educational services and products. As Amsler and Bolsmann argue (2012, p. 287), "Universities that do not fit the Anglo-American research model are compelled to redefine themselves according to the rankings' standard criteria of value—often to the detriment of autonomous identity, local relations and social access."

In the Brazilian and Colombian cases this intensifies social, economic, and epistemological disparities, ensuring that it is generally upper-middle classes and elites that have access to internationally recognized institutions of education, while the poorer sectors of society are offered lower-quality technical courses and diplomas. As noted by Hazelkorn, this is not a specific phenomenon but rather a more generic feature of the educational logics of marketized education in which "evidence suggests rankings are propelling a growing gap between elite and mass higher education with greater institutional stratification and research concentration. HEIs which do not meet the criteria or do not have 'brand recognition' will effectively be devalued" (2007, p. 1).

Institutionally, as the Colombian and Brazilian cases demonstrate, this results in the creation of new epistemic communities of technocrats and managers who are trained in a way that naturalizes these marketized and measurable logics of education. These are the subjects who enact the new disciplinary mechanisms within the concrete contexts of schools, university, and in relation to individual educators and professors. As Rhoades and Slaughter (2004, pp. 38–39) note in relation to HE, but which is applicable across the entire education sector, this results "in the increasing corporatized, top-down style of decision making and management...their faculties have increasingly become 'managed professionals.'" The new managerialism thus extends, via manipulation of the techniques of neoliberal subjectification and the principles and practices of commodification throughout the educational landscape. Through these practices, educators are produced as disciplined subjects enacting particular performances of self with emotional repertoires and embodied enactments. The ideal-type neoliberal subject is grounded in individualization, infinite flexibility, and precarious commitments, and orientated toward survivalist competition and personally profitable exchanges. This produces a space of hierarchy, competition, and individualism through the eradication of spaces of solidarity, care, and community (Baert and Shipman, 2005, pp. 168–170). It blurs the lines between work and home through new temporal-spatial logics as educational laborers are faced with increasing workloads and pressures to perform to unremitting external performance demands. As Morini (2007, p. 47) describes,

> The house and the private area become part of the productive space. They become an explicitly money-related space, where economic subjects can be found...Working hours are changing, which eliminates the difference between time spent at work and free time. One could talk of the end of any separation between the different social times, and to the introduction of a perception of the day where there is practically no end.

This individualizes working relations and thus undercuts, through the resulting exhaustion and fragmentation of solidarity, the conditions where educational workers might contest deteriorating working conditions resulting from definancing of public education. In this context, some subjects and forms of behaving, feeling, and embodying space are empowered and legitimized. Meanwhile, others are delimited, disciplined, and subjected to the dominant logics, allowing some to judge and others to be judged.

Imposed standards of excellence and quality are those to which the ideal subject is produced against and through. Such standards drive the depoliticization and deintellectualization of school educators. For university educators these standards encourage the development of problem-solving theory, which accepts the status quo, yet concurrently oppose critical theory, which disrupts and denaturalizes the market economy. When educators and communities do not perform to these standards they face judgments that are demoralizing and shaming. Lack of performance to these standards means many educators face being moved to the bottom of the pile in terms of workload, working conditions, and precariousness. The threat of job loss is an omnipresent Damoclese sword. And as illustrated forcefully in the Colombia case, even losing their lives for noncompliance to these imposed standards. The violences of marketization are intensely embodied through the production of self-disciplining subjects articulated through abrasive dynamics of power against self and other. As Michalinos Zembylas (2003, p. 110) has observed we must "regulate and control not only our overt habits and morals, but [our] inner emotions, wishes and anxieties." Under these circumstances subjects of the school and university may tend to discipline themselves by not questioning accepted beliefs and ways of acting but simply follow them in order to avoid marginalization and/or violent eradication. Such processes disconnect educators from the very sources of knowledge from which they might derive truths, recuperate critical heritages, and articulate decolonial pedagogical practices with which to speak against the dehumanizing logics of market colonization of being.

Subjectification, Disciplining, and Disarticulation of Students

These epistemological logics that seek to subordinate, delegitimize, and disarticulate education to market logics and rationalities also interpolate students' subjectivities. The key discursive mechanism through which students enter into marketized rationalities is through the positing of education as the means through which to achieve development, democracy, and dignity. In this representation there is enacted, as we have seen in the Colombian and Brazilian cases, an individualization of social ills, in which successes or failures are placed on the individual shoulders of schools, educators, students, and students' families.

As Amsler (2011, p. 71) argues, within this neoliberal discourse, "in order for the state to privatise public universities it must force students to pay, persuade them that they should pay, or convince them that there is no alternative." Accordingly, governments represent public sector education as failing, budgetary constraints as inevitable, and teachers as special interest group defending their privileges when they resist such processes. This creates divisions and mistrust between critical educators and oppressed communities, thereby undercutting the very conditions that might foster a critical and liberatory practice of education. Thus, in the name of equality of consumer choice, processes are enacted that break the power of educators and their ability to articulate alternative pedagogical-political projects, subjects, and horizons, ultimately reinforcing pernicious inequalities.

Such a discourse of democratizing education is articulated through the normalization of systems of external rankings. Through the institutionalization of such systems it is claimed that consumer-students are provided with the information to make informed choices about the educational products best suited to their needs. The responsibility to choose the best educational product to ensure individual success and inclusion is internalized into the students' subjectivity. Such technologies of governance produce in the very desires of the poorest of students the objective of obtaining education as a way out of poverty and naturalization that the only way to ensure such access is through private financing.

Thus, in the name of democracy, processes of the dedemocratization of education occur as transnational representatives of finance capital and intellectual experts of international financial institutions (IFIs) determine standards of quality, excellence, and value in relation to the needs and logics of the global market. As Collini argues (2011, p. 9), "All this talk about 'the student experience' starts to betray the purposes of education is in its focus on a narrow form of short-term box-ticking satisfaction." This legitimizes external unaccountable interventions into the policy-making decisions of Latin American governments, reinforcing the epistemological and political hierarchies of capitalist coloniality in which it is the technical rationalities of the Western white-bourgeois monological imperial subjects that define the contours and possibilities of what it means to know, create knowledge, and ultimately organize society. This removes the possibility of students (and educators) from enacting democratic decision making in relation to pedagogies, educational objectives, and epistemological-political logics. Such dedemocratizing processes thus disarticulate the pedagogical possibilities through which counterhegemonic subjectivities, social relationships, and ways of life might be imagined and articulated.

Indeed, the naturalization in the desires of poor students of the need to pay for educational products and service as a means to become a competitive worker and ensure access to the consumer market embeds more deeply inequities in access and possibility. As we have demonstrated many become indebted to gain access to poor-quality privatized educational services, which offer education as quantifiable skills. They are therefore denied and excluded from educational and pedagogical experiences, which articulate alternative epistemological horizons and readings of the world that could enable a reauthoring of excluded communities as collective agents able to transform their conditions of exclusion into dignity, agency, and social power. This reinforces the reproduction of the colonizer's logics into the self-understandings of the oppressed who come to devalue their knowledges and wisdoms, those of their fellow educators, and instead place their faith and belief in the patriarchal colonial prophets of neoliberal hegemony. The result is to situate the European subject as the center through which all knowledge practice and subject are judged and delegitimized (Agathangelou and Ling, 2004). The epistemological logics of patriarchal capitalist coloniality thus attempt to produce subjects who are removed from their capacity to enact relationships other than those of alienation and power-over. The colonizer's logics become embodied in the self-judgments, enacted as a consequence of the internalization of a discourse of individualization of social ills. The epistemological politics of contemporary capitalist coloniality thus attempts to separate the oppressed from their creative, intellectual, and spiritual capacities through which to unlearn dominant rationalities, social relationships, and subjectivities. The possibilities of learning to produce themselves, social relationships, and their communities differently remain closed under this colonial capitalistic logic.

Decolonizing Epistemological Practices, Projects, and Subjects

Our work to deconstruct the hegemonic practices, representations, and logics of the epistemological politics of neoliberal capitalist coloniality, particularly in the Brazilian and Colombian cases, denaturalizes the current hegemonic contours of educational thinking and practice. In this way it can help open possibilities of critical reflection on the current conditions that we find ourselves in as educators or students, and as those concerned with the question of how to construct alternatives to neoliberal globalization. However, such a practice of critique as negation, as we have attempted to demonstrate through the three case studies of Colombia, Brazil, and Venezuela, is not enough. As hooks (1990, 15) describes,

> In that vacant space after one has resisted there is still the necessity to become—to make oneself anew... That process emerges as one comes to understand how structures of domination work in one's own life, as one invents alternative habits of being and resists from marginal space of difference inwardly defined.

And it is here that the ethical commitments and epistemological practice of decolonial, feminist, and radical educators seem pertinent. For as is suggested by bell hooks, those from the margins—be they internationally marginalized countries in the international division of labor, or oppressed communities and individuals produced on the margins of contemporary forms of patriarchal capitalist coloniality—have epistemic privilege in the reimagining of new forms of emancipatory pedagogical-political practices, projects, and subjectivities. As de Angelis and Harvie (2009, p. 28) argue in relation to HE but which is applicable across broad education,

> A first step is to make our opposition more public and visible, in order to decouple as much as possible the priorities of competitiveness and profit-seeking from those of knowledge and social production. Just as capitalist measure is based on a social process that seeks to define the *how*, the *what*, and the *how much*, and to subordinate these to accumulation, a recomposition of the fragmented struggles in [higher] education must occur on the basis of alternative values and measures of the *what*, *how much* and *how*. (Emphasis original)

Arguably, it is in the practices of Latin American educators, students, and social movements that such decoupling in theory and practice, through the development of alternative pedagogical-political projects, is being created. Through these struggles and pedagogical practices countries, communities, and subjects are learning to produce themselves differently and create the contours, conditions, and practices of a deeply democratic and multiple reimagined twenty-first-century socialism. This, of course, turns on its head the epistemological representations and logics of hegemonic articulations of regimes of knowledge and truth of contemporary capitalism, as it suggests that as opposed to being the passive, uneducated, and underdeveloped underside of Western modernity, Latin America's majorities are at the forefront of reimagining the horizons of social emancipation.

In what follows, I systematize the pedagogical-political projects and practices and the epistemological politics of the counterhegemonic decolonizing practices of educators, students, and social movements in Brazil, Colombia, and Venezuela. I offer these as an invitation to critical reflection through which we might embrace alternative epistemological and pedagogical horizons from the margins that can support our learning to produce ourselves, our communities, and our worlds as alternatives to capitalism, regardless of geography.

Latin American Critical Educators

The pedagogical-political projects that have been developed across the three cases by educators are all embedded in the rich traditions of Latin American decolonizing epistemological and philosophical traditions. Capitalist coloniality is conceptualized as a practice that not only shapes the external economic, political, social, and cultural contours that produce underdevelopment, but also shapes the subjectivities of the colonized. Thus, the struggle for social emancipation is inherently pedagogical as it involves the unlearning of the colonizers' logics and their transformation into decolonizing practices, subjectivities, and emancipatory projects. As Monsignor Jose Joaquin Salcedo Guarin one of the founders of Acción Cultural Popular (Popular Cultural Action) in Colombia explains,

> To open the path to solutions it is necessary to open the mind of man, creating consciousness of their own personal dignity, developing this and putting it to work in the improvement of their life through their personal-community struggles.

Revolution cannot, therefore, happen without an educational and epistemological revolution in the everyday practices of oppressed communities. He continues, "As dreaming doesn't cost us anything, can we vision the consequences of enabling Latin American countries to integrate so as to implement a deep educational revolution to enable the development of human potential."

Traditions of radical education, such as Popular Cultural Action in Colombia and popular education projects in Venezuela and Brazil influenced by Paolo Freire's critical praxis, can be conceptualized as decolonizing practices. Through such educational praxis, critical educators in all three countries have attempted to disrupt the logics of capitalist coloniality in communities of the oppressed. Here, there is a challenge to the epistemological logics of capitalist coloniality through pedagogical practices and projects, which themselves propagate the appearance of subjugated knowledges by decentering the word as separate from the world as the dominant rationality of a disembodied and individualized knowing subject. In stark contrast, critical educational projects are intensely embedded in the present and processes of the embodied experiences of oppression and thus attentive to the concrete and rootedness of community in history, spatiality, cosmology, culture, and social relations.

Critical educational praxis is concerned with creating dialogues of knowledges to foster collective reflection on practice and experience by oppressed communities. Here the contours of good sense become the groundwork from which critical readings of the world in thought and practice can be constructed. As Freire (cited in Cotos, 2013, p. 112) describes, "Dialogue is an existential demand and enables a form of meeting which fosters reflection and action...Dialogue is the terrain which grants meaning to desires, aspirations, dreams, hopes and makes possible an exchange of ideas and critical conversations that emerge from reality...To exist humanly is to speak the world...Dialogue is the meeting of people mediated by the world, which enables such a speaking of the world." Thus, processes of reauthoring ourselves and unlearning colonized beliefs, practices, and relationships between self and other become pivotal to the construction of speaking the world and creating alternative ways of life.

Dialogical construction breaks the domination of monological thought, practice, and being as it opens up the space for multiplicity, for doubts, questions, and discontent with the world as it is (both internal and external). To foster such dialogical spaces involves an ethical commitment to listening to and speaking with the other, within and without. As Anzaldúa articulates,

> We (women of colour) knew we were different, set apart, exiled from what is considered "normal." And as we internalised this exile, we came to see the alien within us and too often, as a result, we split apart from ourselves and each other. Forever after we have been in search of that self, that "other" and each other. (Cited in Keating, 2009, p. ix)

The critical educator thus creates spaces imbued with an ethical commitment to the exiled other within and without, thus nurturing new forms of intimacy, solidarity, and understanding. This as hooks (2001, p. 9) describes means "[to] choose the model of interbeing and interdependency [and] begin the work of restoring integrity and with integrity comes care of the soul."

Thus, the form of knowledge construction that foregrounds the critical educator practices is also decolonized as it enacts a collective coconstruction of knowledges that can support processes of social and subjective transformation. This is often premised on the popular education methodology that involves five steps: describe, thematize, theorize, evaluate, and strategize. Here oppressed communities who are represented by the dominant paradigm as uneducated, failures, delinquents, and underdeveloped, themselves develop intellectual, creative, and critical capacities. In the process they overturn the division of labor of capitalist coloniality in which there are thinkers and doers, knowers and known.

The pedagogical-political projects developed by radical educators are epistemologically committed to the building of knowledge for transformation arising from the experience of oppression and exclusion, and the fragments of good sense and subaltern knowledges, found immanent to these experiences. Thus, culture becomes a nexus that is theorized as the linkage between the pedagogical and the political. The educator thus embraces multiple forms of knowledge and produces pedagogical practices as multiple, interior, and immanent to communities' experiences, beliefs, and traditions. As Boom (2010) explains, "Pedagogical knowledge enriches in its multiplicity by creating nexus between literature, story, music, art, languages."

In the Latin American context this has included recovering and the reclaiming of misnamed popular traditions and everyday religiosities. These include indigenous, Afro-Colombian, Venezuelan, and Brazilian spiritual practices and politicized forms of Catholicism, most notably liberation theology. In all three cases there are invisibilized histories of radical educational practices enacted by critical educators that have built upon these heritages. For example, in the case of liberation theology, radical pedagogical practices—characterized by an ethical commitment to the body of suffering poor, faith realized through action for the oppressed, the Bible reread collectively, a focus on direct access to the word of God, and a commitment to self-actualization of the oppressed through their own liberation—are shaped (Boff and Boff, 1987, pp. 1–9). As Boff and Boff (1987, p. 9) describe, it is a biblical frame of reference in which "knowing implies loving, letting oneself become involved body and soul, communing wholly—being committed."

This has wrought an educational practice that is deeply democratic and decentralized, committed to the flourishing of radical difference and multiplicity that has shaped a new logic of emancipatory politics. Such logics transgress twentieth-century forms of revolutionary praxis, which themselves reinscribed representational and vertical logics of the political, in the process legitimizing the separation of the means of revolutionary struggles from the ends. In contrast to twentieth-century practice, these twenty-first century articulations of revolutionary practice develop through and with subaltern cultural and spiritual traditions. This positions the pedagogical process of transformation as central as the outcomes of such processes. As such, oppressed subjects and communities come to find their dignity, wisdom, and develop the creative capacities to transform their communities and societies. Here processes of mass intellectuality are created, with a conceptualization of intellectuality, which subverts that of capitalist coloniality.

Centrally, such pedagogical practices involve a reconceptualization of the role of the educator and the school. These political-pedagogical practices are often framed as a struggle over creating the conditions and possibilities for "other teachers" and "other schools." Here the educator is conceptualized as an organic intellectual who is ethically and politically committed to developed pedagogies for and with the oppressed. To contest the depoliticizing, deprofessionalizing, and disarticulating logics of contemporary forms of marketized education, educators of revolutionary practice are situated as intellectuals and producers of knowledge, not mere implementers of technical skills and measurable sound bites of consumable knowledge. This seeks to overcome the separation and deintellectualization of teacher practice through the recombining of teaching, research, and political practice.

At the heart of such a practice is resistance to the external implementation of systems of ranking, policies of professionalization, and standardized curriculum development. Radical teachers have been at the heart of challenges to such logics by exposing authoritarian and dedemocratizing intentions that remove the autonomy of educators, communities, and countries to self-determine their economic, political, and social destinies. As workers, critical educators in Brazil and Colombia have been at the heart of union organizing to contest the definancing of public education and destruction of the rights and guarantees of educators. Yet as Boom (2010, p. 4) suggests, critical educators' struggles "cannot be reduced to moments of counter-power or resistance, but also something different, to reconstructing politics in a more productive way."

The affirmative epistemological practice suggested by Boom has occurred but often in the shadows of discussions and reflections about the reconstruction of popular politics in Latin America. These everyday commitments to projects, practices, and networks of radical educators are often invisibilized and devalued in the struggle for social transformation. Yet they have continued throughout the neoliberalization of education in Brazil and Colombia, and have coexisted with the reproduction of a conservative and elitist educational teaching practice in Venezuela, notwithstanding the broader revolutionary political and educational processes set in motion by the election to power of Chávez.

Often, these practices and projects have involved forging spaces of pedagogical possibility within neoliberal hegemonic structures, relationships, and processes of subjectification. They are to be found in the margins of university departments and centers dedicated to radical educational practice, and within school collectives and groups of critical educators who over decades have painstakingly created alternative curriculum and courses. Networks in Colombia, Brazil, and Venezuela have been autonomously cocreated to enable alternative temporalities and spatialities to those of neoliberal educational spatiotemporalities. Here educators have come together to continually reflect on their practices and systematize methodologies, pedagogies, and decolonizing practices. These alternative spatiotemporalities are forged through creating alternative logics of relating, in which dynamics of competition, hierarchy, and discipline are transformed into logics of care, solidarity, and dialogue.

While these pedagogical practices of radical education that foster the creation of critical educators and mass intellectuality often occur within formal educational spaces and sites, they are inherently transgressive of the logics of separation that underpin formal bourgeois education. Such logics of separation seek to reproduce the separation of the word from the world, education from community, and learning from political transformation. Thus, these projects and practices of necessity work in, against, and beyond the school or university. Notions of validity, quality, and objectives are forged in relation to the concrete needs of the communities in which an institution is embedded. The dialogue of knowledges forged in this process therefore brings together educators, students, their families, communities, and social movements. Learning necessarily escapes the classroom walls and is linked to projects of participatory and militant research, which disrupt the dualism between teacher and student, allowing all the potential to become learners and cocreators of knowledge for transformation.

Not surprisingly, critical educators have often been at the center of practices and representations of delegitimization, deprofessionalization, and devalorization. They often face some of the harshest forms of the disciplinary and coercive mechanisms of the neoliberal state. The development of critical educational projects and practices therefore involves constant collective and political struggle to ensure their survival and continuation. Such struggles involve negotiation, navigation, and contestation of the contours of neoliberal hegemony and its contradictions in Brazil and Colombia. In the Venezuelan case, this requires navigation of the contradictions in the process of constructing twenty-first century socialism out of the ashes of twentieth-century neoliberal capitalism.

The three cases discussed in this book are representative of the spectrum of state formations and hegemonic constructions of neoliberalism in the continent. The following paragraphs provide a summary.

The Venezuelan example is a national process of construction of twenty-first century socialism. Here, there is active commitment to the creation of a socialist state and a process of revolutionary transformation that places education for self-liberation at the heart of its political practices. Yet the birth of a new multiple, becoming and deeply democratic revolutionary processes of necessity, comes into tension and contradiction with the old capitalist state and its ideological-educational apparatus. This is concretely manifested in the figure of the educator, for whom many have been trained in the epistemological logics, practices, and subjectivities that reinforces patriarchal capitalist coloniality and which views the popular as lacking, ignorant, and to be filled with the knowledges of the colonizer in order to create civilized and modern subjects of democracy and development. Thus, practices, projects, and subjects of radical education often face barriers and limits to their generalization and socialization from entrenched institutions, practices, and subjects of hegemonic education. However, again it is through the concrete practices of creating "other" schools and "other" teachers that the possibilities of decolonizing epistemological practices are fostered and consolidated, thereby creating processes of self-liberation of the oppressed.

In the Brazilian case the contradictory construction of neoliberal hegemony by the governments of the Workers' Party (PT) has opened a fragmented and often disorientating terrain of struggle for critical educators and subaltern communities. Critical educators find themselves within a broader political-pedagogical state practice that fosters the monological epistemological logics of capitalist coloniality and disarticulates the possibilities for decolonizing pedagogical-political projects. Yet, the popular history of the PT and its linkages to movements and communities in struggle, radical intellectuals, and leftist organizations has also manifested in contradictory possibilities opened up in educational policy, rhetoric, and practice. Such possibilities have only been realized in relation to organized communities able to politicize and radicalize these contradictions. Such counter-hegemonic practices and openings exist within a broader, hegemonic neoliberal epistemological politics, and thus remain fragmented and often disconnected. Yet the possibilities of alternative epistemological-political projects, practices, and social relations are being constructed in the everyday struggles of critical educators. Spaces of possibility are emerging and practices of coconstruction of unlearning of dominant subjectivities, social relationships, and ways of life are being forged.

In the Colombian situation the militarized neoliberal state and governance has fostered a much clearer space of exteriority and otherness for critical educators. This has shaped their educational struggles and practice in a way that is clearly opposed to authoritarian logics and has attempted to maintain and develop autonomous educational spaces of possibility. Interestingly in such adverse macroconditions, the relative level of pedagogical-political consolidation is deeper and more consolidated than in the Brazilian case. The antipopular nature of capitalist hegemony in Colombia has created a terrain of significant possibility for alternative educational-pedagogical projects, practices, and subjects. This has enabled the politicization of the contradictions in neoliberal hegemony with respect to the promises of education as a way to "buy paradise and prosperity." As we have demonstrated this has resulted in the explosion onto the political stage of a new radical student movement to which we now turn.

Students: Reoccupying the Political

Student movements have arisen in the global South and North to contest the promises of neoliberal discourse that dignity, development, and freedom would be theirs through the acquisition of education. Such processes of deepening of marketization and transnational private sector management, design, and coordination of education have often been developed in the name of educational revolutions committed to social justice, democracy, and economic development. Yet such processes have reproduced evermore-egregious inequalities in access to quality education, with the poorest of students having to carry the burden of debt to ensure consumption of educational goods, which often do not result in the promised land of freedom and opportunity. This has created intense and widening fault lines in neoliberal hegemony, where struggles over public education have become struggles over the contours and nature of democratic life and of the political itself. Student movements have been at the forefront of politicizing these fault lines. As De Angelis and Harvie (2009, p. 28) argue, such movements are necessary to socialize and generalize struggles over educational and epistemological paradigms being enacted as

> a recomposition of the fragmented struggles in education...on the basis of alternative values and measures of the *what, how much* and *how*. Here, the "frontline" between these two conceptions of value and measure [marketization vs. emancipatory horizons and practices] must become visible and the object of public, open debate. (Emphasis original)

Student movements in Colombia have arguably made public a critique in body, thought, and practice of the technologies, rationalities, and processes of subjectification of marketized (higher) education. They have done this through developing pedagogies of everyday life in which a reoccupation of the political has been enacted. Such a reoccupation has reverberations throughout the social logics of militarized capitalist coloniality in Colombia and beyond, given that they do not merely articulate a negation of these logics but put into public practice alternative epistemological logics to produce themselves and democratic life differently.

Building on the heritages of popular educational micropractices, these student movements from the onset of Uribe's educational revolution initiated the process of building the conditions to appear as subjects on the political stage. The moment of rupture in which the movement appeared was thus preceded by micropedagogical practices that involved creating the conditions for communities of resistance, structures of feeling, and alternative measures of value from which to articulate a critique of marketized education. Thus, spaces had been created within universities to foster critical discussion and reflection on Uribe's educational revolution and to take seriously the need to recompose the fragmented social and political fabric that was the result of the intensification of militarized neoliberalism, implemented in the name of democratic security from the early 2000s. Therefore, while it is important to recognize the radical breaks that such moments embody, it is equally important to recognize the continuities and traditions of preexisting struggles present in these events for the lessons that can be learnt about the pedagogies of possibility that foster the conditions of possibility for the emergence of new popular political subjects.

The movement was clearly influenced by previous traditions of radical education because their conceptualization of pedagogical struggles is inherently political and connected to the possibilities of producing alternative democratic horizons, practices, and subjects. Thus, from its visible appearance in 2011, it made a set of integral demands that included the working conditions and well-being of all educational workers, the autonomy of educational institutions and educators to develop pedagogical and educational contents, development of curriculum and methodologies, and the necessity of reimaging democracy through creating processes in which "society" could construct educational reforms. The movement also destabilized hegemonic articulations of the knowing subject by dethroning the "expert" disassociated from the needs of ordinary Colombians, and instead embracing the multiplicity of needs and experiences of these subjects and their intellectual capacities and creativity. As part of this, multiple forms of literacy and knowledge were embraced including the pivotal role of the cultural to link the pedagogical and political. Thus, the movement embraced multiple tactics including theatrical representations, occupations, marches, social media, and public parody. Their ethics of practice were committed to the other and therefore embedded in antiauthoritarian logics of dialogue and pluralism contesting the monological authoritarian logics of marketized education and ways of life.

Through these practices they developed affective pedagogies that disrupted the emotional and embodied hierarchies of politics as normal in which control of the emotions, mastery of others, and practices of shaming were dominant. Instead, they used laughter, parody, and affection, for example, to reoccupy and re-create immanently the public space of the political. This also created the conditions for the decolonization of student subjectivities as competitive, instrumental, and individualized subjects, instead creating openings to the possibility of relationships of solidarity, commitment, and care. Alternative grounds of becoming political were fostered through these practices, which decentered the disembodied, monological, and individualized subject of knowledge of neoliberal capitalist coloniality.

The embrace of multiple literacies and knowledges as texts of transformation such as video, dance, music, theater, social media, and text decentered the word separate from the world as the pinnacle of knowing, knowledge, and creating knowledge. In this way, they opened the possibilities for multiple readings and practices of reading their struggle for a democratic, participatory, public, and autonomous education. The processes of creating these tactics were pedagogical in that students and allies developed methods and methodologies with which to coproduce movement materials. As well as decentering dominant literacies, these experiences also created the grounds of becoming political subjects differently.

The use of repertoires of action that involved the occupation of public space fostered possibilities for public enactment of other spatiotemporalities and practices of creating community, however temporarily, that transgressed those of commodified, depoliticized, and militarized Colombian society. In such situations students inevitably had to ask questions about how to put into practice antiauthoritarian logics committed to a radical participatory democracy in which communities governed themselves. Such spaces of experimentation foster qualitative processes of individual and collective learning that consolidate the grounds for the reimagining of democratic life and democratic subjectivities. As Amsler argues in relation to the UK student movement but which is apt for thinking and reflecting about the Colombian and broader experiences of student movement's use of occupation, "It thus bears thinking about occupation not as a model of political action but as one articulation of an ethos of critical experimentation...an attitude toward being that struggles to expand and resignify space and time while inhabiting them with others."

The consolidation of alternative pedagogical-political projects of democratic life, enabled by these experiences, was manifested in the development of a nationwide process of democratic and collective coconstruction of alternative reform proposals. These were in stark contrast to that offered by Santos and to which the students' mass mobilizations had been a response. Here methodologies rooted in popular education were experimented with across the country by thousands of students. From these autonomous local methodological processes of mapping, the major thematics that the alternative proposal should be based upon moved to regional and national spaces again developed through democratic methodologies of reflection and systematization. These processes of systematization were then returned to the local level to be debated, refined, and developed again through the use of methodologies rooted in radical education. The process continues to be refined until the present day (i.e., late 2013). Such a colossal process no doubt has developed the pedagogical skills, practices, and understandings for thousands of students and allies across Colombia. The continued consolidation of such alternative epistemological horizons and pedagogical practices into a popular project of democratization will depend on the ability to link these struggles over value in education to other struggles for social reproduction. Of course, it is here that the systematization of the role of the pedagogical in social transformation enacted by Latin American social movements becomes pivotal in visioning how to consolidate and nurture processes of unlearning of dominant relationships and subjectivities and the learning of new ones.

Pedagogies of Democratic Life: Decolonizing in Thought and Practice

Popular education and radical pedagogies are at the heart of enabling the conditions of emergence of a reinvented emancipatory politics from below and the immanent development of the movement's emancipatory visions, practices, subjectivities, and ways of life. Some of the most complex decolonial pedagogical practices are being developed by those who face multiple oppressions, particularly poor-nonwhite women. This suggests that it is from the epistemological margins that an emancipatory practice for our times is emerging that can decenter the epistemological-political logics of patriarchal capitalist coloniality through negation and affirmative epistemological creation of the world and ourselves differently. Such processes of remembering, re-creating, and reweaving themselves and the world are deeply pedagogical. They suggest that it is time to recognize the inherently pedagogical nature of the political and to declare our commitment to a politicization of the pedagogical.

Processes of informal learning are key in the (re)construction of sociabilities, political subjectivities, and collectivities. The pedagogical here is not merely understood as practices and methodologies that enable the creation of collective readings of the world that can shape political strategy and analysis. Rather the pedagogical becomes an essential part in the coming into being of popular political subjectivities and organizations, of creating the openings, possibilities, and relationships that enable communities often silenced and violently invisibilized to appear as embodied political subjects. Here pedagogies of reoccupying and re-creating space, integrated with affective pedagogical processes, become central.

Like in the case of Mesa Amplia Nacional Estudiantil (MANE) in Colombia, the practices of the Solidarity Economy (SE) enable spaces of communion in which women and men come together and share space, time, and experiences in workshops and meetings in a safe space where all have the right to speak. This is a collective learning process that creates solidarities, collectivities, affinities, and shared histories of coconstruction. SE offers moments of self-reflection that often do not result in immediate outcomes or decisions but rather create alternate temporalities from those of the constant demands of precarity and political organizing, consequently fostering connections of solidarity and care between individuals and communities.

In the movimento dos trabalhadores rurais sem terra (Landless Rural Workers' Movement, MST) there are similar pedagogical processes that have helped create the conditions of possibility for the emergence of a new popular and pluralistic political actor. The occupation and organization of settlements is an intensely pedagogical process that is built upon a dialogue of knowledges in which the cultural becomes the linchpin between processes of informal learning and political and subjective transformation. Through the building of communities of resistance and alternative forms of social reproduction and production, individuals and families unlearn the logics of individualization and survival characteristic of neoliberal capitalism and instead (re)learn practices of mutuality, care, and sharing. This rerooting of communities in their histories and land enable popular political subjects to emerge that forge emancipatory cultural practices, moral economies, emotional landscapes, and ways of life.

The practice of the Escuela demonstrates the importance of creating safe and intimate space of trust through which to enable women that have historically suffered multiple oppressions and who are represented as ignorant and apolitical come to voice and agency. These then foster the conditions of possibility for women to reoccupy the space of the public and in the process reconstruct the political. This opens horizons of hope through which to imagine alternatives to militarized capitalist coloniality. These experiences blur the boundaries between the political (public) and social (private) and the competitive separations between women fostered by patriarchal capitalist coloniality creating the conditions of possibility for new forms of sociability, solidarity, and sisterhood out of which women can build their political power and social autonomy.

Such informal learning processes create the conditions of possibility for the emergence of new popular democratic political subjects and movements. The experiences of the MST, the Escuela, and La Mascara suggest that reoccupations of the space of the public, the private, and the embodied subject are key in these processes. They also suggest that embodied and affective pedagogies that enact practices of coming to voice and active listening are at the heart of the politics of knowledge of emergent popular projects and struggles. The conditions of emergence of new popular emancipatory subjects and movements are therefore inherently dialogical, in which the means and ends of struggle contest the monological logics of capitalist coloniality.

As we have demonstrated, developing alternatives to colonial capitalism involves exceeding the logics of the form of knowledge production constitutive of the geopolitics of knowledge of (neoliberal) capitalist coloniality. Such excess is being actively developed by social movements and collectives across the continent (Ceceña, 2012; Colectivo Situaciones, 2003; Denis, 2012). Collective processes of knowledge production, building on traditions and histories of popular education are important ways in which movements and communities are developing their own theoretical and strategic readings of the world. Such readings begin from the lived experiences and oppressed bodies of the excluded, enabling deeper understanding, the flourishing of multiple literacies and knowledges, and the creation of tools to change their conditions (Motta, 2013c). This involves bringing dignity and agency to those who are otherwise written over by dominant intellectual and political discourses. This rethinking of alternatives challenges the divisions between thinkers and doers, and mind and body that characterizes colonial patriarchal capitalism.

The MST and SE use popular education to combine different knowledges: those of the academy, those of popular culture and philosophy, and those of community experience. From this reflexive dialogue between knowledges, they build strategic coherence within particular MST rural communities and methodologies of the coconstruction of economic cooperatives. These function as lynch pins in producing communities differently from patriarchal colonial capitalism. Such popular education practices have developed into formal educational projects that link the university, state, and communities in struggle, bridging boundaries and borders of knowing and relating. Here subjects from multiple perspectives, experiences, and spaces come together and through a dialogue of knowledges, design and develop curriculum and transferable methodologies around issues and forms of knowledge relevant to MST and solidarity communities' lives and struggles. The objective is to create the conditions of producing their communities and social relationships in ways that transgress capitalism and build the groundwork for a reinvented socialism of the twenty-first century that is deeply democratic, multiple, and epistemologically committed to cocreating knowledges for transformation of and by the oppressed.

Similar to such a pedagogical practice is the work of the Escuela and La Máscara in which women learn to rename the world and speak the world in new ways by building on the lived knowledges and experiences of participants. Here again methodologies based in popular education and theater of the oppressed are developed, experimented with, and systematized with the aim of coconstructing multiple forms of knowledge that can decolonize the hearts, minds, bodies, and social relationships of participants. Both movements share a commitment to exceeding the logics of form of knowledge production of capitalist coloniality through commitments to mass intellectuality, an embrace of multiple knowledges, and multiple pedagogies. Such postrepresentational and prefigurative practices transgress the representational logics of capitalist coloniality that mark and oppress women's lives. They instead nurture the possibilities of reoccupations of the body, heart, and soul, which enable women to contest and radically transform these logics. As we have demonstrated many popular processes of social and political emancipation are premised upon a politicization of knowledge in both its form and content. This means that pedagogies of resistance and transformation have become embedded in the complexities of experience and desire of subaltern urban and rural communities. Thus, the affective and the embodied have been brought to the heart of the praxis of popular transformation. There are two main ways in which this occurs: the development of affective and embodied pedagogies and as a result of these pedagogies, the expansion of the objectives of social and political transformation to include affective and embodied relationships and experiences. The MST develops affective and embodied pedagogies, in a critical reading of the world that involves building learning spaces in which the totality of participants' experiences are engaged with. Thus, the use of mística involves pedagogies of the imagination and pedagogies of the body enacted through cultural practice, which enable critical intimacy and collective trust to develop. Here the wisdom of touch is pedagogical in that it helps form the bonds and openings to intimacies and solidarities that reach beyond competitive individualism (Motta, 2013c).

The Escuela and La Máscara develop a multiplicity of embodied, affective, and spiritual pedagogies, which include creating a dialogue between "ancestral practices, others which are emergent from cultural context and others which are new" (Diáz and Bermúdez, 2009, p. 3). These enable a stepping inward, thereby facilitating awareness of how systems of oppression work to remove the capacity to enact relationships, other than those of alienation and power-over that fragment hearts, minds, and body. These pedagogies enable exploration and conceptualization of how patriarchal capitalist coloniality creates wounds that become embedded in our bodies, distort our emotions, separate us from our souls, and limit our creative capacities.

The feminist decolonial popular educator thus turns toward the other and everyday life by coconstructing the conditions for voice, speaking, and listening. Anzaldúa (2009c, p. 75) explains, "If I'm talking to you but not really listening or observing your body language and I'm not really empathic with you, I don't really hear or see you. It's a multilevel kind of listening...You listen with both outer ear and inner ear. This is the spiritual dimension...which combines activism with inner, subjective listening." Here the power of authorship and knowing cannot be imprisoned in a solitary and abstract mind of the knower, hence the earlier critique of Gramscian interpretation. It is necessarily dispersed in multiple subjects, forms, and communities who come to value and nurture their inner life, their knowing, and their truth as they (we) begin to build the conditions for collective and critical readings of the world that enable their (our) transformation. This sets the grounds for inclusive difference in intimacy in which critique unfolds as lives lived in openness to multiplicity and difference. As Anzaldúa (2009a, p. 49) eloquently describes, it is "a going deep into the self and an expanding out into the world, a simultaneous recreation of the self and a reconstruction of society."

The embodied enactments and affective commitments of such a popular community educator cannot involve practicing knowledge as mastery over the known and control over the unruly emotions and embodied self, as does the knowing-subject of coloniality. Rather she commits to emotional opening and embodied trust through which she finds the courage to make visible (her) embodied experiences and internalized wounds. She thus facilitates practices that support the coconstruction of spaces of communion through nurturing safety and recognition. As hooks (2003, p. 216) explains, "We cannot really risk emotionally in relationships where we do not feel safe."

Central to such performance of critique is an ethics and practice of love. Love not in its individualized, commodified, and bourgeois form as lover of possessions, power over the other, and the disembodiment of desire. In this alternative interpretation, love is perceived as an ethics of affirmation of power with and within. This enables a stepping through anger toward self-love and love for the other. Such a transformation of the pain and anger of denial and devaluation into relationships of becoming, opening, and integrity involves crossings into the borderlands (Anzaldúa 2009b). For Anzaldúa such crossings are multiple and take us to our borders of self and certainty. As she describes (Anzaldúa, 2007, p. 48), "Every increment of consciousness, every step forward is a travesia, a crossing. I am again an alien in new territory. And again, and again."

The affective attributes of enabling such a practice of love cannot involve practices of shaming, which is one of the central ways of creating the distorted masculinities of colonial patriarchal capitalism. Rather as has been demonstrated, such spaces and relationships are enacted through critical practices of affirmation and emotional opening. This is not a denial of the importance of pain, grief, or anger in our coming to voice and agency but rather suggests the development of practices of emotional alchemy that are "difficult...painful" but enable their transformation into joy, courage, and love, "without which there can be no wholeness" (hooks, 2004, p. 156).

Here pedagogies of discomfort are at play, not destructive discomfort but discomfort as a horizon of possibility realized through a politics of care. Such a politics of care implies collectivizing care of the self and other. This ethics of care is not the patriarchal articulation of the caring maternal role through which women are interpolated into individualized and sacrificial roles. Rather, La Máscara and La Escuela foster transgressions in patriarchal femininities toward a feminist ethic of care as a basis from which to forge commitment, responsibility, and sociability that can contribute to the building of the infrastructure of agency of the oppressed.

The ethics and practice of love and politics of care are inherently pedagogical and involve the collective coconstruction of multiple forms of knowledge and ways of weaving the world and ourselves. The affective and embodied pedagogies characteristic of such spaces and enactment of emancipatory praxis are those of the loving eye, the tender touch, the attentive ear, and the knowing heart. Here song, dance, and ritual—in which bodies, hearts, minds, and souls meet— are the epitomes of these revolutionary pedagogies. These threads create a weaving that remembers and honors women's histories and through which novel structures, conceptions of self, and social relationships are reworked.

Conclusion

Pedagogizing the political and politicizing the pedagogical in the multiple and complex ways demonstrated throughout this book push for recognition that epistemological practices and pedagogical-political projects are struggles for decolonization of our hearts, mind, bodies (including the body of the land), and spirits.

This construction of twenty-first century socialism emerges from the margins, from those subjects and communities that have been violently denied, denigrated, and invisibilized by patriarchal capitalist coloniality. As Anzaldúa argues those who are pushed out and have faced multiple oppressions are most likely to develop *la facultad*—the capacity to see in surface phenomena the meaning of deeper realities (2007, p. 60). The ones possessing this sensitivity are "excruciatingly alive to the world" and from critical collective remembering, re-creating, and reweaving these experiences can develop the most complex and multiple forms of liberatory praxis.

This I believe focuses our attention on asking important questions about how might we as critical educators, students, and communities unlearn dominant ways of producing ourselves, our relationships, and communities and learn new ones. Such practices of unlearning and learning cannot be forged with the master's epistemological and pedagogical tools. For as Luce Irigaray argues (Irigaray and Burke, 1980),

> If we continue to speak the same language to each other, we will reproduce the same story. Begin the same stories all over again. Don't you feel it?...Same arguments, same quarrels, same scenes. Same attractions and separations. Same difficulties, the impossibility of reaching each other. Same...Same...Always the same.

Rather we can learn from the radical educational practices and in dialogue with the radical educators from the epistemological margins, disrupting the gaze that focuses on the pedagogical practices and epistemological politics of the powerful. The counterhegemonic practices analyzed in this book are embedded in a number of epistemological, ethical, and political commitments. We have sought throughout the writing of this work to systematize these as a means to offer creative and challenging ways to stimulate reflexive and critical praxis in other spaces of pedagogical innovation and experimentation.

They include a commitment to weave the world and ourselves anew through creating spaces of radical communion that imbue our experiences of oppression and survival with divinity and power. Here the critical educator enters in her nakedness in such spaces not as the liberated or the liberator but as a participant in practices of healing and transformation. Such an affirmative epistemological practice is embedded in an ethics and practice of love and politics of care. It enacts not a stepping outside but a stepping inward to the other, within and without.

This opens our epistemological horizons to multiple knowledges, multiple subjects of knowing, and multiple practices of creating knowledge. Here, the organic intellectuals are one and many, self as other, and speak, write, and become in multiple tongues. This enables a speaking from, and of, the margins as "a new location from which to articulate our sense of the world," which enacts a (collective) speaking of truth to power that in its practice creates us and our society anew.

Annexure 1: MANE Methodology of Programmatic Construction of the Alternative Project of Reform of Higher Education

We have considered the construction of a collective methodology as the means through which we can develop an alternative reform proposal for higher education (HE), beginning from the Minimum Program for Students declaration. This reformed program needs to contain the sentiments of the general Colombian population, including the needs of students. This will be a local and regional convergence process and will be multiethnic, multicultural, and social, including the academic community and all social sectors of the Colombian people.

In this sense, the Mesa Amplia Nacional Estudiantil (MANE) alternative process must be characterized by intensive participation, based on principles of respect and diversity and representative of Colombian students and the popular sectors. Only through these commitments can we establish a coherent and inclusive process and alternative proposal. We know that this process will be built by respecting the dynamics of social processes in terms of time and the contexts of the participating actors at local and regional levels.

This process will have several steps and will be derived from discussions and reflections begun at the grassroots levels. The stages will be as follows:

First, a negotiating table with the government will be set up. This scenario will run *ONLY* once we have chosen national spokespeople for this purpose. This election shall be conducted according to our times and mechanisms as students. The discussion will focus *ONLY on* the following points:

1. MANE is recognized as a unique space for dialogue between students and the government.

2. The government should respect the autonomy of the construction process of the educational community and the people in general, committing all necessary resources for this to occur.
3. The legislation concerning HE will NOT be changed until the end of the construction process of the educational community and all further discussions exhausted (i.e., the fourth and last stage of dialogue).

These conditions are the minimum requirements and basic guarantees needed to enable the initiation of a process of dialogue with the government. We require that the government find a way to reverse the suffocation of the education budget and to respect democratic freedoms and guarantees of autonomy.

Second, the diagnosis and the initial draft of the proposal will be drafted in outline form. This outline will be developed locally and will stimulate democratic and participatory debate about the purpose and objectives of HE.

With the aim of keeping the political debate about HE alive, monthly public debates will be carried out focusing on the key axes developed in the Minimum Programme for Students declaration. These are as follows:

- *University-Society relations*—February
- *University Autonomy*—March
- *University Financing*—April
- *Academic Excellence*—May
- *Welfare and democratic liberties*—June
- *Presentation and Exposition of draft outline* developed by social actors and university community—August

Third, the construction and exposition of the basic statement will then be developed at regional and national levels. Forum will be open to the people and all social sectors that are united in their defense of education as a right and against neoliberalism.

The First Regional Stage will deepen the program and the debate on HE.

- The findings will be systematized by the Academic Committee, which will meet in the month of May.
- The results of this meeting will be presented in a national assessment document and a draft explanatory memorandum. This draft will be also sent to universities and will be again discussed in the *First National Stage*.

The *First National Stage* will be conducted on the 7th, 8th, and 9th June. During this time, the Presentation and Exposition of the Basic Statement will take place and expert committees will be organized. In this meeting the future national programmatic process and methodology will be scheduled and organized.

Fourth, the presentation and exposition of basic statements will be followed by a discussion process that returns to the regional level. The discussion will be based on the draft bill finalized by the Committee of Experts and the National Academic Committee. After returning to the regional stage for changes, discussion, and amendments, a final draft of the bill will be discussed, debated, and amended by a second national meeting.

Once the construction process is finished, we will establish the second stage of dialogue with the national government.

We emphasize that the MANE and the student movement is committed to democratically constructing an alternative reform of HE that will serve the vast majority of people. *This process requires time and organization. Accordingly we request that the government not rush to create a negotiation process and rather respect the mechanisms and the time that the MANE needs to appoint national spokespersons and develop an initial draft of an alternative reform proposal for HE.*

We call out to the society, parents, social and political organizations such as COMOSOL, Polo Democrático, Marcha Patriotica (Patriotic Parade), People's Congress, Defence Committee of the Right to Education, and all the groups that are supporting us in our defense of education as a right, to join us in this democratic construction process of an alternative proposal for education regionally and nationally. In this way we will build the education that Colombian people need.

We are sure that massive *mobilization* was the tool that now puts us in this tactical position. We will continue to develop and strengthen this new political movement. Consequently, the MANE has organized several mobilizations that will enable us to develop and defend this process of construction of our proposal of a new HE bill.

We are committed to deepening a comprehensive, proactive, and creative process of construction and building a movement that respects the contexts and needs of local and regional spaces. However, we highlight the imperative need to strengthen our national-level mobilizations to defend and create a different education in Colombia. The work organized in this IV Meeting of the MANE focused on consensus and consolidation of the principles already developed in our multiple spaces of articulation. This was the necessary condition to guarantee an efficient transparency of information and to facilitate teamwork and collective dialogue. We are seeking to continue with the debate and to strengthen MANE, consolidating this space of unity in diversity of the student movement and for the creation of mechanisms for inclusive, multiscalar, and deliberative organization processes.

Notes

Series Editor's Preface

1. Che Guevara in a letter to Fidel Castro on leaving Cuba in 1967 to continue the struggle in Bolivia.
2. WTO in its most recent manifestation (December 2013) of "agreement" on trade made a small movement and development of the negotiations initiated in Doha 12 years ago. This round attempts to render customs delays less significant in trade fluidity while offering little by way of resolving mutuality of agreement on tariff arrangements by which national economies "defend" their producers against globalized corporate interests, especially in agricultural production. It does little to allay fears of crises of food insecurity and starvation among the poor since initial Doha negotiations.
3. US economy has very significant global trading relationships, not least with Latin and South America. Indicative here is that for Venezuela, 56 percent of its exports are to the United States; for Colombia, 42 percent; and for Brazil, 10 percent.See, *The Observatory of Economic Complexity* at http://atlas.media.mit.edu/country/chn/.
4. Bloch's commentary on Marx's theses on Feuerbach (Bloch, 1959a) is valuable methodological support here, not least on Thesis Three, *educating the educators* in practices of *speculative materialism*. Such inspiration must function to counter, while critically interrogating *capitalist realism* and it generating its very own acquiescent fatalism, in both the "developed" and "developing" worlds and their complex interdynamics.
5. For instantiation of a moment of class struggle manifest in guerrilla journalism as ideology critique for realization of materialist pedagogy of critique of oppressive modes of production in "The 'Fake' Mandela Memorial Interpreter Said It All," see Slavoj Žižek's brief analysis of the liberal "truth" behind the global memorializing of the life of Nelson Mandela. It is emergent in *balm in iconography for the comfort and reassurance of the oppressors* and simultaneously in the yet to be realized *potential of the South African working poor, oppressed, and marginalized* (Žižek, 2013). Developing resonances from the memorializing Mandela project, somewhat similar methods can be applied to

the fleeting "selfie" moment written now in digital stone, of the threesome moment in neoliberal piety of David Cameron (UK) / Helle Thorning-Schmidt (Denmark) / Barack Obama (US), an antidignity moment in microcollective performative fun that shimmers with ambiguities for the global gaze in loss and celebration, of what is, what has been, and what could have been and echoing through time/spaces of class struggles, perhaps, the poignancy among myriad other possibilities of Billie Holliday's performances of Lewis Allen's *Strange Fruit* and the *memorializing lynch photography* that inspired such guerrilla art as popular radical educational idiom, too (Žižek, 2013).

6. Liberal fascism, an essentially contested while positive oxymoron term exposing social and political *differends* (Lyotard, 1979, 1983; Malpas, 1993), and refers here to apparent irreconcilability, its meaning *either* the radical abstract individualism that rejects taking collective responsibility for even the most life threatening of the insecurities of working poor "citizens" who are deemed to have only themselves to blame, *or* to high-handed state unaccountability and flaunting of constitutional individual rights.

7. In this context, as well as recognizing collective powers of noncooperation in capital-forming production and all manner of practices of antistate resistances to oppressive collectivist forms, Latin America has thrown up many inspirational bodies of work for radical movements through the arts of literature and drama, not least *magical realist* literature and activist drama inspired by Freire, for instance, the *Theatre of the Oppressed* movements (Augusto Boal, Panagiotis Assimakopoulos, and Jennifer Hartley). In Boal's words (2000), "This kind of theatre is expressly 'subjunctive'; that is, it represents a version of reality that is experimental, asking 'what would…?' rather than stating 'this is.'" See, Boal (2003) and Hartley (2012).

3 The Bolivarian Republic of Venezuela: Education and Twenty-First Century Socialism

1. "Barrio" is a Spanish word meaning district or neighborhood. In the Venezuelan context, the term commonly refers to the outer rims of big cities inhabited by poor working-class communities. The Venezuelan working class should not be viewed as constituting a traditional industrial proletariat. Some 60 percent of Venezuelan workers are involved in the informal economy (street vendors and so on), primarily in the barrios from where the revolution draws its support (Dominguez, 2010).

2. Vladimir Illyich Ulyanov (commonly known as Lenin), one of the founders of the Russian Revolution, characterized capitalist democracy as the process by which oppressed workers are allowed once every few years to decide which particular representatives of the oppressing class will represent them and repress them in parliament (Lenin, 1917 [2002], p. 95).

4 The Alternative School of Community Organization and Communicational Development, Barrio Pueblo Nuevo, Mérida, Venezuela

1. The subheadings in this section of the chapter reflect the main issues and concerns that arose in Ellis's interviews. The issue of racism was also raised (see Cole, 2011, Chap. 5). Cole (2011) as a whole specifically addresses racism, and Chapter 5 of that volume also considers racism and antiracism in Venezuela (for a more recent analysis of antiracist multicultural twenty-first century socialism in the making, see Cole, 2014).
2. Venezuelanalysis.com, in its own words, is an independent website produced by individuals who are dedicated to disseminating news and analysis about the current political situation in Venezuela. The site's aim is to provide ongoing news about developments in Venezuela, as well as to contextualize this news with in-depth analysis and background information. The site is targeted toward academics, journalists, intellectuals, policy makers from different countries, and the general public.
3. For Paulo Freire, learning environments, as democratic spaces, entail an absence of authoritarianism (Freire, 1987, p. 102, cited in Freire and Shor, 1987). Such an absence is not to be confused with a lack of authoritativeness. As Peter Ninnes (1998) points out, Freire explains the importance of teachers being authoritative, rather than being weak and insecure or being authoritarian. In addition to democracy, dialogic education centralizes the need to develop an open dialogue with students, and requires a balance between "talking to learners and talking with them" (Freire, 1998, p. 63, cited in Ninnes, 1998). Freire maintains that only through talking with and to learners can teachers contribute to the "[development of] responsible and critical citizens" (Freire, 1998, p. 65, cited in Ninnes, 1998). Freire makes a distinction between the progressive and democratic teacher, on the one hand, which he favors, and the permissive or authoritarian teacher, on the other, which he rejects.
4. See Kane (2013) for a discussion of the resonances and dissonances between Latin American traditions of popular education and Orthodox Marxism.
5. Participation Action Research (PAR) involves respecting and combining one's skills with the knowledge of the researched or grassroots communities; taking them as full partners and coresearchers; not trusting elitist versions of history and science that respond to dominant interests; being receptive to counternarratives and trying to recapture them; not depending solely on one's own culture to interpret facts; and sharing what one has learned together with the people, in a manner that is wholly understandable (Gott, 2008).
6. This section of the chapter consists of an analysis of a video (Fundación CAYAPA, 2011) made by some of the students at the school.

7. However, as we have seen from the 2013 interview with Tamara Pearson, twenty-first century socialist content is present in Barrio Pueblo Neuvo as well as twenty-first century socialist practice. While there were undoubtedly socialist teachers talking about socialism in the United Kingdom in the 1960s and 1970s, twenty-first century socialism would by definition not have been a feature of education then.

5 Epistemological Counterhegemonies from Below: Radical Educators in/and the MST and Solidarity Economy Movements

1. For examples of this material, see the series Globalização e Solidariedade [Globalization and Solidarity], http://www.pacs.org.br/2012/12/20/serie-globalizacao-e-solidariedade/.
2. In the municipality of Caucaia, Sítios Novos district, Metropolitan Region of Fortaleza, 63 km from the capital.
3. For comprehensive archive of MST texts see, http://www.landless-voices.org/vieira/archive 05.phtml?rd=MSTPUBLI109&ng=p&sc=3&th=45&se=0.
4. This is also similar to the concept insider-outsiders within which as Lugones (1987, p. 3) names is a world-traveler who "has necessarily acquired flexibility in shifting from the mainstream construction of life where she is constructed as an outsider to other constructions of life where she is more or less 'at home.' This flexibility is necessary for the outsides but it can also be wilfully exercised by the outsider...what I call world-travelling," She continues, "I affirm this practice as a skilful, creative, enriching and, given certain circumstances, as a loving way of being and living. I recognise that much of our travelling is done unwillfullly to hostile White/Anglo worlds."

6 Decolonization in Praxis: Critical Educators, Student Movements, and Feminist Pedagogies in Colombia

1. http://www.fecode.edu.co/index.php/multimedia/revista-educacion-y-cultura

References

Acselrad, H., Mello, C. C. A., & Bezerra, G. (2009). *O que é justice ambiental*. Rio de Janeiro: Garamond.
Agathangelou, A. A., & Ling, L. H. M. (2004). "The House of IR: From Family Power Politics to the *Poisies* of Worldism," *International Studies Review*, 6, 21–49.
Almeida De Carvalho, C. H. (2006). "O PROUNI no Governo Lula e o Jogo Politico em Torno do Aceso ao Ensino Superior," *Educ. Soc.*, Campinas, 27 (96)—Especial, 979–1000.
Althusser, L. (1971). "Ideology and Ideological State Apparatuses," in *Lenin and Philosophy and Other Essays*. London: New Left Books. http://www.marx2mao.com/Other/LPOE70NB.html.
Alves, M. H. M. (1985). *Estado e oposição no Brasil (1964–1984)*. Tradução de Clóvis Marques, 3rd ed. Petrópolis: Vozes.
Amsler, S. (2011). "Beyond All Reason: Spaces of Hope in the Struggle for England's Universities," *Representations*, 116 (Fall), 62–87.
Amsler, S., & Bolsmann, C. (2012). "University Ranking as Social Exclusion," *British Journal of Sociology of Education*, 33 (2), 283–301.
Anzaldúa, G. (2007). *Borderlands/La Frontera: The New Mestiza*. San Francisco: Aunt Lute Books.
Anzaldúa, G. (2009a). "La Prieta," in A. Keating (ed.), *The Gloria Anzaldúa Reader*. Durham, NC, and London: Duke University Press, pp. 38–50.
Anzaldúa, G. (2009b). "Speaking in Tongues: A Letter to Third World Women Writers," in A. Keating (ed.), *The Gloria Anzaldúa Reader*. Durham, NC, and London: Duke University Press, pp. 26–35.
Anzaldúa, G. (2009c). "Spirituality, Sexuality and the Body: An Interview with Linda Smuckler," in A. Keating (ed.), *The Gloria Anzaldúa Reader*. Durham, NC, and London: Duke University Press, pp. 74–96.
Anzola, M., & Pearson, T. (2013). "Alternative Education Can Eliminate Corruption," Venezuelanalysis, August 8. http://venezuelanalysis.com/analysis/9916.
Arruda, M. (1998). "O 'Feminino Criador': Socioeconomia Solidária e Educação," Instituto de Políticas Alternativas para o Cone Sul, Rio de Janeiro.

Arruda, M. (2010). *Potencialidades de la Praxis de la Economía Solidaria.* Laboratorio Internacional Estrategias alternativas al desarrollismo, Buenos Aires, April 12–14, 2010.

Artz, L. (2012). "Venezuela: Making a 'State for Revolution'"—the Example of Community and Public Media," *Links International Jounal for Socialist Renewal.* http://links.org.au/node/2849.

Azzellini, D. (2013). "The Communal State: Communal Councils, Communes, and Workplace Democracy," NACLA, Venezuelanalysis.com, June 30. http://venezuelanalysis.com/analysis/9787.

Baert, P., & Shipman, A. (2005). "University under Siege? Trust and Accountability in the Contemporary Academy," *European Societies,* 7 (1), 157–185.

Ball, S. J. (2002). "Big Policies / Small World: An Introduction to International Perspectives in Education Policy," *Comparative Education, 34* (2) 119–130.

Barreira, C., & De Paula, L. A. M. (1998). "Os assentamentos rurais no Ceará uma experiência a ser seguida?," in *Os assentamentos de reforma agrária no Brasil.* Brasília: UnB.

Bartolome L. (1994). "Beyond the Methods Fetish: Toward a Humanizing Pedagogy," *Harvard Educational Review, 64* (2), 173–195.

Beck, J. (1999). "Makeover or Takeover? The Strange Death of Educational Autonomy in Neo-Liberal England," *British Journal of Sociology of Education, 20* (2), 223–238.

Bercovitch, S. (2013a). "Maduro's First 100 Days in Office Marked by Street Government, Latin American Integration, Economic Debate." http://venezuelanalysis.com/news/9888.

Bercovitch, S. (2013b). "Opposition and PSUV Present Plan for Selecting Candidates for Venezuelan Municipal Elections." http://venezuelanalysis.com/news/9858.

Bercovitch, S. (2013c). "With 'Zero Tolerance to Gringo Aggression,' Maduro Cuts Off Venezuela-U.S. Talks," Venezuelanalysis.com, July 21. http://venezuelanalysis.com/news/9872.

Bermúdez, N. L. (2013). "Cali's Women in Collective Crossing through Three Worlds: Popular Education, Feminisms, and Nonviolence for the Expansion of the Present, Memory and Nurturing of Life," in Sara C. Motta and Mike Cole (eds.), *Education and Social Change in Latin America.* London; New York: Palgrave Macmillan Press, pp. 239–260.

Bernal, M. P. U, Martinez Boom, A., & Medina Bejarano, M. J. (2003). *La expedicíon pedagógica y las redes de maestros: Otros modos de Formación.* Documentos de Sistematización. Bogota: MIMEO.

Bernal, M. P. U., Orozco Cruz, J. C., & Cespedes, A. R. (2001). *Expedición Pedagógica Nacional:Una experiencia de movilización social y construcción colectiva de conocimiento pedagogico.* Bogota: Red Académica.

Bianchi, A., & Braga, R. (2005). "Brazil: The Lula Government and Financial Globalization," *Social Forces, 83* (4), 1745–1762.

REFERENCES

Birchfield, V. (1999). "Contesting the Hegemony of Market Ideology: Gramsci's 'Good Sense' and Polanyi's 'Double Movement,'" *Review of International Political Economy*, 6 (1) (Spring), 27–54.

Bloch, E. (1959a). "Commentary on Theses on Feuerback from *The Principle of Hope*." http://www.marxists.org/archive/bloch/index.htm.

Bloch, E. (1959b). *The Principle of Hope*. Cambridge, MA: MIT Press.

Blough, L. (2010). "Bolivarian Republic of Venezuela: It Is Not Chavez. It Is the People," *Axis of Logic*, April 14. http://axisoflogic.com/artman/publish/Article_59344.shtml.

Boal, A. (2000). *Theatre of the Oppressed, Third Edition*. London: Pluto.

Boal, A., N. (2003). "From *Theatre of the Oppressed*," in N. Wardrip-Fruin and N. Montfort (eds.), *The NewMedia Reader*. Cambridge, MA: MIT, pp. 341–352.

Boff, L., & Boff, C. (1987). *Introducing Liberation Theology*. Maryknoll, NY: Orbis.

Bohorquez, G. J. (2013). "La redes pedagogicas, una posibilidad de formación de maestros en el ejercicio de la docencia." http://www.psi.uba.ar/academica/carrerasdegrado/profesorado/sitios_catedras/902_didactica_general/cartelera/contexto/redes_pedagogicas.pdf (last accessed October 7, 2013).

Boito, A. (1994). "The State and Trade Unionism in Brazil," *Latin American Perspectives*, 21 (1) (January), 7–23.

Boito, A. (2012). "Governo Lula: a nova burguesia nacional no poder," in A. Boito and A. Galvão, *Política e classes sociais no Brasil dos anos 2000*. São Paulo: Alameda, pp. 237–263.

Bolaños, G., & Tattay, L. (2013). "La educación propia, una realidad oculta de resistencia educativa y cultural de los pueblos," in L. Cendales, M. R. Mejía, and M. Muñoz (eds.), *Entretejidos de la educación popular en Colombia*. Bogota: Ediciones desde Abajo, pp. 65–80.

Boom, A. M. (2010). "El Movimiento Pedagógico Colombiano y sus nexus con las politicas educativas." http://issuu.com/amboom/docs/named23594 (last accessed September 20, 2013).

Borges de Souza, A., Conceição Ferreira, da C., & Gritti, S. M. (2008). "Formação de educadores de EJA: possibilidades de formação humana," in C. L. Bezerra Machado, C. S. Soares Campos, and C. Paludo (eds.), *Teoria e práctica da educaçáo do campo: Análises de experiências*. Brasília: MDA, pp. 112–123.

Braga, L. Q. De, Vicente da Silva, M. De L., & Paz Feitosa, M. Da (2011). "Com a palavra, os que lutam: Os movimentos de resistência das comunidades do baixo jaguaribe em defese da terra, do trabalho e de modos de vida," in R. Rigotto (ed.), *Agrotóxicos, trabahlo e saúde: vulnerabilidade e resistência no context da modernização agrícola no Baixo Jaguaribe/CE*. Fortaleza: Edições UFC, pp. 445–488.

Breilh, J. (2011) "La Codicia Agrícola como Modelo de la Muerte," in R. Rigotto (ed.), *Agrotóxicos, trabahlo e saúde: vulnerabilidade e resistência*

no context da modernização agrícola no Baixo Jaguaribe/CE. Fortaleza: Edições UFC, pp. 25–34.
Brittain, J. (2006). "Human Rights and the Colombian Government: An Analysis of State-Based Atrocities toward Non-combatants," August 16, 2006. http://newpol.org/content/human-rights-and-colombian-government-analysis-state-based-atrocities-toward-non-combatants,.
Buci-Glucksmann, C. (1979). "State, Transition and Passive Revolution," in C. Mouffe (ed.), *Gramsci and Marxist Theory*. London: Routledge and Kegan Paul, pp. 207–236.
Cabezas, H., Casas, F. A., & Valencia, A. T. (2011). *La zozobra de la Universidad, entre el desastre y la oportunidad*, El observatorio de la Universidad colombiana, November 9, 2011.
Cadavid, M., Calderon, D. M., Uribe, L. F., & Taborda, D. (2010). "Teacher Education in Colombia: Past, Present and Future," in G. K. Karras and C. C. Wolhuter (eds.), *International Handbook on Teacher Education Worldwide. Training, Issues and Challenges for the Teaching Profession.* Athens: Atrapos Editions, pp. 110–128.
Caderno do MST (1999). "A evolução da concepção de cooperação agrícola do MST," Caderno de Cooperação Agrícola n° 08 (número repetido), São Paulo.
Caldart, R. S. (2000). *Pedagogia do Movimento Sem Terra: Escola é ais do que escola*. Petrópolis: Vozes.
Caldert, R. S., Periera, I. B., Alentejano, L., & Frigotto, G. (eds.) (2012). *Dicionãio la Educação do Campo*. Rio De Janeiro; São Paolo: Escola Politécnica de Saúde Joaquim Venâncio Expressão Popular.
Campo, V. M., & Giraldo, J. E. (2009). "Redito educativo, acciones afirmativas y equidad social en la educacion superior en Colombia," *Revista de Estudios Sociales, 33*, 106–117.
Carvalho, A. I. de, Looi, Y., Saad, F., & Sinatra J. (2013). "Education in Colombia: Is There a Role for the Private Sector?," *Knowledge@Wharton*. http://knowledge.wharton.upenn.edu/article/education-in-colombia-is-there-a-role-for-the-private-sector/ (last accessed March 2, 2014).
Carvalho, S. M. G. de. (2003). "As políticas de Educação de Jovens e Adultos no Brasil: O programa recomeço em questão," in S. L. de Matos Kelma (ed.), *Movimentos sociais, educação popular e escola: A favor da diversidade*. Fortaleza: UFC, Coleção Diálogos, n. 13.
Carvalho, S. M. G. de. (2006). *Educação do campo: Pronera, uma política pública em construção*. Tese (Doutorado em Educação). Programa de Pós-Graduação em Educação Brasileira da Universidade Federal do Ceará (UFC), Fortaleza, Brasil.
Catani, A. M., & Gilioli, R de. S. (2005). "O PROUNI na encruzilhada: entre a cidadania e a privatização," *Linhas Críticas*, Brasília, *11* (20), 55–68.
CB (Caribbean Business) Online Staff (2013). "Maduro Wants PR in CELAC Bloc," *Caribbean Business*. http://www.caribbeanbusinesspr.com/news/maduro-wants-pr-in-celac-bloc-87456.html.

Ceceña, A. E. (2012). "On the Complex Relation between Knowledges and Emancipations," *South Atlantic Quarterly, 111* (1), 111–132.
Cendales, J., & Muñoz, L. (2013). "Antecedentes y presencia del CEAAL en Colombia: Elementos para la reconstrucción de la historia de la educación popular en Colombia," in L. Cendales, M. R. Mejía, and M. Muñoz (eds.), *Entretejidos de la educación popular en Colombia*. Bogota: Ediciones desde Abajo, pp. 33–53.
Cendales, L., Mejía, M. R., & Jairo Muñoz, M. (eds.) (2013). *Entretejidos de la educación popular en Colombia*, CEAAL. Bogota: Ediciones desde Abajo.
Cepeda, U. F. (2003). "Alvaro Uribe: Dissident," Inter American Dialogue Working Paper, no. xi.
Chávez, H. (2010). "Coup and Countercoup: Revolution!" April 11. http://venezuelanalysis.com/analysis/5274.
Ciccariello-Maher, G. (2013). *We Created Chávez: A People's History of the Venezuelan Revolution*. Durham, NC, and London: Duke University Press.
Cole, M. (2009). "The State Apparatuses and the Working Class—Experiences from the United Kingdom: Educational Lessons from Venezuela," in D. Hill (ed.), *Contesting Neoliberal Education: Public Resistance and Collective Advance*. New York and London: Routledge, pp. 219–241.
Cole, M. (2011). *Racism and Education in the U.K. and the U.S.: Towards a Socialist Alternative*. New York and London: Palgrave Macmillan.
Cole, M. (2014). "Austerity/Immiseration Capitalism and Islamophobia or Twenty-First Century Multicultural Socialism?," *Policy Futures in Education, 12* (1), 86–101.
Colectivo Situaciones (2003). "On the Militant-Researcher." http://eipcp.net/transversal/0406/colectivosituaciones/en/base_edit (last accessed March 14, 2013).
Collini, S. (2011). "From Robbins to McKinsey. Review of *Higher Education: Students at the Heart of the System*," *London Review of Books, 33* (16) (August 25), 1–15.
Conte, I. I. (2006). *A Educação como proceso de de formaçã de sujeitos*. Veranópolis: ITERRA/UERGS.
Conte, I. I. (2011). "Mulheres camponesas em luta: resistência, libertação e empoderamento." Programa de pós-graduação em educação nas ciências. Universidade regional do noroeste do estado do rio grande do sul.
Coté, M., Day, R., & de Peuter, G. (2007). "Utopian Pedagogy: Creating Radical Alternatives in the Neoliberal Age," *Review of Education, Pedagogy, and Cultural Studies, 29* (4), 317–336.
Cotos, A. G. (2013). "Formar en investigación desde la perspectiva de la educacion popular," L. Cendales, M. R. Mejía, and M. Muñoz (eds.), *Entretejidos de la educación popular en Colombia*. CEAAL. Bogota: Ediciones desde Abajo, pp. 100–130.
Davies, N. (2004). "O Governo Lula e a Educaco: A Desercao do Estado Continua?," *Educacion e Sociedad, 25* (86), 245–252.

de Almeida, L. P., Pingas, M. R., Pinto, P. E., Knijnik, G. (2008). "Discutindo a cultura camponesa no processo de ensino-aprendizagem em três escolas do sul do Brasil," in C. L. Bezerra Machado, C. S. Soares Campos, and C. Paludo (eds.), *Teoria e práctica da educação do campo: Análises de experiências*. Brasília: MDA, pp. 100–109.
De Angelis, M., & Harvie, D. (2009). "'Cognitive Capitalism' and the Rat-Race: How Capital Measures Immaterial Labour in British Universities," *Historical Materialism*, 17, 3–30.
De Ferranti, David, Perry, Guillermo E., Ferreira, Francisco H. G., & Walton, Michael (2004). "Inequality in Latin America, Breaking with History?" Washington, DC: World Bank.
de Janvry, A., Frederico, F., Sadoulet, E., Nelson, D., Lindert, K., Bénédicte de la Brière, B., & Lanjouw, P. (2005). "Brazil's Bolsa Escola Program: The Role of Local Governance in Decentralized Implementation." World Bank Institute, Discussion Paper, No. 0542, 1–52. http://siteresources. worldbank.org/SOCIALPROTECTION/Resources/SP-Discussion -papers/Safety-Nets-DP/0542.pdf.
De Paula, M. de. F. (2009a). "A perda da identidade e da autonmia da universidade brasileira no contexto do neoliberalismo," ALEPH—Formação de Professores, 1–17. http://www.uff.br/aleph/textos_em_pdf/a_perda _da_identidade_da_universidade.pdf.
De Paula, M. de. F. (2009b). "Reforma da Educação Superior do Governo Lula: as políticas de democratização do acesso em foco," *Revista Argentina Educacon Superior*, 1 (1), 152–173.
De Paula, M. de. F., & Avezedo, M. D. (2006). "Politícas e Practícas de Privatiação do Publico na Universidade: O caso UPF," *Avaliação Revista de Avaliação da Institutional da Educação Superior*, 11 (3), 91–111.
de Souza, E. J., Ferreira de Andrade, E., Mendes de Lima, G. A., & Bezerra Machado, C. L. (2008). "Limites e possibilidades: Um olhar sobre o projeto politico pedagogico na perspectiva da educação do campo," in C. L. Bezerra Machado, C. S. Soares Campos, C. Paludo (eds.), *Teoria e práctica da educação do campo: Análises de experiências*. Brasilia: MDA, pp. 44–58.
Denes, C. (2003). "Bolsa Escola: Redefining Poverty and Development in Brazil," *International Education Journal*, 4 (2), 137–157.
Denis, R. (2012). "The Birth of an 'Other Politics' in Venezuela," *South Atlantic Quarterly*, 111 (1), 81–93.
Departmento Nacional Planeacion (2003). "lan nacional de desarrollo 2002–2006," *Hacia un estado comunitario* (no 8025–43–5), Bogota.
Díaz, G. C., & Bermúdez, N. L. (2009). "Travesía hacia el encuentro de tres mundos: sistematización de la Escuela política de Mujeres Pazíficas, una experiencia de educación popular en clave de feminismos y nonviolencia," *Informe de Investigacion: Maestria en educacion—enfasis educacion popular y desarrollo comunitario*, Universidad del Valle, Instituto de eduacion y pedagogia, Santiago de Cali.

Dienst, R. (2011). *The Bonds of Debt: Borrowing against the Common Good.* London: Verso.
Diniz, A. S., & Gilbert, B. (2013). "Socialist Values and Cooperation in Brazil's Landless Rural Workers' Movement," *Latin American Perspectives,* Special Issue edited by S. C. Motta and L. Chen, Reinventing the Lefts from Below, *40* (4), 19–34.
Dominguez, F. (2010). "Education for the Creation of a New Venezuela," Paper delivered at Latin America and Education, Marxism and Education: RenewingDialogues XIII, Institute of Education, University of London, July 24.
Dominguez, F. (2013). "Education for the Creation of a New Venezuela," in S. C. Motta and M. Cole (eds.), *Education and Social Change in Latin America.* New York and London: Palgrave Macmillan, pp. 123–137.
Dorado Cardona, O. (2008). "25 años del movimiento pedagogico en Colombia."
Elias, D. (2003). "Agronegócio e desigualdades soioespacias," in D. Elias and R. Pequeno (eds.), *Difusão do agronegócio e novas dinâmicas socioespaciais.* Fortaleza: Banco do Nordeste do Brasil, pp. 25–82.
Ellis, E. (2010). "Fieldwork Notes Taken at Barrio Pueblo Neuvo." unpublished.
Ellner, S. (2013). "Just How Radical Is President Nicolás Maduro?," Venezuelanalysis.com, July 11. http://venezuelanalysis.com/analysis/9841.
Escobar de Almeida, A., Barreto, E. M., Braga, I. C., Alves Xavier, L. A., & Pazetti, M. (2008). "Educação, escola, movimentos sociais e comunidade," in C. L. Bezerra Machado, C. S. Soares Campos, and C. Paludo (eds.), *Teoria e práctica da educação do campo: Análises de experiências.* MDA: Brasília, pp. 156–170.
Esteves, A. M. (2013). "Experiential and Relational Dimensions in the Pedagogical Practice of Solidarity Economy: Insights from Brazil," in Sara C. Motta and Mike Cole (eds.), *Education and Social Change in Latin America.* New York; London: Palgrave Macmillan, pp. 203–220.
Femia, J. V. (1975). "Hegemony and Consciousness in the Thought of Antonio Gramsci," *Political Studies, 23* (1), 29–48.
Ferreira Rosa, I., Matos Pessoa, V., & Rigotto, R. M. (2011). "Introdução: agrotóxicos, saúde humana e os caminhos do estudo epidemiológico," in R. Rigotto (ed.), *Agrotóxicos, trabalho e saúde: vulnerabilidade e resistência no context da modernização agrícola no Baixo Jaguaribe/CE.* Fortaleza: Edições UFC, pp. 217–256.
Feitosa, M. D. A. (2002). "Participação: Ainda uma trilha na reforma agrária do Ceará: estudo de caso no Assentamento Santa Bábara." Dissertação (Mestrado em Educação Brasileira)—Programa de Pós-Graduação strito sensu em Educação. Universidade Federal do Ceará, Fortaleza.
Fischman, G. E., & McLaren, P. (2005). "Intellectuals or Critical Pedagogy, Commitment, and Praxis Rethinking Critical Pedagogy and the Gramscian

and Freirean Legacies: From Organic to Committed," *Cultural Studies <=> Critical Methodologies*, 5 (4), 425–446.
Fonseca, da C., Lourenço de Souza, Santin L. M., Rodrigues, T. M., & Mazzini, V. L. (2008). "A organização do processo educativo," in C. L. Bezerra Machado, C. S. Soares Campos, and C. Paludo (eds.), *Teoria e práctica da educação do campo: Análises de experiências*. MDA: Brasília, pp. 58–69.
Freire, P. (1993) [2006]. *Pedagogy of the Oppressed*. New York: Continuum Books.
Freire, P. (1998). *Teachers as Cultural Workers: Letters to Those Who Dare Teach*, trans. Donaldo Macedo, Dale Koike, and Alexandre Oliveira. Boulder, CO: Westview Press.
Freire, P., & Shor, I. (1987). *A Pedagogy for Liberation: Dialogues on Transforming Education*. London: Macmillan Education.
Frigotto, G., Ciavatta, M., & Ramos, M. (2005). "A Politíca de Educação Profissional no Governo Lula: Um Percurso Histórico Controvertido," *Educ. Soc.*, Campinas 26 (92), 1087–1113.
Fuenmayor, R. (1989). *Interpretive Systemology: Its Theoretical and Practical Development in a University School of Systems in Venezuela*. Hull: Department of Management Systems and Sciences, University of Hull.
Fundación CAYAPA (2011). "La Escuelita: (ENGLISH) The Alternative School of Barrio Pueblo Nuevo." Mérida, Venezuela, Video, December. http://www.youtube.com/watch?v=mHG89aHxHIo.
Gadelha de Carvalho, S. M., & Mendes, E. (2011). "The University and the Landless Movement in Brazil: The Experience of Collective Knowledge Construction through Education Projects in Rural Areas," in S. C. Motta and A. G. Nilsen (eds.), *Social Movements in the Global South: Dispossession, Development and Resistance*. London; New York: Palgrave Macmillan.
Garces, G. J. F., & Jaramillo, I. J. (2008). "De la autonomía a la evaluacion de calidad: gestion educative, reformas legislativas e investigacion de los maestros y las maestras en Colombia (1994–2006)," *Revista Educacion y Pedagogia*, 20 (51), 175–187.
Garcia, M. C. (2012). "Movilizacion estudantil por la defensa de la educacion superior en Colombia," *Anuari del Conflicte Social*, 1, 449–466.
Gindin, S., and Panitch, L. (2013). *The Making of Global Capitalism: The Political Economy of American Empire*. London: Verso.
Gonçalves-Fernandes, A., Alves de Sousa, E., Conte, I. I., Maggioni, L., Vanusa de Abreu, M., & Riberio, M. (2008). "A Pedagogia e as prácticas educativas na educação do campo," in C. L. Bezerra Machado, C. S. Soares Campos, and C. Paludo (eds.), *Teoria e práctica da educação do campo: Análises de experiências*. Brasília: MDA, pp. 26–43.
Gott, R. (2008). "Orlando Fals Borda: Sociologist and Activist Who Defined Peasant Politics in Colombia," *The Guardian*, August 26. http://www.guardian.co.uk/world/2008/aug/26/colombia.sociology.

Graeber, D. (2012). *Debt: The First 5,000 Years*. New York: Melville House.
Gramsci, A. (1971). *Selections from the Prison Notebooks of Antonio Gramsci*, ed. and trans. [from the Italian] Q. Hoare and G. Nowell Smith. London: Lawrence and Wishart.
Gramsci, A. (1985). *Selections from Cultural and Political Writings*, ed. D. forgacs and G. Nowell-Smith, trans. W. Boelhower. Cambridge, MA: Cambridge University Press.
Griffiths, T. G. (2008). "Preparing Citizens for a 21st Century Socialism: Venezuela's Bolivarian Educational Reforms," Paper presented at the Social Educators Association of Australia National Biennial Conference, Newcastle, Australia.
Griffiths, T. G. (2013). "Higher Education for Socialism in Venezuela: Massification, Development and Transformation," in T. G. Griffiths and Z. Millei (eds.), *Logics of Socialist Education: Engaging with Crisis, Insecurity and Uncertainty*, Explorations of Educational Purpose. Dordrecht: Springer, pp. 91–109.
Griffiths, T. G., & Williams, J. (2009). "Mass Schooling for Socialist Transformation in Cuba and Venezuela," *Journal for Critical Education Policy Studies*, 7 (2), 30–50. http://www.jceps.com/index.php?pageID=article&articleID=160.
Guevara, C. (1965) [2005]. "Socialism and Man in Cuba," *The Che Reader*. Minneapolis, MN: Che Guevara Studies Center and Ocean Press. http://www.marxists.org/archive/guevara/1965/03/man-socialism.htm.
Guimarães, J. (2004). *A Esperança Equilibrista: O Governo Lula em tempos de transição*. Sao Paulo: Editora Fundação Perseu Abramo.
Gutiérrez, R. (2012). "The Rhythms of the Pachakuti: Brief Reflections Regarding How We Have Come to Know Emancipatory Struggles and the Significance of the Term Social Emancipation," *South Atlantic Quarterly*, 111 (1), 51–64.
Hall, Anthony (2006). "From Fome Zero to Bolsa Família: Social Policies and Poverty Alleviation under Lula," *Journal of Latin American Studies*, 38 (4), 689–709.
Hartley, J. S. (2012). *Applied Theatre in Action: A Journey*. Stoke-on-Trent: Trentham.
Harvey, D. (2005). *A Brief History of Neoliberalism*. Oxford, UK: Oxford University Press.
Hazelkorn, E. (2007). "How Do Rankings Impact on Higher Education?," *IMHE Info. Journal of the OECD Programme on Institutional Management in Higher Education, December*. http://www.oecd.org/dataoecd/8/27/39802910.pdf.
Hernandez, I. (2004). "Las privatizaciones en Colombia," *Apuntes del Cenes*, November, 55–92.
Hill, D. (ed.) (2013). *Immiseration Capitalism and Education: Austerity, Resistance and Revolt*, Brighton: Institute for Education Policy Studies.
hooks, b. (1990). *Yearning: Race, Gender and Cultural Politics*. Cambridge, MA: South End Press.

hooks, b. (2000). *Feminist Theory: From Margin to Center*. New York; London: Pluto Press.
hooks, b. (2001). *Salvation: Black People and Love*. New York: Harper Collins.
hooks, b. (2003). *Communion: The Female Search for Love*. New York: William Morrow & Company.
hooks, b. (2004). *The Will to Change: Men, Masculinity and Love*. Washington, DC: Washington Square Press.
Interview at *La Mascara Theatre*, December 13, 2010, author with Isabella and Elizabeth, participants in Aves de Paraíso, Theatre Group, Comuna 14, Santiago de Cali, Colombia.
Interview at *La Mascara Theatre*, December 13, 2010, author with Pilar Restrepo, participant and cofounder of *La Mascara Theatre*.
Irigaray, L., & Burke, C. (1980). "When Our Lips Speak Together," *Signs*, 6, 69–79.
Janicke, K. (2008). "Chavez Supporters and Opposition Commemorate Overthrow of Venezuela's Last Dictatorship," Venezuelanalysis.com, January 23. http://venezuelanalysis.com/news/3096.
Janicke, K. (2010a). "Venezuela Creates Peasant Militias, Enacts Federal Government Council," Venezuelanalysis.com, February 22. http://venezuelanalysis.com/news/5150.
Janicke, K. (2010b). "Venezuela Celebrates 'Day of the Bolivarian Militias, the Armed People and the April Revolution,'" Venezuelanalysis.com, April 14. http://venezuelanalysis.com/news/5276.
Jessop, B. (1990). *State Theory: Putting the Capitalist State in Its Place*. Cambridge, UK: Polity Press.
Jessop, B. (2002). *The Future of the Capitalist State*. Cambridge, UK: Polity Press.
Jessop, B. (2014). *The State: Past, Present, Future*. Cambridge, UK: Polity Press.
Kane, L. (2013). "Marxism and Popular Education in Latin America," in S. C. Motta and M. Cole (eds.), *Education and Social Change in the Americas*. New York; London: Palgrave Macmillan.
Keating, A. L. (ed.) (2009). *The Gloria Anzaldúa Reader*. Durham, NC, and London: Duke University Press.
Keck, M. E. (1995). *The Workers' Party and Democratization in Brazil*. New Haven, CT: Yale University Press.
Kliman, A. (2012). *The Failure of Capitalist Production: Underlying Causes of the Great Recession*. London: Pluto.
Laval, C. (2004). *A escola não é uma empresa: O neoliberalismo em ataque ao ensino público*. Londrina: Planta.
Laval, C. (2005). "A escola não é uma empresa—O neoliberalismo em ataque ao ensino público," *Eccos Revista Científica*, 7(1) (junho), pp. 175–177.
Lenin, V. I. (1917) [2002]. *On Utopian and Scientific Socialism*. Amsterdam: Fredonia Books.
Libâneo, J. C. (2008). "Alguns Aspectos da Política Educacional do Governo Lula e sua Repercussão no funcionamento das escolas," *Revista HISTEDBR On-line*, Campinas, 32, 168–178.

REFERENCES

Light, D., Manso, M., & Noguera, M. (2009). "An Educational Revolution to Support Change in the Classroom: Colombia and the Educational Challenges of the Twenty First Century," *Policy Futures in Education*, 7 (1), 88–101.
Lopes, A. C. (2005). "Políticas de currículo: mediação por grupos disciplinares de ensino de Ciências e matemática," in A. C. Lopes and E. Macedo (Org.), *Currículo de Ciências em debate*. Campinas: Papirus.
Lopes, A. C. (2006). "Discursos nas políticas de Currículo," *Currículo sem Fronteiras*, 6 (2), 33–52.
Lorde, A. (2000). *The Uses of the Erotic: The Erotic as Power*. Tucson, AZ: Kore Press.
Lugones, M. (1987). "Playfulness, 'World'-Travelling, and Loving Perception," *Hypathia*, 2 (2), 3–19.
Lyotard, J-F. (1984). *The Postmodern Condition: A Report on Knowledge* (first published in French, 1979). Minneapolis: University of Minnesota Press.
Lyotard, J-F. (1989). *The Differend* (first published in French, 1983). Minneapolis:University of Minnesota Press.
Macedo, D. (1994). "Preface," in P. McLaren and C. Lankshear (eds.), *Conscientization and Resistance*. New York: Routledge, pp. 1–8.
Maia, L. A. (2008). *Mística, educaçã o e resistência no movimento dos sem terra: MST*. Fortaleza: UFC.
Mallett-Outtrim, R. (2013a). "Venezuela's Maduro Seeks Enabling Law to Combat Corruption, Assures PSUV 'Will Never Be Homophobic,'" Venezuelanalysis.com, August 16. http://venezuelanalysis.com/news /9943.
Mallett-Outtrim, R. (2013b). "Venezuela's New Culture Law Promotes 'Decolonisation Thought,'" Venezuelanalysis.com. August 15. http://venezuelanalysis.com/news/9942.
Malpas, S. (1993). *Jean-François Lyotard*. London: Routledge.
MANE (2011a). "Programa Mínimo del Movimiento Estudiantil Universitario Colombiano." http://manecolombia.blogspot.com.au/2011/10/programa-minimo-del-movimiento.html (last accessed October 3, 2013).
MANE (2011b). "Documentos base de la Mesa Amplia Nacional Estudiantil de Colombia." http://manecolombia.blogspot.com.au/2011/10/doc umentos-base-de-la-mesa-amplia.html (last accessed October 3, 2013).
MANE (2011c). "Mesa Amplia Nacional Estudiantil—Jan Farid Chen Lugo." http://manecolombia.blogspot.com.au/2011/10/mesa-amplia-nacional-estudiantil-jan.html (last accessed October 3, 2013).
MANE (2011d). "Convocatoria Encuentro Programático Nacional Estudiantil—13 y 14 de Noviembre." http://manecolombia.blogspot.com. au/2011/11/convocatoria-encuentro-programatico.html (last accessed October 3, 2013).
Mansell, J., & Motta, S. C. (2013). "Re-articulating Dissent: Representing the Working Class from Third Way to New Right in Britain and Chile," *Political Studies*, 61 (4) (December), 748–766.

Marques, R. M. (2005). "As limitações da política de combate à pobreza no governo Lula." Colóquio Latinoamericano de economistas políticos, October 27–28, 2005, Anais, México.

Marrero, A., & Hernandez, F. J. (2005). "Las reformas educativas de las ultimas decadas: privatizacion y privacion," *Anuario de Servicios Publicos*, 1–10. http://www.tni.org/sites/www.tni.org/archives/books/yearb-05education-s.pdf (last accessed March 2, 2014).

Martínez, J., & Díaz, A. (1996). "Chile: The Great Transformation," The United Nations Research Institute for Social Development. Washington: The Brookings Institution.

Martinez, C., Fox, M., & Farrell, J. (2010). *Venezuela Speaks! Voices from the Grassroots*. Oakland, CA: PM Press.

Marx, K. (1863–1883). *Capital*, Vol. 3 (Compiled by Engels, 1894 from Marx's posthumous documents), Chap. 29 available at http://www.marxists.org/archive/marx/works/1894-c3/.

Meade, B., & Gershberg, A. (2008). "Restructuring towards Equity? Examining Recent Efforts to Better Target Education Resources to the Poor in Colombia," UNESCO: Education for All Global Monitoring Report. http://unesdoc.unesco.org/images/0018/001804/180411e.pdf.

Medina, T., & La Máscara, (2010). *El Teatro de Género: Memoria del proceso*. Medellin: Editorial Lealon.

Mejía, R. M. (2002). "La calidad de al educación en tiempos de globalización," *Una mirada crítica desde la educación popular*, Congreso Pedagógico Nacional de Fe y Alegría Nicaragua, 21–22 de octubre de 2002.

Mencebo, D. (2004). "Universidade para Todos: Privatização em Questão," VI meeting of Pesquisa em educacao da regiao sudeeste, May 3–6, 2004, Rio de Janeiro. http://www.proposicoes.fe.unicamp.br/~proposicoes/textos/45-dossie-%20mancebod.pdf.

Mendieta, E. (2008). "Prologue: The Liberation of Politics: Alterity, Solidarity, Liberation," in Enrique Dussel, *Twenty Theses on Politics: Latin America in Translation*, trans. George Ciccariello-Maher. Durham, NC: Duke University Press.

MercoPress (2009). "To School for Reading Classes with Karl Marx and Che Guevara," MercoPress, May 17. http://en.mercopress.com/2009/05/17/to-school-for-reading-classes-with-karl-marx-and-che-guevara.

Mignolo, W. D. (2009). "Epistemic Disobedience, Independent Thought, and De-colonial Freedom," *Theory, Culture and Society*, 26 (7–8), 1–23.

Mills, C. Wright (1956). *The Power Elite*. New York: Oxford University Press.

Ministerio del Poder Popular Para la Educación (2007). "Currículo Nacional Bolivariano: Diseño Curricular del Sistema Educativo Bolivariano." http://www.redalyc.org/articulo.oa?id=35603920

Morales, A. A. (2010). "A 200 anos de herencias y herejias en la Universidad publica colombiana," *Revista Colombiana de Education*, 5, 206–226.

Moreno, S., & Jardilino, J. (2007). "Acción Cultural Popular en los albores: la filosofía del movimiento pedagógico y la educación popular en Colombia," *Eccos Revista Científica*, 9 (2), 409–415.

Morini, C. (2007). "The Feminization of Labour in Cognitive Capitalism," *Feminist Review*, 87, 40–59.
Morton, A. D. (2007). *Unravelling Gramsci: Hegemony and Passive Revolution in the Global Political Economy*. London: Pluto Press.
Motta, S. C. (2008). "The Chilean Socialist Party (PSCh): Constructing Consent and Disarticulating Dissent to Neo-liberal Hegemony in Chile," *British Journal of Politics and Industrial Relations*, 10 (2), 303–327.
Motta, S. C. (2010). "Aves de Paraiso: Theatre of the Oppressed in Cali, Colombia." *Nottingham Critical Pedagogy*, Exploring Alternatives to Neoliberal Higher Education. http://nottinghamcriticalpedagogy.word press.com/2010/12/26/aves-de-paraiso-theatre-of-the-oppressed-in-cali-colombia/.
Motta, S. C. (2011a). "Notes towards Prefigurative Epistemologies," pp. 178–199 in S. C. Motta and A.G. Nilsen (eds.), *Social Movements in the Global South: Dispossession, Development and Resistance*. London: Palgrave Macmillan.
Motta, S. C. (2011b). "Pedagogies of Resistance and Anti-Capitalist Creation in Latin America," *Roundhouse Journal: Reimagining the University*, 64–73. http://www.scribd.com/doc/54768353/Roundhouse-Journal.
Motta, S. C. (2013a). "Brazil: Anatomy of a Crisis," Beautiful Transgressions, *Ceasefire*. http://ceasefiremagazine.co.uk/brazil-anatomy-crisis/ (last accessed October 13, 2013).
Motta, S. C. (2013b). "Introduction: Exploring the Role of Education and the Pedagogical in Pathways to Twenty-First Century Socialism in Latin America," in Sara C. Motta and Mike Cole (eds.), *Education and Social Change in Latin America*. New York and London: Palgrave Macmillan, pp. 1–15.
Motta, S. C. (2013c). "On the Pedagogical Turn in Latin American Social Movements," in Sara C. Motta and Mike Cole (eds.), *Education and Social Change in Latin America*. London; New York: Palgrave Macmillan, pp. 53–70.
Motta, S., and Cole, M. (2013). *Education and Social Change in Latin America*. New York: Palgrave Macmillan.
MST (2001). "Pedagogia do Movimento Sem Terra; acompanhamento às escolas," Boletim da Educação n°08, São Paulo.
Muhr, T. (2010). "Counter-hegemonic Regionalism and Higher Education for All: Veneuela and the ALBA," *Globalisation, Societies and Education*, 8 (1), 39–57.
Munarim, A. (2007). "Secretaria Nacional de Economia Solidária—SENAES: superação do capitalismo?," Thesis from the Universidad Federal de Santa Catarina, Specializing in Marxist Economy and Solidarity Economy.
Navarro, L. H. (2013). "Nicolas Maduro—The Bus Driver," Venezuelanalysis.com, La Jornada, March 29. http://venezuelanalysis.com/analysis/8415.
Neill, A. S. (1960). *Summerhill: A Radical Approach to Child Rearing*. New York: Hart Publishing Company.

Neves, D. P. (1997). *Assentamento rural: Reforma agrária em migalhas*. Niterói: EDUFF.

Neves de Sousa, D. (2008). "Reestruturação capitalista e trabalho: notas críticas acerca da economia solidária," *Revista Katálisis*. Florianópolis, *11* (1), 53–60.

Ninnes, P. (1998). "Freire, Paulo," in *Teachers as Cultural Workers: Letters to Those Who Dare Teach*, trans. D. Macedo, D. Koike, and A. Oliveira, Boulder, CO: Westview Press, *Education Review*, August 4. http://www.edrev.info/reviews/rev28.htm.

Novelli, M. (2009). *Colombia's Classroom Wars: Political Violence against Education Sector Trade Unions in Colombia*. Brussels: Education International.

Novelli, M. (2010). "Education, Conflict and Social (In)justice: Insights from Colombia," *Educational Review*, *62* (3), 271–285.

Oliveira, D. (2009). "As políticas educacionais no governo Lula: rupturas e permanências," *RBPAE*, *25* (2), 197–209.

Oliveira, F. de (2007). "The Lenin Moment," *Mediations*, *23* (1), 83–125.

Ossa, J. A. (2011). "Las verdaderas intenciones del gobierno Santos en la reforma a la educacion superior," *Edicion Especial Ley*, *30*, 24–34.

Otranto, R. C. (2006). "Desvendando a Política da Educação Superior do Governo Lula," *Revista Universidade e Sociedade—ANDES-SN*, *16* (38), 18–29.

Pacheco, P. A. (2011). "La verdadera reforma, detras de la publicitada reforma de la educacion superior," *Revista de la Educacion Superior*, *41* (4), 123–133, 164.

Pearson, T. (2009). "Venezuela Opens National Art Gallery and Launches National Reading Plan," Venezuelanalysis.com, April 28. http://venezuelanalysis.com/news/4402.

Pearson, T. (2011). "Venezuela's Dreams and Demons: Has the Bolivarian Revolution Changed Education?," Venezuelanalysis.com, March 18. http://venezuelanalysis.com/analysis/6072.

Pearson, T. (2012). "Planning the Next 6 Years of Venezuela's Bolivarian Revolution," Venezuelanalysis.com, July 6. http://venezuelanalysis.com/analysis/7091.

Pearson, T. (2013). "Understanding the Venezuelan Presidential Election Outcome," Venezuelanalysis.com, April 15. http://venezuelanalysis.com/analysis/8638.

Pequeno Marinho, A. M., Ferreira Carneiro, F., & Almeida, V. E. (2011). "Dimensão socioambiental em area de agronegócio: A complexa teia de riscos, incertezas e vulnerabilidades," in R. Rigotto, (ed.), *Agrotóxicos, trabalho e saúde: vulnerabilidade e resistência no context da modernização agrícola no Baixo Jaguaribe/CE*. Fortaleza: Edições UFC, pp. 166–214.

Pequeno Marinho, A. M., Araújo Teixeira, C. A. De, Ferrera Monteiro, M., Silva de Castro, F., Braga, S. F., de, & Mattei Maciel, H. R. (2011). "Agronegócio, agricultura familiar, assentamento e comunidade agroecológica: quem são estes trabalhadores?," in R. Rigotto (ed.),

Agrotóxicos, trabahlo e saúde: vulnerabilidade e resistência no context da modernização agrícola no Baixo Jaguaribe/CE. Fortaleza: Edições UFC, pp. 273–295.

Pinilla, P. A. (2012). "El fin de al educacion y la deificacion de la formacion del capital humano." http://orlandopulidochaves.blogspot.com. au/2011/06/el-fin-de-la-educacion-y-la-deificacion.html (last accessed October 3, 2013).

Piper, S. (2007). "After the Elections: A New Party for the Venezuelan Revolution," Socialist Resistance: SR41, January 2007. http://international viewpoint.org/spip.php?article1188

Pontes Furtado, E. D. (2003). "A educação de Jovens e Edultos no Campo: Uma Análise a Luz do PRONERO," in K. S. Lopes de Matos (ed.), *Movimentos Sociais, Educaçã0 Popular e Escola: a favour da diversidade.* Fortaleza: Editora UFC, pp. 198–211.

PRONERA (2007a). "Practica de Ensino: Curso de Formação de Educadores e Educadoras nas Áreas de Assentamentos de Reforma Agrária no Ceará." Fortaleza: Pronera, UECE.

PRONERA (2007b). "Metologia do Trabahlo Científico—Modulo 1." Fortaleza: Pronera and UECE.

PRONERA (2008). "Formação de Educadores: Fundamentos Sociológicos da Educação." Fortaleza: Pronera, UECE.

Raby, D. L. (2006). *Democracy and Revolution: Latin America and Socialism Today.* London: Pluto Press.

Ramírez, E. (2010). *Venezuela posee la quinta matrícula universitaria más alta del mundo.* Caracas: Correo de Orinoco.

Ramirez, F. (2005). *The Profits of Extermination: How US Corporate Power Is Destroying Colombia.* Monroe, ME: Common Courage Press.

Restrepo, P. (1998). *La Máscara, la Mariposa y la Metáfora: Creación Teatral de Mujeres.* Santiago de Cali: Teatro La Máscara.

Reyes, A. (2012). "Revolutions in the Revolutions: A Post-counterhegemonic Moment for Latin America?," *South Atlantic Quarterly, 111* (1), 1–27.

Rhoades, G., & Slaughter, S. (2004). "Academic Capitalism in the New Economy: Challenges and Choices," *American Academic, 1* (1), 37–59.

Rikowski, G. (2012). "Monthly Guest Article (September): Critical Pedagogy and the Constitution of Capitalist Society," September 15. http://www.flowideas.co.uk/?page=articles&sub=Critical%20Pedagogy%20and%20 Capitalism.

Robertson, E. (2013a). "Venezuela: Workers' Control Congress: 'Neither Capitalists Nor Bureaucrats, All Power to the Working Class.'" *Links International Journal of Socialist Renewal.* http://links.org.au/node/3415.

Robertson, E. (2013b). "Venezuela's Nicolas Maduro Sworn in, Promises 'a Revolution of the Revolution,'" Venezuelanalysis.com, April 19. http://venezuelanalysis.com/news/8703.

Robertson, E. (2013c). "Maduro Demands Greater Government Support for Venezuela's Communes," Venezuelanalysis.com, August 16. http://venezuelanalysis.com/news/9948.

Robertson, E. (2013d). "20 New Communes to Launch in Venezuelan Capital," Venezuelanalysis.com, August 19. http://venezuelanalysis.com/news/9957.
Rodas, F. C. (2012). "La privatización de la Universidad pública significa su desnaturalizacion," *Instituto de Filosofia*, 1–9. http://www.udea.edu.co/portal/page/portal/bActualidad/Principal_UdeA/noticias2/reformaLey30/La%20privatizaci%C3%B3n%20de%20la%20universidad%20p%C3%BAblica%20significa%20su%20desnaturalizaci%C3%B3n (last accessed March 2, 2014).
Rodriguez, E. C. (2013). "La reforma de la educacion superior y las protestas estudiantiles en Colombia," *Postdata*, *18* (1), 1–12.
Rose, N. (1993). "Government, Authority and Expertise in Advanced Liberalism," *Economy and Society*, *22* (3), 283–299.
Royston, J. (2013). "Sick Prez Chavez Dies at 58," *The Sun*, March 6. http://www.thesun.co.uk/sol/homepage/news/4826757/Sick-prez-Chavez-dies-at-58.html.
Sabadini, M. S. (2005). "A política econômica do governo Lula: reformismo e submissão ao capital financeiro." http://pendientedemigracion.ucm.es/info/ec/jec10/ponencias/714Sabadini.pdf (last accessed October 15, 2013).
Salcedo, J. R. (2013). "La forma neoliberal del capital humano y sus efectos en el derecho a la educación," *Actual. Pedagog*, *61* (enero-junio del 2013), 113–138.
Salter, L., & Weltman, D. (2011). "Class, Nationalism and News: The BBC's Reporting of Hugo Chavez and the Bolivarian Revolution," *International Journal of Media and Cultural Politics*, 7 (3), 253–273.
Schugurensky, D. (2000). "Adult Education and Social Transformation: On Gramsci, Freire, and the Challenge of Comparing Comparisons," *Comparative Education Review*, *44* (4), 515–522.
Sheehan, C. (2010). "Transcript of Cindy Sheehan's Interview with Hugo Chavez," March 30. http://venezuelanalysis.com/analysis/5233.
Shor, I., & Freire, P. (1987). "What Is the 'Dialogical Method' of Teaching?," *Journal of Education*, *169* (3), 11–31.
Showstack Sassoon, A. (1982). "Passive Revolution and the Politics of Reform," in A. Showstack Sassoon (ed.), *Approaches to Gramsci*. London: Writers and Readers, pp. 127–148.
Socialist Outlook Editorial (2007). "Chavez: 'I Also Am a Trotskyist,'" *Socialist Outlook* 11, Spring. http://www.marxist.com/chavez-trotskyist-president120107.htm.
Spronk, S., & Webber, J. R. (2012). "'Open Horizons': An Interview with Roland Dennis," Venezuelanalysis.com, The Bullet, August 25. http://venezuelanalysis.com/analysis/7202.
Stiglitz, J. (2010). *Freefall: Free Markets and the Sinking of the Global Economy*. London: Allen Lane.
Stokes, D. (2005). *America's Other War: Terrorizing Colombia*. London: Zed Books.

Suggett, J. (2010). "Chávez's Annual Address Includes Minimum Wage Hike, Maintenance of Social Spending in Venezuela." http://venezuelanalysis.com/news/5077 (last accessed August 5, 2010).
Székely, M. (2001). "The 1990s in Latin America: Another Decade of Persistent Inequality, but with Somewhat Lower Poverty." Working Paper 454. Washington, DC: Inter-American Development Bank, Research Department.
Tamayo Valencia, A. (2006). "El movimiento pedagogico en Colombia," *Revista HISTEDBR On-line, Campinas*, 24, 102–113.
Teivanen, T. (2002). *Enter Economism, Exit Politics: Experts, Economic Policy and the Political*. London: Zed Books.
Thompson, P., and Žižek, S. (2013). *The Privatization of Hope: Ernst Bloch and the Future of Utopia*. Durham, NC; London: Duke University Press.
Tiriba, L. (2004). "Ciência econômica e saber popular: reivindicar o 'popular' na economia e na educação," in L. Tiriba and I. Picanço (eds.), *Trabalho e Educação: arquitetos, abelhas e outros tecelões da economia popular solidária*. São Paulo: Idéias e Letras, pp. 75–102.
Tygel, A. F., & Souza de Alvear, C. A. (2011). "The Development of an Information System for the Solidarity Economy Movement," *Journal of Community Informatics*, Special Double Issue: The Internet and Community Informatics in Brazil, 7, 1–2.
United Nations Development Programme Report (2011). http://hdr.undp.org/en/reports/global/hdr2011/download/.
UPTM Kleber Ramirez (2013). http://www.uptm.edu.ve:8080/iute/website/estudios/pea.
Valencia, M. (2013). "Language Policy and the Manufacturing of Consent for Foreign Intervention in Colombia," *PROFILE*, 15 (1), 27–43.
Victor, M. P. (2009). "From Conquistadores, Dictators and Multinationals to the Bolivarian Revolution," Keynote speech at the Conference on Land and Freedom, of The Caribbean Studies Program, University of Toronto, October 31. Venezuelanalyis.com, December 4. http://www.venezuelanalysis.com/analysis/4979.
Vulliamy, E. (2002). "Venezuela Coup Linked to Bush Team," *The Oberver*, Sunday, April 21. http://www.theguardian.com/world/2002/apr/21/usa.venezuela.
Wilpert, G. (2007). *Changing Venezuela by Taking Power: The History and the Policies of the Chávez Government*. London: Verso.
Wilpert, G. (2010). "Prologue," in C. Martinez, M. Fox, and J. Farrell (eds.), *Venezuela Speaks: Voices from the Grassroots*. Oakland, CA: PM Press.
Wirth, I. G., Fraga, L. S., & Novaes, H. T. (2011). "Educação, Trabalho e Autogestão: limites e possibilidades da Economia Solidária," in E. L. Batista and H. Novaes (eds.), *Trabalho, educação e reprodução social: as contradições do capital no século XXI*. Bauru: Canal 6, pp. 180–206.
Woods, A. (2009). "First Extraordinary Congress of the PSUV—Chavez Calls for the Fifth International," in *Defence of Marxism*, November 23. http://www.marxist.com/first-extraordinary-congress-psuv.htm.

World Bank (2013). "Bolsa Família: Changing the Lives of Millions in Brazil." http://go.worldbank.org/3QI1C7B5U0.
Yogev, E., & Michaeli, N. (2011). "Teachers as Society-Involved 'Organic Intellectuals': Training Teachers in a Political Context," *Journal of Teacher Education*, 62 (3), 312–324.
Young, C., & Franco, J. (2013). "No Matter Who Wins in Venezuela, Chavez's Legacy Is Secure," *Reuters*, April 12. http://blogs.reuters.com/great-debate/2013/04/12/no-matter-who-wins-in-venezuela-chavezs-legacy-is-secure/.
Zapata, V. (2012). "La uni-pluri-versidad esta en peligro de desparecer en Colombia," *Uni-pluri/versidad*, 11 (1), 1–2. Facultad de Educación—Universidad de Antioquia. Medellín, Col.
Zembylas, M. (2003). "Interrogating 'Teacher Identity': Emotion, Resistance and Self-Formation," *Educational Theory*, 53 (1), 107–127.
Žižek, S. (2013). "The 'Fake' Mandela Memorial Interpreter Said It All," *Guardian*, December 18.

Index

21st century, 7, 15, 16, 65, 66, 67, 72, 74, 87, 89, 108, 110, 111, 112, 113, 115, 141, 171, 182, 187, 188, 195, 198, 207, 208
  advance to, 101
  anti-, 87
  Bolivarian, 74, 83
  as common word, 99–100, 111
  commune, 76
  construction of, 77, 100
  curriculum, 111
  democratic, 91, 108
  economically productive, 91
  education for, 80, 82
  exchange, 81
  habits, 111
  indigenous, 101
  mode of living, 91
  motherland, 81
  of MST, 136
  praxis, 99
  pro-, 107, 111
  revolutionary, 11, 79, 99, 107, 112, 113
  seen as authoritarian, 100
  state, 75, 188
  substance of, 111
  territorial, 91
  thinking, 79
  transformation, 113, 131
  values, 99, 110, 111
  ways of life, 139
  see also anticapitalism, collectivism, counterhegemony, Marxism, postcapitalism, resistance
23 de Enero barrio, 68, 91
24 Hours (TV show), 73

A Ávore (poem), 134
A carta do Ciço (text), 134

Abrams, Elliot, 86
abstraction, 130, 196, 206
  conceptual, 13, 111, 156
academia, 37, 38, 49, 62–4, 79, 82–3, 79, 85, 115, 118, 124, 149, 150, 176, 195, 201, 202–3, 207
  see also universities
ACCES (Access with Quality to Higher Education), 35
Acción Cultural Popular (Popular Cultural Action), 144, 183
accumulation, 48, 114, 182
  by dispossession, 118
  model of, 48
  primitive, 48
  strategy of, 9, 21
  see also capitalism
Acevedo, Marybel, 157
Acselrad, Mello, and Bezerra, 49
activism, 33, 49, 77, 83, 99, 100, 110, 118, 122, 123, 137, 156, 167, 196, 206
  knowledges of, 123
  nonviolent, 33
AD. *See* Democratic Action
Adrian, Tamara, 90
adult education. *See* education
aesthetics, 167
affect/emotion, 2, 4, 5, 6, 11, 12, 13, 14, 27, 28, 30, 40, 45, 51, 83, 118, 119–20, 123, 124, 125, 127, 128, 129, 133, 136, 140, 141, 151, 155, 156, 157, 159, 160, 161, 163, 166, 167, 168, 169, 170, 171, 178, 179, 191, 193, 194, 196–8
affection, 106, 109, 119, 191
  binary with intellect, 168
blockages, 13
chains of affection, 153

affect/emotion—*Continued*
    control of, 14, 191, 197
    deep knowledge, 171
    distortion of, 13, 170, 196
    emotional alchemy, 197
    emotional palette, 170, 178
    emotionality, 13, 120
    hierarchy of, 191
    landscapes of, 194
    see also anger, anxiety, courage, greed, humour, joy, love, stress, trauma, trust
affirmation, 8, 15, 37, 121, 170, 171, 186, 193, 197, 199
affirmative action, 37, 59, 62
affirmative concepts. *See* authenticity, autonomy, becoming, border-thinking, care, coconstruction, communion, cooperation, desire, dialogue, dignity, dreaming, emancipation, empowerment, erotic, experimentation, flourishing, flow, friendship, good sense, healing, hope, horizons, imagination, immanence, joy, listening, love, nurturing, openness, oppression, personalization, potentiality, prefiguration, reciprocity, reflection, solidarity, storytelling, utopia, voice, weaving
Afro-Brazilians, 63, 123, 185
Afro-Colombians, 158, 162, 185
Afro-Venezuelans, 66, 69, 70, 72, 79, 90, 111, 185
anti-racism in Venezuela, 207
Agathangelou and Ling, 13–14, 140, 181
agroindustry, 48, 49, 50, 138
agrotoxins, 48–9
Aguablancas, 160
ALBA (Alianza Bolivariana para los Pueblos de Nuestra América), 71
alcoholism, 102
alienation, 1, 6, 12, 13, 14, 15, 119, 120, 123, 168, 169, 170, 181, 196
    affective alienation, 12
    from body, 12–13
    dealienation, 168
    disarticulation, 4, 10, 19–23, 27, 32–4, 38, 40, 44, 45, 46, 47, 50, 51, 54, 55, 56, 61, 63, 139, 144, 149, 176, 177, 179–80, 186, 188
    disassociation, 171, 190
    estrangement, 171

fragmentation, 3, 4, 10, 19, 27, 34, 36, 40, 43, 45, 46, 50, 51, 58, 59, 60, 61, 63, 122, 129, 139, 145, 146, 170, 178, 182, 185, 188, 189, 190, 196
    of human experience, 168
    inner, 184
    isolation, 7, 106, 146, 148, 151, 163
    as liberation, 197
    segmentation, 60, 133
    separation, 3, 6, 7, 12, 13, 14, 30, 45, 51, 61, 119, 121, 123, 135, 140, 145, 151, 169, 170, 171, 176, 177, 178, 181, 183, 185, 186, 187, 191, 194, 196, 199
    transgression of, 119, 169–70
    see also forms of oppression, fragmentation
Allen, Lewis, 206
Almeida de Carvalho, 59–60
Alternative School of Community Organization and Communicational Development, 97–115, 207–8
Althusser, Louis, 78–9
Alvaredo, Cornelio, 67
Alves, 44
Amontada, 125
Amsler, 179, 192
Amsler and Bolsmann, 177
AN. *See* National Assembly
ancestral practices, 196
Andes, 98
anger, 158, 170, 197
Anglos, 177, 208
antagonism, 10
anticapitalism, 84, 107, 111, 169
    see also socialism
anxiety, 179
Anzaldúa, Gloria, 13, 120, 141, 184, 196, 197, 198
Anzola, Myriam, 97, 106
    and Pearson, 97, 98, 99, 114, 115
architecture, 10
Argentina, 4, 87
army, 24, 69, 78, 83
    see also coups, militarization
Arrango, Jose Roberto, 23
Arruda, Marcus, 119–21, 123–4
art, 71, 124, 135, 145, 156, 160, 185, 206
    guerrilla, 206
    of living, 122

INDEX

Articulação de Esquerda, 45, 50
articulation, 5, 9, 10, 15, 19, 20, 21,
    23, 40, 43, 44, 45, 46, 49, 51,
    54, 56, 64, 82, 105, 118, 119,
    120, 121, 123, 139, 149, 150,
    151, 152, 156, 157, 162, 166,
    169, 175, 179, 180, 182, 184,
    185, 190, 192, 198, 199, 203
  of consent, 19, 22, 44, 63
  counterhegemonic, 29, 58
  cultural, 64
  epistemological, 44, 121
  hegemonic, 5, 19, 190
  patriarchal, 198
  rearticulation, 51
  of socialism, 15, 80, 119–20
  spaces of, 203
  by state, 10
  see also disarticulation, hegemony
Artz, 75
assessment, 29, 30, 34, 89, 202
  see also ranking, surveillance
Assimakopoulos, Panagiotis, 206
assimilation, 11
Ataco, 24
AUC (Autodefensas Unidas de
    Colombia), 20
austerity, 21, 22
  see also neoliberalism
authenticity, 79, 82, 168
  see also affirmative concepts
authoritarianism, 21, 100, 144, 148,
    151, 169, 186, 189
  anti-, 19, 101, 191
  versus authoritativeness, 104,
    110–11, 207
  in education, 15, 83, 100, 104, 140
  see also forms of oppression
Autodefensas Unidas de Colombia. See
    AUC
autogestion, 120, 122
  see also solidarity economy
autonomy
  of community governance, 11, 122
  in critical pedagogy, 121, 139, 146
  financial, 36, 61
  in Marxism, 79
  in neoliberalism, 37, 61
  of particular educational projects, 99,
    128, 131, 189, 202
  in relationships, 139
  relative, 145
  reproductive, 48

  self-government, 75, 76, 119,
    122, 169
  social, 47, 74, 131, 169, 187, 194
  in social movements, 154, 192
  of subject, 7, 55, 56, 86
  of teachers, 32, 35, 190
  of universities and schools (from
    neoliberalism), 149, 150,
    152, 176, 177, 186, 191, 202
  see also affirmative concepts
autoreduction, 68
Aves de Paraíso, 158, 163
Aymara, 168
Azzellini, Dario, 74–8

Baert and Shipman, 178
Bahia, 48
Ball, 57, 58
banalization, 61
  see also forms of oppression
Bank of Brazil, 47
banking education, 101, 121
Barreira e De Paula, 127
Barrio Adentro, 85, 103
Barrio Pueblo Neuvo, 66, 84,
    97–115, 207–8
Barros Monteiro, Maria Ocília, 126
Bartolome, Lillia, 136
Baruta barrio, 93
base militants, 46
BBC (British Broadcasting
    Corporation), 87
Beck, 176
becoming, 7, 16, 63, 121, 136, 141,
    185, 187, 188, 191, 197, 199
  see also affirmative concepts
Belen, Mérida, 110
Bercovitch, 89, 92
Bermúdez, Norma, 20, 164,
    166–8, 196
Bernal et al, 148
Bernardo, 120
Bernstein, 176
Bianchi and Braga, 46, 50, 51
biodiversity, 24, 48
Birchfield, 10
black feminism, 8, 13, 14, 119
black people, 6, 69. See also Afro-
    Brazilians, Afro-Colombians,
    Afro-Venezuelans
Blair, Tony, 1
Bloch, Ernst, 93, 205
body. See embodiment

INDEX

bodywork, 156
Boff and Boff, 185
Bohorquez, 147, 148
Boito, 45, 49
Bolaños and Tattay, 148
Boli-bourgeoisie, 88
Bolivar (town, Colombia), 24
Bolivarian process, 75–6, 109, 114, 115
Bolivarian Revolution, 65, 66, 73, 74, 80, 82, 83, 85, 86, 88, 109
Bolivarian Revolutionary Movement (MBR), 69
Bolivariano, El, 67
Bolivia, 4, 5, 205
Boloña, Lucy, 157
Bolsa Escola, 52–4
Bolsa Familia, 51, 52–5, 56, 63
book, purpose of, 1, 7, 15
Boom, 145, 185, 186
border-thinking, 124, 136, 140, 195, 197
  see also affirmative concepts
Borges de Souza, Conceição Ferreira, and Gritti, 138
boundaries, 7, 136, 166, 194, 195
bourgeoisie, 9, 23, 75, 91, 180, 187, 197
  Boli-, 88
  petty, 89
  see also capitalism
Braga, Vicente da Silva, and Paz Feitoso, 46, 48, 49
brand recognition, 177
Bravo, Douglas, 66, 67, 79, 89
Bravo, Napoleón, 73
Brazil, 4, 7, 8, 15, 43–64, 117–41, 169, 175, 177, 179, 181, 182, 183, 185, 186, 187, 188, 189, 205
Brecht, 157
Breilh, 48
Brittain, 21
Bruce, 70
Buci-Glucksmann, Christine, 9
Buenaventura, Enrique, 156
bureaucracy, 2, 9, 45, 46, 50, 55, 63, 76, 77, 79, 84, 88, 89, 93, 113, 114, 115, 119, 120, 176.
  See also state concepts
burnout, 136, 137
Bush, George W., 24, 111

Cabezas, Casas, and Valencia, 149
Cadavid et al., 22, 31, 34, 35
Caixa Economica Federal, 53
Caldera Rodríguez, Rafael, 69
Caldert, Periera, Alentejano, and Frigotto, 124
Cali, 143, 146, 157, 160, 162, 163
Cameron, David, 206
Campo and Giraldo, 36, 37
Canada, 24
Cano Likmon-Covenas, 24
capacity building, 29–31, 35–6, 49
capital
  agricultural, 48, 131
  (*see also* agroindustry)
  finance, 4, 36, 40, 47, 64, 180
  (*see also* debt)
  formation of, 206
  forms of, 5
  human, 26, 38
  national, 38
  power of, 145
  private, 61
  structural power of, 10
  trans/multi/international, 2, 27, 28, 38, 47, 48, 49, 138, 177
capitalism, 77, 78, 82, 91, 100, 109, 168, 169, 170, 182
  academic, 27
  alternatives to, 8, 15, 23, 77, 82, 93, 111, 120, 123, 141, 182, 194, 195
  (*see also* anticapitalism, socialism)
  capitalist realism, 205
  colonial, 57, 130, 133, 166, 170, 181
  (*see also* coloniality)
  colonial patriarchal, 1, 13, 119, 120, 121, 123, 138, 140, 143, 144, 148, 155, 158, 170, 175, 195, 197 (*see also* coloniality)
  development of, 2, 49
  education, 110, 131
  epistemologies of, 86, 140, 182, 188
  exploitation, 2
  forms of, 8, 12, 20, 113
  global, 175 (*see also* globalization)
  heartlands of, 87, 109
  hegemonic form of, 10, 189
  imaginary of, 81
  imperatives of, 82
  logic(s) of, 12, 26, 176, 181, 188, 194
  militarized, 143, 155, 158, 190, 194
  neoliberal, 1, 2, 14, 15, 23, 25, 26, 41, 49, 61, 62, 65, 68, 71, 72, 138,

155, 159, 164, 175, 181, 187, 191, 194 (*see also* neoliberalism)
patriarchal, 14, 119, 157, 165 (*see also* gendered division of labour, patriarchy)
production, 26, 170
reproduction of, 8–9, 20 (*see also* social reproduction)
social relations of, 168
society as, 72, 78, 107, 109, 113, 128
state as, 75, 78, 82, 188, 206
structures of, 86, 123
thinking of, 81, 182
values of, 82, 101
word, 111
world system of, 87 (*see also* international division of labour)
see also accumulation, bourgeoisie, capital, efficiency, imperialism, instrumentality, marketization, profit
Capriles Radonski, Henrique, 90, 93
Caracas, 68, 73, 83, 91–3, 109
Caracazo (1989), 65–9
Cardoso, 47, 52, 57, 59, 129
care, 125, 127, 137, 140, 178, 184, 187, 191, 193, 194, 197–8
ethics of, 130, 198
politics of, 16, 123, 197, 199
see also affirmative concepts
careerism, 7
Caribbean, 68, 70, 71
Carmona, Pedro, 73, 86
carnavalesque, 153
Carroll, Rory, 87
Carta ao Povo Brasileiro, 46–7
Carter, Jimmy, 87
Carvalho, Sandra, 125–6, 127, 132
Castañeda, Nora, 68–9
Castro, Fidel, 69, 205
Catani and Gilioli, 60
Catholicism, 67, 72, 185
see also religion
Cauca, 147, 162
Caucaia, 125, 208
CAYAPA, 98, 112, 207
CCTV, 151
Ceará, 48, 49, 57, 125, 127, 131, 132, 136
Ceceña, 6, 127, 166, 168, 194
CEID (Centros de Estudios e Investigaciones Docentes), 146

CELAC (Community of Latin American and Caribbean States), 71, 92
Cendales and Muñoz, 144
Cendales et al, 6
Central Bank, 23, 47
Central Única dos Trabalhadores (CUT), 25, 59
Cepeda, 22, 23, 25
charisma, 74
Chávez, Hugo, 4, 65–75, 77–89, 92–3, 99, 108, 109, 111, 112, 115, 186
see also Bolivarian Revolution
Che Guevara Collective, 68
Chicana writers, 13
Chile, 87
Chocó, 158, 162
choice, 4, 27, 28, 29, 35, 36, 37, 39, 57, 92, 105, 130, 175, 179, 180
see also neoliberalism
Christ, Jesus, 67, 111
see also religion
Christian Democratic Party. *See* COPEI
Christianity, 67
see also Catholicism, liberation theology, religion
Ciccariello-Maher, 66, 67, 68, 69, 72, 73, 74, 75, 76, 78, 79, 87, 88, 114
Ciclos
de Calidad, 30
de escolarização, 57
circus, 157
civil society. *See* society
class, 8, 9, 10, 20, 21, 22, 23, 25, 37, 43–54, 60, 63–4, 66, 69, 70, 72, 77, 78, 99, 100, 118, 123, 128, 132, 133, 139, 166, 168, 177, 205, 206
see also bourgeoisie, informal working class, peasants, organized working class, working class
clientelism, 61, 88
closure. *See* openness
CNN (Central News Network), 71
Coco. *See* Solzana
coconstruction, 16, 129, 140, 151, 153–6, 170, 184, 188, 192, 193, 195–8
see also affirmative concepts
coercion, 19, 21, 33
see also forms of oppression, violence
cognition, 5, 6, 26, 141
Cole, Mike (other works), 78, 207

INDEX

Colectivo Situaciones, 194
collectivism, 120, 206
  see also socialism
Collini, 180
Colombia, 1, 5, 7, 8, 15, 19–41,
  143–71, 175, 177, 179, 181, 182,
  183, 185, 186, 187, 188, 189, 190,
  191, 192, 193, 201–4, 205
  constitution of 1991, 21–2
colonialism, 123
coloniality
  capitalist, 2, 25, 27, 29, 34, 38, 41,
    57, 132, 137, 140, 143, 155, 166,
    169, 170, 176, 180, 181, 183, 184,
    185, 188, 190, 191, 194, 195
  knowing subject of, 197
  paradigms of, 15
  patriarchal capitalist, 6, 8, 15, 16,
    141, 144, 148, 169, 181, 182,
    188, 193, 194, 196, 198 (*see also*
    capitalism)
colonization, 179
colonized, 171, 183
  beliefs, 184
colonizers, 6, 181, 188
Columbus, Christopher, 111
Comites de Tierra Urbana
  (Venezuela), 5
commitment, 1, 3, 5, 6, 7, 11, 16, 37,
  46, 47, 51, 56, 59, 77, 89, 91, 99,
  113, 118, 120, 121, 127, 129, 130,
  132, 133, 136, 137, 138, 139, 140,
  148, 150, 151, 152, 153, 154, 156,
  157, 167, 169, 170, 171, 178, 182,
  184, 185, 186, 188, 189, 191, 193,
  195, 197, 198, 199, 201, 202, 203
commodities and commodification, 2,
  19, 26, 34, 57, 63, 66, 124, 125,
  136, 140, 151, 155, 175, 176, 178,
  191, 197
  see also forms of oppression
common sense, 9–11, 14, 87, 133, 145,
  149
  see also false consciousness, good
  sense, hegemony, ideology
communal councils, 65, 69, 74, 75,
  75–6, 77, 78, 80, 83, 91, 110
communes, 65, 74, 76, 78, 80, 91
communication, 2, 20, 50, 79, 81, 97,
  98, 99, 100, 104, 105, 152
communion, 170, 185, 193, 197, 199
  see also affirmative concepts
communities, 31, 122, 193, 194
  academic, 62, 150, 151, 176,
    201, 202
  activism, 99, 100
  autonomy of, 186
  business, 23
  capacities of, 160
  communal enterprises/production,
    77, 81, 118, 138
  communal libraries, 80, 103
  communal meals, 100
  community as a value, 109, 112, 113
  community development, 160
  community facilitators, 158
  community legal centre, 85
  community radio, 103
  community theatre, 158, 162
  community vision, 103
  construction/production of, 6,
    40, 108, 157, 160, 170, 181,
    182, 185, 191, 195, 198
  as contexts, 98
  culture of, 49
  democratization of, 108
  destruction of, 159, 164, 178
  displaced, 159, 160
  domination of/in, 167, 183
  educational work in, 46, 54, 61,
    83–4, 100, 122, 130, 197
  epistemic communities/knowledge
    in communities, 30, 36, 56,
    147–8, 162, 177, 195
  exclusion of, 21, 37, 48, 125, 127,
    158, 159, 160, 181
  experience of, 21, 185
  grassroots, 207
  identification with, 110
  improvement of, 112, 183
  indigenous, 51, 101
  inequality between, 2
  knowledge exchange in, 114
  of managers, 30
  marginalized, 103, 160, 198
  multiple, 196
  needs/interests/realities of, 57, 62,
    75, 84, 124, 128, 130, 133, 145,
    147, 187
  oppressed, 3, 7, 34, 140, 141, 145,
    158, 170, 171, 179, 182, 183,
    184, 185
  organizing of, 110, 115, 124, 126,
    128, 129, 138, 188
  peasant, 133
  as (pedagogical) spaces, 7, 40, 140, 159

politicization of, 123
poor, 4, 32, 36, 99, 206
power of, 78, 80, 85
relationship to educators, 32, 61, 83–4, 102, 110, 111, 112, 137, 140, 146, 150, 169, 187
of resistance, 27, 62, 151, 155, 190, 193
responsible for education, 22
re-weaving of, 143
role of women in, 165
rural, 49, 124, 125, 126, 130, 132, 133, 195, 196
self-construction of, 6, 119, 123, 128, 130, 140, 148
self-government of, 5, 11, 126, 127, 186, 191 (see also communes, communal councils)
service to, 77, 83, 85, 100, 102
shaming of, 178
sharing with, 167
situated, 124
struggles, 4, 7, 16, 124, 130, 133, 135, 145, 188, 195
subaltern, 4, 54, 117, 128, 140, 167, 188, 193
as subjects, 193
of teachers, 30, 202
traditions of, 124, 162, 183, 194
visibility and voice of, 164
COMOSOL, 203
competencies, 26, 30, 31, 38
 see also skills, education for skills
competitiveness, 2, 3, 26, 29, 35, 37, 39, 56, 62, 63, 64, 83, 114, 151, 155, 177, 180, 182, 191, 194, 196
complexity, 5, 7, 8, 12, 15, 20, 49, 74, 118, 122, 123, 160, 168, 170, 171, 193, 196, 198, 205
Comuna 14, 160, 162
conditional transfers, 51–2, 60
conflict resolution, 161
CONPES, 23
conscientization, 101
consent/consensus, 9, 10, 12, 19–22, 24–5, 28, 33, 34, 40, 44, 45, 63, 138, 154, 203
constitution
 Brazil, 58
 Colombia, 21–2, 25, 29, 35, 146
 Venezuela, 69, 73
consumer society, 27

consumerism, 27, 82
 see also commodities and commodification, neoliberalism
consumers, 2, 3, 19, 26, 27, 35, 39, 40, 41, 49, 59, 63, 148, 151, 176, 177, 179, 180
consumption, 26, 27, 38, 100, 176, 186, 189
Conte, 128, 138
contradictions, 5, 8, 10, 14, 19, 21, 41, 43, 44, 45, 46, 47, 51, 62, 64, 107, 108, 118, 122, 123, 127, 129, 130, 132, 139, 145, 149, 187, 188, 189
Contreras, Hellen, 104, 105
Contreras, Ruby, 104
Convergence (party), 69
CONVIVIR, 20
cooperation, 100, 109, 111, 206
 see also affirmative concepts
cooperative education facilitators, 99
cooperative games, 101, 103
cooperative learning, 114
cooperatives (economic), 25, 72, 118, 120, 122–3, 124, 135, 140, 195
co-optation, 118, 119, 146
Coordinadora Nacional de Estudiantes Universitarios (CNEU), 151
Coordinadora Simón Bolívar, 68.
COPEI, 66, 69
corruption, 22, 34, 61, 76, 88, 89, 90, 91, 111, 114, 131, 151
Cortez, Miguel, 97, 107, 108, 111
cosmologies
 5, 6, 14, 67, 117, 119, 123, 140, 183
 see also epistemology
Coté et al., 2, 7, 11
Cotos, 184
counterhegemonic
 articulations, 29
 decolonial, 8, 12, 182
 education, 32, 38, 44, 82, 86, 139. 144, 146, 152, 169
 epistemological, 15, 26, 51, 120, 140, 144
 practices, 44, 58, 188, 199
 resistances, 56
 subjectivities, 12, 14, 21, 26, 34, 40, 58, 155, 180
counterhegemony, 7, 8, 10, 12, 14, 15, 16, 35, 46, 47, 64, 65, 73, 85, 101, 117, 128, 146, 151, 169
 see also socialism
counterinsurgency, 21

coups
  by Chávez (1992), 65, 67, 69
  against Chávez (2002), 65, 72–4, 86–7, 93
  in Chile (1973), 87
courage, 136, 140, 170, 197
CPM, 144–6, 151
cracks, 4, 118, 149
  see also contradictions
creativity, 2, 6, 56, 86, 90, 98, 101, 109, 148, 152, 153, 155, 156, 157, 158, 160, 163, 168, 170, 175, 181, 184, 185, 191, 196, 199, 203, 208
crime, 89
criminalization, 33, 149, 175
  see also forms of oppression
criminology, 100
crisis, 9, 22, 136, 167, 205
critical theory, 178
CTV (Venezuelan Labour Confederation), 72
Cuba, 69, 84, 92, 111, 205
curriculum, 2, 3, 28, 29, 31, 34, 35, 55, 57–8, 63, 98, 115, 122, 130, 132, 133, 139, 140, 147, 150, 186, 190, 195
  alternative, 187
  Bolivarian, 81–3, 97, 107, 111
CUT. See *Central Única dos Trabalhadores*
cycles of schooling, 57

dance, 98, 100, 102, 105, 135, 145, 156, 157, 162, 168, 170, 191, 198
Davies, 60, 62
de Almeida, Pingas, Pinto, and Knijnik, 128, 137
de Angelis and Harvie, 2, 175, 182, 189
De Ferranti et al, 52
de Janvry et al, 52, 53, 54
De Paula, 59, 60, 61, 62, 63, 127
  and Avezedo, 61
de Souza et al, 130, 132, 138
death squads, 86, 87, 158
death threats, 3, 21, 33, 158
debt, 3, 4, 27, 37, 62, 64, 68, 73, 149, 180, 189
  see also financialization, capital, finance
decentering, 16, 141, 156, 183, 191, 193
decentralization, 5, 29, 30, 48, 50, 54, 79, 185

decoloniality and decolonization, 4, 7, 8, 12, 13, 14, 15, 16, 90, 95, 120, 133, 140, 141, 143, 155, 169, 170, 171, 179, 181, 182, 183, 184, 187, 188, 191, 192, 193, 195, 196, 198
deconstruction, 8, 13, 14, 15, 29, 40, 147, 181
dedemocratization, 23, 50, 51, 55, 176, 180, 186
Defence Committee of the Right to Education, 203
dehumanization, 4, 125, 179
  see also forms of oppression
deintellectualization, 3, 40, 136, 155, 178, 186
delegitimation, 1, 13, 23, 29, 32, 34, 35, 76, 88, 149, 158, 179, 181, 187
  see also forms of oppression
delinking, 45, 51
Democracia Socialista, 45
democracy, democratic and democratization, 6, 22, 23, 29, 33, 35, 37, 43, 44, 45, 51, 54, 55, 56, 58, 59, 60, 62, 63, 65, 82, 83, 85, 86, 87, 92, 100, 128, 131, 132, 140, 143, 144, 145, 148, 149, 150, 151, 152, 153, 154, 155, 169, 179, 180, 182, 185, 186, 188, 189, 190, 191, 192, 195, 203, 207
  capitalist, 206
  freedoms, 202
  learning environments, 101, 207
  liberal, 176
  methodologies, 192
  participatory, 69, 72, 82, 100, 105, 108, 110, 113, 153, 191, 202
  pedagogies, 140
  representative, 76, 82
  revolution, 91
  social, 72, 75, 113
  spaces, 207
  subjectivity, 192, 194
  values, 99
  workplace, 74, 76–7
Democratic Action, 66
Democratic Republican Union, 66
demonization
  of Chavez as dictator, 86–7
  of communities, 160, 162
  see also forms of oppression
denaturalization, 8, 178, 181
Denes, 52

INDEX 235

Denis, 194
dengue, 107
Dennis, Roland, 75
dependency
   global, 27, 45, 57 (*see also*
     international division of labour,
     capitalist world system)
   inter-, 184
   social, 63
depoliticization, 3, 19, 29, 30, 31, 34,
   40, 46, 51, 55, 57, 138, 139, 149,
   178, 186, 191
deprofessionalization, 3, 19, 40, 155,
   186, 187
deregulation, 3, 21, 48
desertion, 31–2
desire, 13, 27, 28, 34, 37, 121,
   125, 126, 136, 149, 154,
   155, 157, 164, 165, 168,
   180, 184, 196, 197
   see also affirmative concepts
determinism, 8
development, 4, 13, 27, 28, 57, 144, 149,
   153, 175, 179, 188, 189, 205
   capitalist, 2, 8
   community, 160
   democratising, 128, 150
   dependent, 45, 57
   economic, 26
   educational, 36, 139
   endogenous, 82, 84, 86, 115
   human, 26, 53, 71, 183
   human capital, 26, 38
   inclusive, 43
   infrastructural, 31
   integral, 122, 123
   neoliberal, 19, 24, 27, 29, 31, 43, 47,
     48, 49, 52, 55, 148
   of production, 48
   resource, 24, 150
   rural, 70, 128, 129
   self, 122
   social, 49, 133, 152
   social movement, 5, 10, 48, 51, 64,
     122, 128, 138, 192, 203
   socialist, 78, 82, 84, 86, 91,
     108, 139
   sustainable, 129
   technological, 29, 115
   under-, 13, 40, 130, 182, 183,
     184, 205
   urban, 118
developmentalism, 20, 21, 139

Dezim, 127
dialectics, 11, 65, 73, 74, 87, 112
dialogue, 15, 16, 101, 119, 121, 123,
   124, 126, 132, 133, 140, 145,
   146, 148, 151, 152, 156, 157,
   159, 163, 164, 165, 167, 183,
   184, 187, 191, 193, 194, 195, 196,
   199, 201, 202, 203, 204, 207
   see also affirmative concepts
Diáz and Bermúdez, 196
Díaz, Luis, 105
difference, 98, 126, 146, 148, 151, 181,
   185, 197
differend, 206
dignity, 3, 27, 37, 115, 133, 135,
   136, 146, 149, 158, 160, 162,
   165, 170, 175, 179, 181, 183,
   185, 189, 195, 206
   see also affirmative concepts
Diniz and Gilbert, 124, 127
dirty wars, 86
disability, 98
discipline, 2, 3, 4, 20, 25, 26, 28, 29,
   30, 31, 32, 40, 51, 54, 56, 57, 62,
   63, 64, 83, 84, 101, 105, 122, 134,
   139, 140, 176, 177, 178, 179, 187
   see also forms of oppression
discomfort, 124, 158, 197
discrimination, 60, 123, 162
   see also forms of oppresion
displacement, 21, 33, 158, 159, 160,
   162, 163, 167
   see also forms of oppression
dispossession, 118, 124, 125
   see also forms of oppression
docility, 25, 26, 28, 34, 40, 155
Doha, 205
domination, 5, 7, 8, 9, 10, 11, 12, 14,
   15, 16, 19, 20, 21, 34, 35, 45, 50,
   64, 78, 87, 105, 113, 119, 121,
   125, 128, 131, 136, 141, 144, 149,
   167, 168, 169, 176, 178, 181, 183,
   184, 188, 191, 192, 195, 198, 207
   see also forms of oppression
Dominguez, 70, 81, 92, 206
Dorado Cardona, 146
dreaming, 128, 136, 155, 163, 164,
   168, 183, 184
   see also affirmative concepts
drugs, 20, 21, 23, 24, 102, 109
dualisms, 14, 121, 127, 166, 168, 170,
   187
   see also forms of oppression

INDEX

ECLAC, 70
ecology, 24, 98, 112, 119, 121
  agroecology, 48, 98, 111
Ecuador, 5
education/pedagogy/learning
  access to, 3, 27, 32, 40, 60, 64, 83
  active, 111
  adult, 7, 129, 131, 132, 138, 144, 147
  affective, 5, 14, 121, 125, 127, 128, 133, 151, 155, 157, 159, 160, 166, 167, 169, 180, 190, 191, 193, 194, 196, 198
  alternative, 4, 15, 32, 34, 66, 84, 98, 108, 109, 114, 115, 128, 143, 144, 148, 150, 152, 153, 154, 169, 176, 182, 189, 203
  Alternative School of Community Organization and Communicational Development, 97–115, 107–8
  and enjoyment, 104
  and epistemology, 1, 5, 7
  and work, 129
  anti-authoritarian, 19
  anti-capitalist, 107
  anti-methods, 136
  for art of living, 122
  articulation of, 51, 149
  authoritarian, 15, 104, 105, 111, 140, 148, 207
  authoritative, 111, 207
  autogestion as, 120
  autonomous, 128, 139, 145, 176, 189, 190, 191
  banking, 101, 121
  basic, 37
  from below, 11, 95
  bourgeois, 187
  capitalist, 26, 55, 86, 110, 131, 187, 188
  caring, 137
  classed and raced orientations to, 52
  collective, 5, 63, 101, 127, 136, 141, 152, 163, 191, 193
  commodified, 2, 19, 26, 59, 140, 151, 176, 178
  for common good, 114
  competitive, 62, 114
  concrete, 129
  connections, 124
  conservative, 83, 110, 186
  of construction, 152
  consumerist, 26, 39, 40, 175, 176, 180, 189
  conventional, 83
  cooperative, 114
  counterhegemonic, 8, 12, 15, 16, 32, 38, 44, 82, 86, 101, 117, 124, 139, 140, 144, 145, 152, 169, 180, 182
  creative, 101, 119, 151, 160
  credit, 36
  critical, 7, 8, 15, 19, 38, 40, 62, 63, 82, 100, 131, 136, 144, 145, 147, 148, 151, 152, 155, 179, 187
    for critical thinking and practice, 31, 145
    of crossing, 168
  cultural, 158
  decentralized, 29–30, 57
  decolonizing, 143, 171, 179, 188, 193
  de-democratization of, 176, 180
  deep, 152, 163, 170, 183, 185, 193, 196
  definition of pedagogy, 5
  deintellectualization of, 186
  demands on, 3
  democratic, 16, 33, 54, 55, 56, 58, 60, 62, 83, 85, 92, 100, 128, 140, 148, 149, 152, 153–4, 180, 185, 190, 192
  depoliticized, 7, 29, 31, 138, 178
  desertion, 32, 70
  design of, 57
  for development, 26, 84, 133, 150, 179, 189
  dialogical, 101, 122, 126, 133, 145, 151, 161, 167, 187, 207
  didactic, 104
  disciplinary, 2, 31
  of discomfort, 197
  distance learning, 38, 56, 57
  do campo/countryside, 117, 128–34, 137–9
  dominant, 144, 198–9
  as domination, 5
  for economy, 27, 56, 57, 58, 61, 107
  educated subject, 28
  education, education, education, 1
  educational revolution, Colombian, 1, 27, 31, 34, 40, 41, 150, 151, 189, 190
  educational revolution, deep, 183
  effective, 104–5
  elitist, 186

emancipatory, 6, 7, 22, 131, 132, 133, 137, 138, 139, 140, 158, 179, 183, 188
embodied, 5, 14, 121, 135, 160, 164, 169, 194, 196, 198
for empowerment, 112
of everyday life, 190
exclusion from, 54, 180
experiences, 26, 81, 120, 135, 145, 167
experimental/innovative, 15, 140, 147, 199
of fear, 136, 176
feminist, 143, 155, 164, 165, 170, 196
formal, 7, 10, 22, 40, 65, 81, 82, 92, 115, 121, 127, 131, 139–40, 143, 144, 151, 187, 190, 193, 195
free, 26, 70, 85, 150
free schools, 113
funding, 4, 32, 34, 39, 40, 55, 56, 57, 58, 59, 83, 84, 131, 179, 186, 202
further, 44, 60
health, 107
hegemonic, 10, 136, 169, 181, 188
higher, 7, 35, 36, 38, 39, 52, 59, 60, 70, 84, 85, 135, 144, 152, 154, 176, 177, 182, 190, 201–4
high-quality (as demand), 27, 54, 57, 104, 122, 149, 152, 177
homogenization of, 55, 57, 151
hope, 27
horizontal, 6, 100, 148
human capital, 26, 38
humanist, 115
of the imagination, 196
inclusion, 34, 60
indigenous, 2, 40, 44, 79, 176
informal, 73, 97, 115, 124, 127, 151, 164, 165, 166, 193
institutional, 26, 56, 60, 177
instrumental, 56, 175, 176
insubordinate, 22
integral, 28, 31, 61, 105
internationalization of, 36, 38–9, 40, 57, 154
as ISA, 9, 10, 78, 188
for liberation, 6
liberatory, 140
as liberatory process, 80
lifelong learning, 38, 80
local approaches to, 2, 29, 155
logics, 25, 140, 177

low-quality, 27, 37, 56, 60, 61, 69, 130, 149, 177, 180, 189
management of, 39, 63
managerial class in, 31–2
market in, 3, 28, 39
marketization of, 2, 4, 10, 52, 56, 58, 135, 151, 175, 177, 179, 186, 190, 191
materialist, 205
meaningful, 115, 145, 151
mechanisms, 12
memory of, 134
methodologies, 11, 83–4, 110, 144, 184, 190
ministry of, 32, 53, 58, 90, 98, 99, 107, 110, 129
misiones, 70
mística as, 135
model schools, 83, 99
models of, 32, 99, 150
modernization, 26, 32, 35, 36, 144
monological, 140
movement, 118, 132, 135, 147
MST, 127, 130–4, 138, 193
multicultural, 154
multiple, 124, 135, 143, 146–147, 148, 151, 153, 156, 168, 185, 195
mutual, 124
national, 31, 56
neoliberal project of, 1, 2–3, 5, 15, 19, 26, 27, 28–9, 33, 36, 40, 55, 57, 58, 62, 64, 131, 136, 148, 187
networks, 147
noninstrumental, 166
occupations, 153
"other," 28, 130, 140, 143, 144, 148, 186, 188
paradigms, 29, 31–2
parallel, 84
parastate, 22
participatory, 98, 99, 105, 110, 187
in party organizing, 46, 50
passive, 85
pedagogia da terra (pedagogy of the land), 128, 130, 133
Pedagogical Movement, 33
pedagogical-political projects, 3, 7, 15, 16, 40, 44, 56, 139, 140, 145, 146, 147, 148, 150, 151, 153, 155, 169, 170, 180, 182, 183, 185, 188, 192, 198
performance management in, 7, 30, 31

education/pedagogy/
  learning—*Continued*
  for personal goals, 114
  philosophies of, 38, 56, 110, 130,
    120, 125, 138, 144, 145, 164, 181
  physical, 105
  plan for, 28–9, 30
  play as, 104–5
  politicization of, 1, 4, 7, 8, 14, 64,
    82, 86, 127, 130, 131, 132, 135,
    139, 145, 147, 153, 185, 189, 191,
    193, 198
  policy, 30, 51, 54, 55, 56, 58, 64,
    117, 130, 145, 186, 188, 189
  popular, 6, 33, 65, 66, 82, 84, 117,
    121, 122, 123, 129, 138, 144, 154,
    159, 164, 168, 170, 183, 184, 190,
    192, 194, 195, 197, 206, 207
  of possibility, 136, 150, 151, 164,
    169, 180, 186, 190, 193
  practices, 5, 13, 15, 25–6, 28, 35, 44,
    56, 57, 117, 119, 121, 122, 130,
    137, 139, 140, 146, 151, 158, 167,
    170, 176, 182, 183, 185, 186, 187,
    192, 195, 199
  primary, 31, 44, 52–3, 60, 110, 112,
    115, 130, 131, 132, 144
  private, 28, 31, 32, 37, 55, 59, 60, 64
  privatization of, 3, 4, 40, 82, 180
  for proactivity, 100
  problem-solving, 109
  as "product," 1
  progressive, 113
  project, Venezuelan, 71, 74, 81, 83,
    86, 113, 115
  public, 2, 3, 22, 31, 32, 37, 39, 40, 53,
    54, 55, 56, 58, 62, 84, 99, 131, 144,
    152, 153, 178, 179, 186, 189, 191
  as public good, 27, 82, 149
  quality discourse, 26, 28, 30, 41
  radical, 6, 29, 121, 131, 137, 183,
    185, 187, 188, 190, 192, 199, 206
  ranking of, 31, 57, 60, 62, 63, 176,
    178, 180
  for recovery of traditions, 79
  reform, 7, 25, 28, 33, 34, 35, 38, 39,
    55, 56, 58, 115, 145, 149, 150,
    151, 190
  relationship to community, 83–4, 98,
    102, 111, 112, 130, 145, 187
  resistance, 44, 118, 152, 196
  responsibility, 29, 57
  restructuring, 29, 55, 144
  results, 19, 31, 54, 57, 58, 63
  revolutionary, 14, 66, 67, 73, 107,
    110, 113, 115, 186, 198
  role of, 7, 21, 146, 186
  rural, 31, 34, 110, 124, 129, 130, 133
  secondary, 31, 34, 44, 52–3, 60, 89,
    92, 109, 112, 127, 130, 131, 144,
    149
  sector, 44, 47, 175, 177
  to see power structures, 171
  seeds of, 146
  self-, 5, 11, 27, 79, 92, 98, 113, 126,
    132, 181, 182
  self-education of the people, 65, 66,
    79, 115
  separation from knowledge
    production, 179
  separation from life, 7, 121, 130, 135,
    169, 177, 187
  separation from social critique, 176,
    177
  services, 4, 27, 31, 34, 38, 40, 60,
    150, 177
  situated, 129
  for skills, 26, 30, 61, 62, 177, 180
  social, 127
  for social order, 26
  for socialism, 80, 81, 84, 100, 107,
    111, 112, 139, 208
  society as "giant school," 80, 89
  sociology of, 133, 134
  as source of inclusion/success, 27, 37,
    115, 179, 180, 189
  as source of values, 83
  spaces of, 139–40, 187, 189
  spiritual, 5, 196
  state role in, 59, 133
  struggles, 12, 26, 64, 117, 144, 145,
    153, 186, 189, 190, 192
  subaltern, 6, 15, 117, 122, 186
  for subjectification, 12, 15, 34, 57,
    121, 123–4, 125, 129, 164
  subjectivities of, 33, 62, 152, 155,
    178
  subordination to power, 176, 179
  success discourse, 30
  surveillance, 30
  technical, 27, 29, 152
  as techniques, 177
  traditional, 104, 105, 110, 114
  transformative, 7, 44, 118, 124, 129,
    132, 133, 185, 187, 192, 196
  uncritical, 82

uneducated, 1, 40, 130, 133, 182, 184
university, 7, 60, 140, 154, 178
unlearning, 5, 8, 11, 15, 107, 119, 125, 141, 153, 155, 158, 165, 181, 183, 184, 188, 192, 194, 198
vanguard of, 91
Education and Culture (journal), 146
educators/teachers
  activist, 137
  as actors, 146
  attempts to control, 32
  authoritarian, 207
  autonomy of, 186
  collectives of, 30, 148, 187
  competitive, 64
  complicit, 40
  conservative, 83, 100, 110, 186
  critical, 1, 3, 7, 8, 15, 22, 32, 35, 40, 63, 129, 131, 132, 136, 139, 145, 147, 148, 179, 183, 184, 185, 186, 187, 188, 189, 198, 199
  democratic, 207
  denied recognition, 35
  deprofessionalized, 3, 40
  devaluation of, 181
  dignity of, 145
  disarticulated, 34, 63
  disciplining of, 34, 140, 177
  dualism with students, 187
  educating the educators, 205
  emancipatory, 7
  empowerment of, 112
  exclusion of, 32, 39
  experiences of, 147–8
  extra work on critical projects, 135
  as facilitators, 92, 99
  figure of, 188
  in Freire, 120
  as functionaries, 33, 35
  hegemonic, 19
  held responsible/blamed for outcomes, 3, 27, 30, 31, 32, 34, 179
  as implementers of neoliberal reforms, 31–2
  individual, 14
  as instructors, 35
  instrumental, 64
  as intellectuals, 33, 145
  isolation of, 148
  as knowledge co-creators, 33, 35, 121, 144, 145, 147, 156, 185, 191, 198
  lack of managerial sympathy for, 30, 57
  as learners, 35, 103, 109, 187
  misnaming of, 29
  mobilization of, 136
  as motivators, 101
  movement, 132, 137
  organic intellectual as, 11
  other-, 131, 140, 144, 148, 169, 186, 188
  perspectives of, 32
  political platform of, 146
  political role of, 56
  popular, 44, 117, 131, 132, 135, 136, 167
  power of, 34, 179
  precarization and stress of, 58, 178
  production of, 132
  professionalism of, 32
  progressive, 207
  proletarianization of, 33, 40
  protests by, 32
  radical, 139, 144, 169, 182, 185, 186, 199
  reflection by, 146, 147, 148
  relationship to communities, 32
  relationship to movement, 118, 137–8
  relative autonomy of, 145
  repression of, 3, 22
  researchers, 145
  respect for students, 107, 207
  revolutionary, 99
  role of, 11, 21, 56, 135, 145, 146, 148, 180, 186
  self-disciplining, 64
  skills of, 192
  socialist, 208
  supportive, 102, 207
  teacher-subjects, 3, 179
  training of, 2, 7, 29, 31, 32, 40, 55, 56, 63, 85, 108, 115, 127, 130–4, 137, 148
  violence against, 33, 151
  voice of, 146
  volunteer, 100, 101
  as workers, 35, 145, 178, 190
  working conditions, 34, 56, 83, 135, 178, 186
Educators and Democracy, 92
efficiency, 2, 6, 29, 30, 31, 34, 89, 203
  see also capitalism, neoliberalism
EGERH (Estrategia de Gestión Del Recurso Humano en Colombia), 28

INDEX

Elias, 48
elitism, 9, 22, 23, 60, 84, 186, 207
　see also forms of oppression
Elizabeth, 158–60, 162, 163
Ellis, Edward, 97, 99, 102, 107, 111, 207
Ellner, 89
emancipation, 1, 3, 5, 6, 7, 15, 16, 21, 22, 23, 44, 56, 63, 80, 119, 120, 121, 123, 124, 125, 129, 131, 132, 133, 137, 138, 139, 140, 158, 165, 166, 167, 182, 183, 185, 189, 192, 193, 194, 195, 198
　multidimensional, 125
　social, 158
　see also affirmative concepts, liberation
embodiment, 5, 6, 7, 12, 13, 14, 16, 30, 68, 73, 76, 120, 121, 122, 123, 125, 126, 135, 141, 143, 153, 156, 157, 158, 159, 160, 162, 164, 168, 169, 170, 178, 179, 181, 183, 185, 190, 191, 193, 194, 195, 196, 197, 198, 206
　and memory, 164
　see also affect, affective concepts
emotion. *See* affect
empire, 72, 92, 111
empowerment, 98, 99, 103, 112, 127, 156, 176, 178
　see also affirmative concepts
end of history, 1, 175, 176
enlightenment, 13, 14
epistemology, 1–8, 10, 11–16, 19, 22, 23, 25–6, 27–30, 33–40, 43–4, 51, 55–7, 58, 61, 62, 64, 86, 120, 121, 123, 132, 133, 137, 139–41, 143, 144, 146, 148, 151–3, 155, 157, 166, 167, 169, 170, 171, 175, 176, 177, 179, 180–3, 185–6, 188–90, 192, 193, 195, 198, 199, 208
　see also knowledge, cosmologies, politics of knowledge
EPSC (Enterprises of Communal Social Property), 76–7
erotic, 168, 171
　see also affirmative concepts
Escobar, 6
Escobar de Almeida et al., 137
Escuela Política de Mujeres Pazíficas, 143–4, 163–8, 170, 194–6, 198
Esmad, 151

ethics, 5, 6, 7, 11, 16, 91, 120, 121, 132, 140, 146, 157, 167, 182, 184, 185, 186, 197, 199
　of care, 130, 198
　ethico-cultural revolution, 90
　of everyday practice, 123, 191
　of love, 16
Euclidean geometry, 6
Eurocentrism, 67, 79
Europe, 18, 13, 28, 55, 80, 181
European Commission, 55
evaluation, 2, 3, 4, 28, 30, 31, 32, 34, 35, 38, 39, 55, 57, 58, 61, 62, 77, 126, 127, 135, 150, 184
　see also assessment, ranking, surveillance
everyday life, 2, 9, 10, 12, 16, 21, 25, 27, 100, 120, 122, 123, 130, 133, 155, 162
　traditional education separate from, 135
excellence, 29, 30, 60, 61, 178, 180, 202
　see also quality, neoliberalism
exclusion, 2, 3, 4, 13, 19, 20, 27, 28, 30, 33, 37, 40, 50, 54, 57, 64, 127, 149, 158, 164, 175, 181, 185
　gendered, 122, 138
　see also forms of oppression
exhaustion, 16, 136, 137, 147, 163, 178, 202
experience, 1, 4, 5, 6, 16, 19, 21, 26, 38, 46, 81, 85, 98, 102, 109, 110, 118, 119–26, 128–30, 132, 133–6, 140, 141, 143, 144, 145, 147, 148, 151, 152, 155, 157–65, 167–9, 180, 183, 185, 191, 192–9
　lived, 143, 194
experimentation, 5, 15, 16, 156, 159, 191, 192, 199, 206
　see also affirmative concepts
exploitation, 2, 24, 66
　see also forms of oppression
extension, 49, 60, 61, 131, 150, 165
extradition, 23

factionalism, 72
facultad, la, 198
Falklands/Malvinas, 87
false consciousness, 9
　see also common sense
family, 3, 4, 10, 22, 26, 30, 35, 37, 48, 52, 53, 54, 57, 63, 71, 76, 78, 85, 89, 92,

102, 109, 115, 121, 124, 125, 126, 129, 145, 149, 157, 165, 167, 179, 187, 194
  see also gender, patriarchy
FARC, 21, 23
Farrel, Jojo, 79
favelas, 123
FECODE (Federación Colombiana de Educadores), 32, 146, 147
Fedecámaras (Federation of Chambers of Commerce), 72
Federacion Colombiana de Educadores, 144
Feitosa, 125, 126
Femia, Joseph, 10
feminism, 5, 8, 13, 14, 15, 119, 182, 196, 198
  Colombian, 143, 155–8, 163–5, 167, 170
feminization, 13, 120
Ferreira Rosa, Matos Pessoa and Rigotto, 49
Feuerbach, Ludwig, 205
Fifth Socialist International, 88
figuration, 11, 12
financialization, 4, 27, 36–7, 40, 49, 64
  see also debt, neoliberalism, (finance) capital
Fischman and McLaren, 9, 11
flexibility, 34, 35, 37, 62, 64, 97, 100, 177, 178, 208
  see also neoliberalism
Flores, Wilber, 104
flourishing, 5, 124, 147, 164, 168, 169, 185, 194
  see also affirmative concepts
flow, 2, 38, 155
  see also affirmative concepts
Fonseca et al., 135
food sovereignty, 70, 167, 205
foquismo, 79
forging, 1, 15, 16, 119, 121, 136, 140, 166, 186, 187, 188, 194, 198
forms of oppression
  see alienation, authoritarianism, banalization, coercion, commodities and commodification, criminalization, dehumanization, delegitimation, demonization, discipline, discrimination, displacement, dispossession, domination, dualisms, elitism, exclusion, exploitation, fragmentation, hierarchy, homogenization, humiliation, impoverishment, individualization, inequality, invisibilization, militarization, monologism, naturalization, normalization, openness/closure, poverty, power-over, privilege, precariousness/ precarity, proletarianization, shaming, silencing, sovereignty, stereotypes, surveillance, violence, wounding
Fortaleza, 49, 56, 208
forum theatre, 156, 161
Fourth Republic, 88
Fox, Michael, 79
fragmentation, 3, 4, 10, 19, 27, 34, 36, 40, 43, 45, 46, 50, 51, 58, 59, 60, 61, 63, 122, 129, 139, 145, 146, 170, 178, 182, 185, 188, 189, 190, 196
  see also forms of oppression, alienation
fraud, 34
Free School Movement, 113
Freire, Paolo, 100, 101, 104, 120, 136–7, 183, 184, 206, 207
friendship, 92, 100, 105, 125, 127, 137, 165, 166
  see also affirmative concepts
Frigotto, Ciavatta and Ramos, 56, 124
Fuenmayor, 98
Fuerzas Armadas Revolucionarias de Colombia. *See* FARC
functionalism, 50, 121
Fundación Paz y Bien, 160

Gadelha, Sandra, 49, 127, 132, 134
Garces and Jaramillo, 29, 33
Garcia, 150, 151, 153, 154
gas, 24, 68, 71
gender, 8, 13, 55, 70, 90, 111, 120, 122, 123, 138, 139, 157, 164, 166, 167, 168
gendered division of labour, 123, 139, 167
gendered subjectivities, 12, 14
gendered violence, 157
  see also patriarchy
geopolitics, 20, 21, 194
Gerardo, 99–103, 107
Giroux, Henry, 7

globalization, 26, 29, 31, 33, 56, 123, 149, 176, 177, 205
neoliberal, 29, 55, 181
see also neoliberalism
God, 67, 185
see also religion
Gonçalves, Porto, 168
Gonçalves-Fernandes et al., 131
good sense, 10–11, 14, 122, 130, 145, 184, 185
see also affirmative concepts, common sense
Gott, 207
governance, 85, 118
conditions of, 7
good, 39
logics of, 45
microdisciplinary, 54
technologies of, 1, 40, 180
governmentality, 2, 37, 59, 63, 137, 176
Gramsci, Antonio, 8–12, 14, 67, 122, 128, 145, 196
grassroots, 45, 50, 75, 89, 91, 115, 201, 207
see also activists, communities, social movements
greed, 114
Griffiths, Tom, 83, 84, 86
Griffiths, Tom, and Jo Williams, 82, 85, 86
Guardian, The (newspaper), 87
guerrillas, 20, 24, 33, 65–7, 68, 72, 78, 79, 158, 159, 164–5, 205, 206
Guevara, Ernesto "Che," 67, 68, 106, 205
Guimarães, 47
Gutiérrez, 6, 168

Haddad, Fernando, 58
Halls, 54
Harken Energy, 24
Hartley, Jennifer, 206
Hazelkorn, 177
healing, 16, 163, 199
see also affirmative concepts
health, 53, 69, 70, 85, 103, 107, 109, 150
hegemony, 1, 7, 8, 9–10, 11, 12, 14, 19, 20, 21, 22, 23, 24, 27, 28, 33, 38, 44, 45, 51, 55, 62, 66, 71, 72, 128, 136, 144, 181, 186–9, 190
articulation, 5, 175, 182
epistemological, 8, 15, 16, 139
limits in Colombia, 33
logics, 29, 181
mechanisms, 34, 149
pedagogical nature of, 169
subjectivity, 12, 14, 30, 34, 153, 155, 157
Hemispherism, 86
Hernandez, 22, 23, 36
hierarchy, 13, 14, 120, 121, 123, 140, 166, 178, 180, 187
affective, 170
embodied, 191
epistemological, 132, 148
raced, classed and gendered, 166
see also forms of oppression
higher education. *See* education
Hill, Dave, 82
historic bloc, 10, 20, 21, 22, 23, 33, 43, 44, 55, 56, 63, 139, 176
historicization, 8, 12
Holliday, Billie, 206
homelessness, 162
see also displacement
homo economicus, 26
homogenization, 12, 13, 55, 118, 151
see also forms of oppression
hooks, bell, 13, 120, 170, 171, 181, 182, 184, 197
hope, 5, 8, 15, 27, 43, 76, 99, 109, 115, 118, 162, 184, 194
see also affirmative concepts
horizons, 1, 4, 5, 6, 10, 21, 23, 27, 32, 40, 44, 58, 117, 119, 212, 127, 140, 152, 169, 180, 182, 189, 190, 192, 194, 197, 199
see also affirmative concepts
horizontality, 100, 148, 166
see also autonomy
hug-ins, 153
human capital, 26, 38
human rights, 20, 33, 69, 86, 90, 150, 160, 162, 167, 206
humanism, 79, 82, 115
humanization, 165
humiliation, 162
see also forms of oppression
humour, 134, 157, 158, 159, 164, 191
hunger, 162, 205

ICETEX (Colombian Institute of Technical Studies), 36
ideology, 10, 19, 43, 44, 45, 66, 87, 110, 205

INDEX 243

ideological state apparatuses (ISAs), 72, 78–9, 87, 188
  see also common sense
illiteracy. *See* literacy
imaginary, capitalist, 81
imagination, 4, 16, 133, 155, 156, 157, 175, 196
  see also affirmative concepts
immanence, 5, 7, 8, 10, 11, 15, 16, 132, 145, 147, 153, 185, 191, 192
  see also affirmative concepts
imperialism, 65, 66, 79, 80, 82, 86, 111
  anti-, 79, 89, 92, 93, 111
  see also capitalism, international division of labour
impoverishment, 13, 32, 53, 69, 160
  see also forms of oppression
in, against and beyond, 17, 44, 51, 118, 140, 144, 187
incentives, 31, 38, 48, 49, 52, 59
inclusion, 3, 4, 9, 26, 27, 28, 34, 43, 55, 57, 67, 85, 123, 127, 155, 180, 196, 197, 201, 204
  see also exclusion
Incubadores de Cooperativas Populares, 118
indigenous groups/knowledges, 2, 4, 6, 40, 44, 51, 63, 66, 67, 69, 70, 72, 76, 79, 80, 83, 88, 90, 92, 101, 111, 117, 176, 177, 185
  land rights, 69
individualism, 13, 39, 82, 101, 114, 119, 196, 206
individualization, 3, 4, 13, 14, 19, 27, 28, 30, 37, 40, 46, 51, 54, 57, 62, 63, 83, 118, 136, 151, 175, 176, 178, 179, 180, 181, 183, 191, 194, 197, 198
  see also forms of oppression
inequality, 1, 2, 3, 19, 20, 27, 30, 32, 36, 40, 48, 50, 54, 55, 57, 60, 64, 70, 122, 177, 180, 189
infanticide, 157
Infocentros, 81
informal sector, 22, 44–5, 46, 51, 54, 63, 72, 126, 206
Inner London LEA, 113
institutions, 10, 12, 19, 22, 26, 30, 31, 45, 54, 76–7, 126, 127, 130, 135, 153, 166, 188
  parallel, 75

Instituto Políticas Alternativas para o Cone Sul. *See* PACS
instrumentality, 1, 3, 13, 45, 46, 56, 62, 63, 64, 119, 140, 151, 160, 162, 166, 175, 191
  see also capitalism
insurrection, 171
international division of labour, 27–9, 36, 37, 40, 57, 177, 182
  see also coloniality, dependency, imperialism
international financial institutions, 2, 180
  IMF, 22, 27, 36, 71
  World Bank, 27, 29, 36, 39, 51, 52, 53, 55, 60, 61, 62, 71
internationalization of education, 29, 36, 59
Internet, 81
interpellation, 40, 87, 157, 179, 198
  see also ideology, ideological state apparatuses
interpretive systemology, 98
intersectionality, 123
invisibilization, 13, 29, 125, 164, 185, 186, 193, 198
  see also forms of oppression
Iran, 92
Irigaray and Burke, 199
Isabella, 158, 160, 162, 163
Izarra, Isamar, 104

James, 112
Janicke, 66, 78
Jessop, Bob, 78
Joshua, 107, 112
joy, 104, 114, 157, 168, 170, 171, 197
JPSUV, 110, 111
judgement, 13, 161, 176, 178, 181
  see also ranking, responsibility
juridical controls, 33

Kane, 207
Keating, 184
Keck, 44
kiss-ins, 153
knowledge/s, 1, 11, 14, 22, 32, 62, 143, 162, 164, 165, 168, 175, 181, 182, 195
  activist, 123, 155
  affective, 4, 13, 124
  codified, 176

knowledge/s—*Continued*
  collective, 133, 167, 169, 194
  colonial, 15, 188
  concrete, 140
  constructed for oneself, 105
  consumption of, 2, 28, 186
  counterpolitics of, 133
  creation, construction, production of, 12, 13, 14, 36, 61, 77, 105, 120, 121, 129, 132, 145, 148, 155, 166, 168, 169, 176, 177, 180, 184, 186, 191, 194, 195, 199
  deep, 168
  dialogue of, 122, 126, 145, 148, 156, 167, 183, 187, 193, 195
  emancipatory, 166
  embodied, 13
  exchange of, 80, 114, 126
  geopolitics of, 194
  indigenous, 176, 177
  inscribed, 168
  levels, 134
  lived, 167, 195
  local, 29, 34, 130
  marginal, 6
  material, 168
  measurable, 177
  movement-relevant, 195, 207
  multiple, 6, 124, 133, 140, 141, 169, 191, 194, 195, 198, 199
  multiplicity of, 120, 125, 132, 169
  neutral, 3, 40
  oral, 13, 145
  other, 14
  -over, 168, 197
  passive reception of, 28, 177
  pedagogical, 146–8, 185
  politicization of, 196
  politics of, 4, 6, 7, 14, 28, 35, 40, 44, 55, 133, 139, 151, 194
  popular, 13, 120
  as power, 80
  quality, 177
  regimes of, 182
  revolutionary, 12
  self, 133
  situated, 130, 140
  socialization of, 61, 77
  sources of, 179
  spiritual, 13
  subaltern, 167, 185
  subjugated, 171, 183
  teachers', 35, 145
  traditional, 124
  transformative, 14, 124, 169, 185, 187
  -with, 168
  of women, 160
  see also epistemology

Labour Party (UK), 1, 113
land reform, 20, 49, 70, 72, 89, 125, 128, 132, 138
Landless Rural Workers' Movement. *See* MST
Lara State, 111
latifundia, 124
Latin America, 2, 4, 5, 7, 8, 12, 15, 52, 60, 66, 67, 68, 70, 71, 79, 84, 87, 90, 92, 107, 111, 112, 117, 120, 173, 175, 177, 180, 182, 183, 185, 186, 187, 192, 205, 206, 207
  see also particular countries
Laval, 55, 57
law, 78–9, 85
  see also coercion, repression
Law 30, 39, 149
Law 715, 34
Law 798, 25
Law 1450, 38
Law 2002, 36
Law 3627/04, 62
Law on Communal Councils, 75
learning. *See* education
legitimation, 9, 22, 23, 70, 77, 150
Lenin, 206
Leninism, 67, 75
Ley General de Educación, 146
LGBT rights (lesbian, gay, bisexual and transgender), 90
Libâneo, 55
liberal fascism, 206
liberation, 22, 71, 81, 111, 125, 136, 145, 146, 156, 159
  self-, 7, 103, 117, 123, 159, 185, 188 (*see also* emancipation, affirmative concepts)
liberation theology, 6, 66, 79, 81, 117, 144, 185. *See also* religion
libraries, 80, 103, 132
Light, Manso and Noguera, 26, 29, 30, 31
Lisbeida, 102–3, 106, 112, 113
listening, 67, 111, 133, 157, 161, 184, 196
  active, 137, 166, 194
  inner, 196
  see also affirmative concepts

literacy, 57, 58, 70, 80, 81, 83, 101, 113, 130
dominant, 141, 191
multiple forms of, 191, 194
literature, 145, 185, 206
locality, 2, 3, 20, 29, 30, 31, 34, 40, 45, 46, 49, 54, 57, 75, 76, 77, 84, 85, 99, 107, 108, 114, 118, 138, 146, 151, 152, 154, 155, 177, 192, 201, 202, 203
looting. *See* autoreduction
Lopes, 56, 58
Lopez, Jeaneth, 101
Lorde, Audre, 13, 120, 168
love, 16, 47, 92, 03, 102, 104, 106–7, 111, 112, 119, 120, 136, 137, 140, 162, 165, 170, 197, 198, 199
see also affirmative concepts, affect
loyalty, 43, 47, 51, 72, 88
Lugones, 208
Luis, 112
Lula (Luiz Ignácio da Silva), 4, 5, 43, 46–50, 58, 59, 61, 62, 118, 129
Luxemburg, Rosa, 67
Lyotard, 206

Macedo, Donaldo, 136
Machado, Antonio, 136
Maia, Lucíola, 135
Mallett-Outtrim, 90–1
Malpas, 206
management, 2, 23, 25, 30, 31, 32, 39, 51, 54, 63, 75, 77, 98, 111, 113, 136, 150, 151, 177, 189
managerialism, 7, 177
Mandela, Nelson, 205
MANE, 149–52, 153–4, 193, 201–4
Mansell and Motta, 23
Mao Tse-Tung [Zedong], 67
Maoism, 79
mapping, maps, 8, 15, 109, 147, 192
Marcha Patriotica, 203
Margarida Esteves, Ana, 122
marginality, 6, 7, 16, 33, 86, 103, 132, 140, 143, 160, 179, 181, 182, 186, 193, 198, 199, 205
marketing, 46–7
marketization, 2, 4, 10, 16, 26, 48, 40, 44, 46, 47, 52, 56, 57, 58, 61, 135, 151, 175, 177, 179, 186, 189, 190, 191
see also capitalism, neoliberalism
marking, 156, 195. *See also* evaluation
Marques, 54

Marrero and Hernandez, 35, 36, 39
Martinez, 33
Martinez, Carlos, 79
Martinez et al., 68, 69, 73, 74, 79, 88
Marx, Karl, 205
Marxism, 9, 67, 75, 79, 86, 89
   orthodox, 78
   see also socialism
Máscara, La, 143, 155–63, 165, 194
masculinity, 13, 170, 197
mass intellectuality, 6, 11, 16, 65, 74, 81, 89, 115, 132, 133, 146, 169, 185, 187, 195
massacres, 24, 68, 129
   Brazil, 129
   Venezuela 2002, 72–3
massage, 168
mastery, 6, 191, 197, 198
mathematics, 31, 101
Mato Grosso, 131
MBR. *See* Bolivarian Revolutionary Movement
McLaren, Peter, 9, 11
Meade and Gershberg, 29, 32, 34
mechanization of intellectualism, 136
media, 9, 60, 71, 73, 81, 87, 93, 152, 158, 162
   in alternative schooling, 98, 100
   as ISA, 78–9
   role in coup against Chavez, 73
   in SE presentations, 123
   social media, 191
Medina and La Máscara, 160
Meirelles, 47
Mejía, 26, 45, 148, 160
memory, 68, 98, 134, 140, 164, 202, 205–6
Mencebo, 60
Mendes, Ernandi, 56, 57–8, 63, 134
Mendieta, 23
MercoPress, 81, 82
Mérida, 66, 84, 97–115, 207
Mesa Amplia Nacional Estudiantil. *See* MANE
mesas amplias locales (MALES), 154
micromanagement, 30, 54, 63
micropolitics, 146
microproduction, 118, 120
Mignolo, Walter, 6, 166
militarization, 3, 7, 19–23, 35, 38, 40, 41, 143, 144, 148, 150, 151, 155, 158, 168, 170, 188, 190, 191, 194
   on campus, 150
   see also forms of oppression

militias, Bolivarian, 65, 72, 74, 77–8
Ministry of Culture, 81, 90
Ministry of Education, 53, 98, 99, 107, 129
Ministry of Work, 118
Miraflores Palace, 72, 73
Mision Barrio Adentro. See *Barrio Adentro*
Mision Ribas, 70
Mision Robinson, 70
Mision Sucre, 70, 110
Misiones, 70, 71, 72, 103, 113
misnaming, 23, 29, 149, 185
mistica, 135, 196
mobilization, 49, 25, 129, 131, 136, 138, 149, 150, 151, 152, 155, 175, 192, 203
modernity, 4, 6, 13, 27, 33, 37, 182
modernization, 1, 3, 23, 28, 29, 31, 32, 35, 336, 57, 144
see also neoliberalism
monkey insult, 87
monoculture, 48–9
monologism, 1, 2, 7, 8, 13, 14, 15, 16, 19, 28, 29, 40, 44, 139, 140, 143, 148, 155, 157, 163, 169, 175, 180, 184, 188, 191, 194
see also dialogue, forms of oppression, silencing
Monroe Doctrine, 71
moral economy, 10, 117, 124, 149, 194
Morales, Evo, 4, 35
Moreno and Jardilino, 144
Morini, 178
Morton, Adam, 12
motherhood, 106, 109, 157, 158, 165, 198
Motta, Sara (other works), 45, 117, 124, 127, 158, 195, 196
Movement for a Fifth Republic (MVR), 69
movimento dos trabalhadores rurais sem terra (Brazil). *See* MST
Movimento Pedagogico en Colombia. *See* CPM
MST, Caderno do, 129
Muhr, 84
multiculturalism, 82, 90–1, 201, 207
multiplicity, 5, 6, 7, 11, 14, 15, 16, 33, 50, 51, 59, 63, 109, 118, 120, 121, 123, 124, 125, 127, 131, 132, 133, 135, 140, 141, 143, 145, 146, 147, 148, 151, 153, 154, 155, 156, 157, 158, 159, 163, 164, 166, 168, 169, 170, 176, 182, 184, 185, 188, 191, 193, 194, 195, 196, 197, 198, 199, 203
Munarim, 118, 119
music, 71, 104, 105, 109, 111, 112, 134, 135, 145, 153, 156, 162, 168, 170, 185, 191, 198
MVR. *See* Movement for a Fifth Republic

Nariño, 158, 162
National Assembly (AN) (Venezuela), 90
National Plan for Economic and Social Development, 2007–2013, 76
National Plan of Development, 29, 38
National Secretariat of the Solidarity Economy, 118
National Security Council, 86
National University in Bogota, 25, 146
nationalization, 24, 70
naturalization, 3, 8, 9, 10, 24, 28, 30, 56, 61, 62, 64, 177, 178, 180, 181
see also common sense, ideology, forms of oppression
Navarro, Luis Hernández, 89
negation, 181, 190, 193
Neill, A. S., 113
neo-Gramscianism, 8
neoliberalism, 1, 2, 3, 5, 8, 10, 12, 14, 15, 19–31, 33–8, 40–1, 43, 45–7, 51–2, 54, 55–7, 59–63, 65, 68, 69, 71, 72, 118, 130, 131, 135, 136, 137, 139, 148, 151, 155, 159, 164, 167, 168, 175, 176, 178, 179, 181, 186, 187, 188, 189, 190, 191, 194, 202, 206
anti-, 46, 119, 202
of desire, 27
discourse, 189
epistemology of, 37–8
expansion of, 2
governmentality, 176
historic bloc of, 23, 44, 55, 176
labour, 140
model of education, 2–3, 26–7, 57, 58, 131, 140
paradigm, 3
popular face, 43
project, 2, 4, 49
restructuring, 7, 20, 21
violence of, 158
see also austerity, choice, consumerism, excellence, financialization, flexibility,

globalization, marketization, modernization, performance, privatization, precariousness/precarity, productivity, quality (discourse of), quantification, responsibility, revolution, security, stability, standardization, Washington Consensus
neo-Marxism, 79
Neves, 126
Neves de Sousa, 119
New Theatre in Colombia, 156
NGO's, 129, 147, 148, 149, 163
Ninnes, 207
nonviolence, 5, 33, 153, 163, 164, 167
normalization, 12, 33, 34, 61, 64, 180. *See also* forms of oppression
North, global, 2, 29, 36, 40, 176, 819
Novelli, 20, 21, 22, 33, 34, 35
nurturing, 7, 120, 122, 167, 170, 184, 192, 195, 196, 197. *See also* affirmative concepts

Obama, Barack, 92, 206
Observer, The (newspaper), 86–7
Occidental Petroleum, 24
OECD, 55
Ojeda, 66
oligarchy, 45, 66, 69, 72, 78, 80
Oliveira, 47, 49, 50, 51, 56, 57
ontology, 4, 14, 23, 29, 40, 125
openness/closure (of horizons, spaces, bodies, etc), 1, 2, 5, 6, 7, 8, 10, 11, 13, 16, 28, 33, 40, 44, 56, 64, 97, 99, 103, 110, 112, 120, 121, 125, 127, 129, 135, 137, 140, 147, 150, 153, 155, 156, 157, 160, 161, 164, 165, 166, 168, 169, 170, 181, 183, 184, 188, 189, 191, 193, 194, 196, 197, 199, 202, 207
see also forms of oppression, affirmative concepts
oppression, 4, 100, 121
action for the oppressed, 185
capacities of the oppressed, 181
class, 123, 168, 206
experiences of, 6, 16, 183, 185, 194, 199
gender, 123, 138, 158, 167, 168, 195 (*see also* patriarchy)
internalized, 123, 125, 166

modes of production of, 205
multiple, 123, 157, 159, 168, 193, 194, 198
oppressed, the/oppressed communities, 3, 4, 7, 32, 34, 72, 115, 120, 130–1, 140, 141, 145, 157, 158, 170, 171, 179, 181, 182, 183, 184, 185, 186, 198, 205
oppressive collectivism, 206
oppressor, the, 168, 205, 206
race, 123, 168 (*see also* Afro-Brazilians, Colombians, Venezuelans)
representations of, 170
self-liberation from, 159, 185, 188, 195
situations of, 132
spaces of, 6
systems of, 170, 196
theatre of the oppressed, 143, 155–6, 159, 160, 195, 206
wounds of, 170
see also forms of oppression
oral histories, knowledges, etc., 6, 13, 14, 124, 141, 145, 163
organic intellectual, 11–14, 99, 132, 133, 146, 186, 199
Organic Law of the Armed Forces, 77–8
organicity, 9, 9–10
Organization of American States, 86
organization of social life, 1, 8, 90–1, 119, 121, 122, 180
organized popular classes/working class, 43, 44, 45, 46, 50, 51, 59, 77, 128
Ossa, 37, 39
other/s, 1, 6, 8, 13, 14, 15, 16, 19, 23, 34, 44, 109, 119, 121, 126, 127, 129, 131, 133, 135, 136, 140, 143, 144, 148, 151–3, 160, 164, 166, 168, 169, 178, 184, 186, 191, 192, 196, 197, 199, 208
another world is possible, 86, 164
becoming-other, 136, 141
otherness, 148, 157, 188
self and, 121, 140, 155, 168, 179, 184, 198, 199
othering, 14, 32
Otranto, 61, 62

Pacheco, 38
Pacific Ocean, 158, 162
PACS, 119, 122–3

PAE (Programa de Alimentacion escolar), 110
Palocci, 47
paradigms, 20, 34, 45, 49, 189
  alternative, 29, 189
  capitalist, 101
  colonial, 15, 101
  dominant, 184
  neoliberal, 3, 31–2
paramilitaries, 3, 20–1, 24, 158, 159
Paraipaba, 125
participation, 9, 11, 38, 39, 43, 45, 53, 54, 55, 56, 57, 60, 61, 74, 76, 81, 82, 83, 85, 89, 98, 99, 100, 101, 102, 105, 106, 107, 111, 112, 120, 121, 122, 123, 125, 126, 127, 132, 133, 135, 146, 149, 150, 152, 154, 155, 156, 158, 160–3, 167, 168, 191, 195, 196, 199, 201, 202
Participatory Action Research (PAR), 84, 102, 207
participatory research, 122, 187
participatory budgeting, 45, 76
participatory democracy, 69, 72, 100, 105, 108, 110, 113, 150, 153, 191
Partido Socialismo e Liberdade (PSOL), 51, 131
Partido Trabajadores (Brazil), 4, 5, 7, 43–52, 54–6, 58, 60, 62, 63, 64, 118, 119, 129, 130, 132, 137, 139–40, 188
  in, against and beyond, 44, 51, 118
party form, 11, 44, 46, 50–1
  mass party, 45
Party of the Venezuelan Revolution (PRV), 67
passive revolution, 9, 19–21
passivity, 2, 19, 28, 29, 35, 85, 159, 165, 177, 182
patriarchy, 12, 13, 170, 198
  anti-, 154
  capitalist, 157
  see also capitalism, patriarchal, coloniality, patriarchal, gender
Pazíficas Women's Collective, 143, 163
PDVSA (Petróleos de Venezuela), 72
Pearson, Tamara, 80, 83–4, 92, 93, 97, 98, 99, 101, 108–11, 113, 114–15, 208
peasantry, 48, 51, 72, 78, 124, 133, 159

pedagogization, 1, 4, 8, 15, 140, 153, 170, 198
pedagogy. *See* education
People's Congress, 203
Pequeno Marinho, Ferreira Carneiro and Almeida, 48, 49
Perdomo, Luis, 88
Pérez Jiménez, Marcos, 66
Pérez Rodríguez, Carlos Andrés, 67–9
performance/performativity, 7, 14, 176, 206
  in the arts, 109, 156, 157, 161, 206
  assessment, 2, 30–2, 51, 57, 62, 178
  of critique, 197
  as individualizing, 57–8
  -related pay, 62, 64
  of self, 178
  see also neoliberalism
Pernambuca, 48
personalism, 88
personalization, 23, 46, 61, 175
  see also individualization, responsibility, forms of oppression
Petrocaribe, 71
PETROSUR, 71
petty bourgeoisie, 89
philosophy, 11, 38, 98, 110, 122, 130, 143, 144, 183, 195
Pingas, 128
Pinilla, 28
pink tide, 4, 5, 137
Piper, 75
pizza making, 108
Plan Colombia, 24
platypus, 47–8
play-based learning, 104–5, 111, 160, 166
  free play, 159
pluralism/plurality, 5, 67, 79, 125, 146, 151, 152, 153, 155, 159, 191, 193
poetry, 134, 135, 136, 156, 157, 162, 163, 164
police, 68, 78, 129, 150, 151, 152
Política Nacional de Irrigação no Nordeste Brasileiro, 48
politicizing
  of Catholicism, 185 (*see also* liberation theology)
  of common sense, 11, 130
  of knowledge, 196
  of pedagogy, 1, 4, 7, 8, 15, 82, 130, 131, 135, 140, 153, 193, 198
  of people, 86

of the private, 14, 123, 137
of social contradictions, 1, 41, 64, 137, 139, 188, 189
of social policy, 54
politics/political, 8, 23, 27, 34, 35, 47, 50, 56, 77, 87, 88–9, 110–11, 118, 125, 128–9, 133, 134, 135, 148, 152, 156, 157, 162, 164, 183, 186, 189, 192, 203, 207
actors/agency, 10, 12, 47, 127, 154, 166, 176, 193
and private sector, 23
and war, militarization of politics, 20, 21, 165, 170
as antagonism, 10
art, 156
articulation, 43, 44, 45, 46, 49, 51, 52, 63, 169
authoritarian, 148
becoming-, 191
capacities, 153
of care, 16, 123, 197, 198
class, 8, 43, 45, 47, 49, 50, 66
closure of, 7, 10, 14, 16
commitments to, 6, 7, 121, 133, 186, 199
consciousness, 84
counterhegemonic, 73
crisis of, 22
cultural work, 145, 156, 158
decision-making, 69
dialogue, 145
differends of, 206
discourse of, 195
of education, 5, 25, 29, 34, 55, 56, 64, 82, 83, 110, 127, 140, 144, 145, 146, 165, 185, 188, 190, 202
electoral/parliamentary, 21, 82
elite, 20, 22, 34, 39, 43, 46, 50, 51, 52, 63
emancipatory, 5, 125, 185, 192, 195
embodied, 193
end of, 23, 34, 175
energy, 138
epistemological/of knowledge, 1, 4, 5, 6, 7, 8, 12, 13, 14, 15, 28, 35, 38, 39, 40, 43, 44, 51, 55, 57, 64, 133, 139, 140, 148, 151, 166, 169, 171, 175, 176, 177, 180, 181, 182, 188, 193, 194, 199
exclusionary, 50
feminist, 165

force, 152
fragmentation of, 45, 63, 190
friendship and, 127, 137, 166
heritage, 146
hierarchical, 180
history of, 44
horizons, 10, 32, 40, 127
ideology, 66
imaginations, 16, 141
inclusionary, 85
institutional, 50
internal party, 50, 138
as ISA, 78–9
left, 45, 51
legitimacy, 150
logic, 11, 14, 16, 34, 185
mainstream, 164
manoeuvres, 10, 22
micro-, 147
of motherhood, 165
music, 111
national, 149
as normal, 149, 165, 191
as one of three types of power, 80
ontology of, 14
"other," 23, 168
patriarchal, 12, 164, 165
pedagogical nature of, 193
pedagogizing, 15, 140, 153, 170, 198
personalized, 46
platform, 146
poetic, 164
political class, 22, 23, 50
political economy, 8, 20, 21, 27, 28, 39, 59, 85, 118, 123, 130, 138–9
political ethics, 90–1
popular, 5, 16, 47, 49, 51, 64, 137, 169, 186, 193, 194
populist, 63
possibility of, 2, 4, 16
of poverty, 50
practice, 10, 43, 46, 118, 128, 132, 153, 186
prefigurative, 169
public, 166, 191, 194
radical, 156
reconstructing, 186, 194
reinvention of, 158
reoccupation of, 190
representational, 169, 185
of SE, 118
seeds of, 146
situated, 5

politics/political—*Continued*
  sociopolitical, 43, 48, 52
  state, 69
  struggle, 8, 10, 12, 129, 131, 187, 189
  subjectivities, 118, 120, 124, 125, 127, 129, 139, 164, 165, 166, 190, 191, 193, 194
  traditions, 144
  transformative, 117, 131, 171, 177, 187, 193, 196
  violence, 20, 21, 24, 33, 92, 158
  see also social movements, state, particular movements/parties
Polo Democrático, el, 149, 203
Pontes Furtado, 129, 133
populism, 7, 19, 22, 23, 50, 63, 151
postcapitalism, 141, 143
postcolonialism, 55, 120
postgraduate education, 61, 62
potentiality, 129
  human, 183
  see also affirmative concepts
poverty, 4, 6, 19, 27, 28, 36, 37, 38, 40, 48, 50, 51, 52, 53, 54, 55, 59, 60, 61, 63, 64, 68, 70, 72, 73, 81, 83, 89, 93, 99, 103, 110, 118, 149, 158, 177, 180, 185, 189, 193, 205, 206
  absolute, 51
  see also forms of oppression
power, 2, 4, 5, 6, 7, 9, 10, 22, 23, 25, 27, 35, 38, 44, 45, 46, 47, 50, 51, 54, 56, 73, 77, 78, 79, 80, 86, 87, 88, 91, 113, 118, 121, 122, 123, 128, 132, 137, 139, 140, 144, 145, 146, 149, 152, 159, 160, 164, 165, 168, 169, 176, 179, 181, 186, 194, 196, 199, 206
  coercive, 20
  constituted, 76
  counter-, 159, 186
  epistemological, 34
  erotic, 171
  gendered, 138, 139, 157
  grassroots, 91
  labor, 34
  multidimensional, 159
  patriarchal, 13
  power-over, 13, 14, 120, 123, 132, 170, 181, 196, 197
  power-with, 197
  speaking truth to, 199
  structural, 10
  see also forms of oppression
Poyo, José, 88
praxis, 14, 16, 28, 33, 40, 99, 100, 117, 121, 122, 135, 136, 138, 143, 144, 144, 158, 160, 176, 183, 185, 196, 198, 199
  feminist, 157
  revolutionary, 121, 185
precariousness/precarity, 3, 4, 32, 40, 48, 50, 56, 64, 130, 132, 177, 178, 179, 193
  see also forms of oppression, neoliberalism
prefiguration, 16, 169, 195
  see also affirmative concepts
prisons, 78, 196
privatization, 3, 4, 21, 22, 23, 25, 30, 32, 35, 38, 40, 59, 60, 61, 64, 82, 150, 179, 180
  see also neoliberalism
privilege, 3, 20, 49, 85, 114, 140, 156, 160
  defence of, 179
  epistemic, 120, 121, 132, 182
  of Mike Cole, 85
  unlearning, 11
  see also forms of oppression
problem-solving theory, 178
process, 2, 3, 4, 5, 6, 7, 9, 10, 11, 12, 14, 15, 16, 29, 30, 31, 33, 34, 40, 44, 45, 48, 49, 50, 51, 53, 54, 56, 58, 61, 62, 63, 64, 66, 67, 73, 74, 75, 77, 79, 80, 81, 83, 84, 85, 87, 88, 100, 101, 102, 103, 104, 107, 112, 113, 114, 115, 118, 121, 124, 125, 126, 127, 128, 129, 130, 131, 132, 133, 134, 135, 138, 139, 146, 147, 148, 149, 151, 152, 153, 155, 157, 158, 159, 160, 161, 162, 163, 164, 165, 166, 167, 168, 170, 171, 176, 177, 179, 180, 181, 182, 183, 184, 185, 186, 187, 188, 189, 190, 191, 192, 193, 194, 195, 201–4, 206
  see also becoming
production, 38, 48, 77, 81, 82, 91, 126, 152, 170
  capital-forming, 206
  co-, 132
  collective, 126, 134
  community, 138
  conditions of, 48

cooperative, 135
education as, 26
food/agricultural, 48, 124, 128, 205
intellectual, 166, 168
of knowledge, 61, 120, 169, 194, 195
labor, 107
of mass intellectuality, 133
means of, 76, 78
micro-, 118
mixed, 127
modes of, 205
non-capitalist, 123
in private space, 178
self-managed, 111
social, 182, 193–4
for social needs, 70
of subjectivities, 140, 179
theatrical, 156
of theory, 6, 168
productivism, 55, 56
productivity, 26, 29, 35, 57, 62, 115
  see also neoliberalism
profanation, 127, 166
profit, 20, 24, 28, 39, 48, 60, 62, 70, 77, 149, 178, 182. *See also* accumulation, capitalism
Programa de Alimentacion Elemental, 110
Programa Minima, 149, 152, 201–2
Programa Residencia Agraia, 130
Programa Universidade para Todos (PROUNI), 59
Proinclusion de Voluntad Popular, 90
proletarianization, 40, 64
proletariat, 11, 206. *See also* working class
PRONERA (Programa Nacional de Educação na Reforma Agrária), 129, 130. 131, 132, 137, 138
prophet, the (figure), 1, 14, 16, 175, 176, 181
protagonism, 82, 102
PRV. *See* Party of the Venezuelan Revolution
PSUV. *See* United Socialist Party
PT. *See Partido Trabajadores*
public transport, 68
public-private divide, 14, 127, 164, 166, 194
  blurred by neoliberalism, 178
  see also gender, patriarchy
pueblo, el, 68, 72–4, 87, 89, 92–3, 115
Puerto Rico, 92

Punto Fijo, 66, 69
Putumayo, 24

quadro, 45
quality, 25, 54, 70, 151–2, 189
  discourse of, 26–30, 35–9, 41, 58, 60–1, 151, 177, 178, 180, 187
  (*see also* neoliberalism)
  distinct from quantity, 56–7
  lacking in technical/private schools, 4, 27, 37, 56, 57, 60, 64, 149, 177, 180
  qualitative, 31, 67, 71, 152, 191
  self-determined, 150
quantification, 2, 26, 31, 54, 56, 57, 58, 62, 71, 180
  see also neoliberalism

Raby, 72, 73
racism, 69, 87, 123, 207
Ramirez, 24
Ramírez, Isidro, 66–7, 79
Rangel, Lisbeida, 100
ranking, 2, 19, 26, 27, 48, 57, 62, 63, 84, 97, 135, 136, 150, 176–7, 180, 186
  see also evaluation, surveillance
rationality/ies, 13, 120, 136
  bureaucratic, 2
  disembodied, 14, 183
  dominant, 12, 15, 181
  instrumental, 1, 3, 63
  irrationality, 1, 13, 120
  marketized, 179, 190
  masculinized, 13
  neoliberal, 2, 44
  other, 7
  technical, 180
  unlearning, 15, 181
  versus emotional, 13–14
  see also epistemologies
realism
  capitalist, 205
  magical, 206
  recipes, 167
reciprocity, 24, 107, 119, 120, 122
  see also affirmative concepts
recovered (occupied) factories, 4
recuperation (of heritages, power, etc), 145, 179
Red de Cualificación de Educadores en Ejercicio (RED CEE), 148
Red de Investigacion Educativa (ieRed), 147

INDEX

Redes Pedagogicas, 147
referenda, 22, 87
reflection, critical, 82, 115, 123, 124, 126, 127, 133, 134–5, 138, 145, 146, 147, 148, 151, 156, 157, 159, 160, 161, 164, 165, 167, 181, 182, 183–4, 186, 187, 190, 192, 201
  self-, 15, 157, 193
  see also affirmative concepts
reflexivity, 11, 15, 33, 35, 163, 195, 199
relationality, 12
  see also social relations
religion, 9, 10, 66, 69, 78, 79, 110, 118, 185
  see also Catholicism, Christ, Christianity, God, liberation theology, spirituality, theology
rentism, 78
representation, 1, 2, 3, 5, 9, 11, 12, 14, 15, 16, 20, 22, 23, 24, 25, 27, 33, 35, 43, 45, 47, 49, 50, 54, 56, 59, 61, 62, 63, 71, 76, 82, 88, 93, 98, 121, 125, 126, 129, 130, 132, 133, 149, 155, 157, 159, 160, 162, 163, 165, 167, 169, 170, 175, 176, 177, 179, 180, 181, 182, 184, 185, 187, 191, 194, 195, 201, 206
  see also knowledge, epistemology, rationality
repression(s), 13, 21, 22, 68, 206
repressive state apparatuses (RSAs), 72, 78
reproduction, 14, 22, 27, 40, 43, 45, 46, 50, 57, 60, 63, 64, 138, 177, 181, 186, 187, 189
  of capitalism/neoliberalism, 2, 3, 8, 12, 22, 26, 29, 59, 61, 62, 168
  of gender inequality, 139, 170
  of hegemony, 1, 7, 12, 62
  of narratives, 199
reproductive rights, 160
social, 9, 48, 119, 120, 126, 128, 134, 139, 192, 193
  see also gender, patriarchy
resistance, 27, 32, 44, 56, 62, 77, 80, 92, 118, 128, 135, 151, 152, 155, 163, 186, 190, 193, 196, 206
  to change, 114
responsibility
  caring, 123, 132
  personal(ized), 3, 22, 27, 29, 37, 54, 57, 59, 63, 180, 206

self-blame/blame of others, 4, 27, 28, 31, 34, 40, 54, 57, 206
of students, 100, 107, 114
as value, 160, 198, 207
  see also neoliberalism
Restrepo, Pilar, 156, 157, 158, 159, 160
restructuring, 2, 7, 20, 21, 22, 29, 55, 57, 58, 59, 62, 91, 144
results, education of, 19, 31, 36, 54, 55, 56–7, 58, 62, 63, 83
revolution
  from above and below, 74
  Bolivarian, 65, 66, 73, 74, 80, 82, 83, 85, 86, 88, 109
  as common word, 100, 111
  counter, 81, 90
  democratic, 91, 188
  educational (radical), 183, 189
  educational (Uribe), 1, 27, 31, 34, 41, 150, 151, 190
  ethical-cultural, 90
  passive, 9, 19, 20, 21
  of the poor, 93
  Russian, 206
  social, 145
  socialist, 11, 73, 79, 91, 93, 107, 110, 113
  state for, 75
  see also revolution
revolutionary
  capacity, 68
  critique, 14
  education/pedagogy, 14, 66, 73, 99, 110, 112, 183, 186, 198
  epistemological, 169, 183
  government, 65, 88
  ideas, 86
  Jesus as, 111
  knowledge, 12
  legacy, 89
  love, 106–7, 136
  movements, 73, 74
  parties, 67, 69
  praxis/practice, 185, 186
  principles, 82
  process, 67, 80, 114, 115
  struggles, 185
  subjects, 139
  transformation, 16, 75, 103, 114, 158, 188
  truth, 11
Revolutionary Reading Plan, 80

Reyes, Alvaro, 7
Rhoades and Slaughter, 177
right to education, 22, 27, 58, 59, 60, 69, 86, 149, 150, 152, 153, 154, 202, 203
Rikowski, 107
Rio Grande do Norte, 48
risk, 49, 106, 136, 140, 197
ritual, 14, 124, 168, 170, 198
Rivas Davila School, 110
Robertson, Ewan, 77, 89, 91
Rodas, 39, 152
Rodriguez, 149, 150, 151, 152
Rodriguez, Simon, 6
romanticism, 154–5
Rose, 2
Roussef, Dilma, 43
Royal Spanish Academy, 72
Royston, 87
rupture, 1, 7, 41, 67, 140, 148, 149, 157, 165, 176, 190
rural struggles, 21, 49, 115, 124, 125, 133, 134. *See also* MST, land reform
Russia, 92, 206

Sabadini, 46
Salcedo, 26–7, 33
Salcedo Guarin, Monsignor Jose Joaquin, 183
Salter and Weltman, 87
Sampaio, Plinio, 118
Samper, 20
Sánchez, Emmanuel, 104
Sánchez, Lilibeth, 106
Santa Barbara, 125–6
Santos, 19, 23, 25, 28, 29, 33, 38, 39, 40, 149, 153, 155, 192
satire, 134
Schugurensky, 12
science, 10, 11, 14, 22, 31, 98, 103, 154, 207
social, 31
SE. *See* solidarity economy
security, 23, 32, 62, 64, 77, 190, 205, 206
see also neoliberalism, militarization
self, 140
 and collective knowledges, 133
 and other, 121, 140, 155, 168, 179, 184, 198, 199
 borders of, 197
 conceptions of, 153, 171, 198
 embodied, 197
 liberation of, 136
 misperceived as source of system, 9
 practices of, 125, 178
 (*see also* subject)
 reoccupation of, 125, 197
self-actualization, 185
self-administration, 75
self-determination, 159, 162, 186
self-development, 122
self-disciplining, 2, 40, 64, 179
self-education, 27, 65, 79, 89, 115
self-emancipation, 3, 103, 117, 159, 188
self-esteem, 162
self-expression, 162
self-government, 75, 76, 119, 122, 169
selfies, 206
self-interest, 3, 32, 45
selfishness, 114
self-judgements, 181
self-love, 197
self-management, 98, 111
self-organization, 77, 128, 131
self-sufficiency, 121
self-understandings, 181
self-valorization, 157
self-worth, 4
see also subjectivity, personalization, individualization
self-defence groups. *See* CONVIVIR, AUC
sex work, 157
sexual harassment, 123
sexuality, 90, 157, 160, 167
shaming, 4, 13, 120, 141, 170, 178, 191, 197
see also judgement, demonization, forms of oppression
Sheehan, 67, 80
Shor and Freire, 136, 207
Showstack Sassoon, Anne, 9
Sierra Nevada de Mérida, 97–8
Sierra's Head, 98
silence/silencing, 1, 13, 29, 33, 34, 125, 143, 155, 157, 164, 165, 176, 193
see also, forms of oppression
SINAES (O Sistema Nacional de Avaliação da Educação Superior), 62
Sítios Novos, 208

INDEX

skills, 3, 26, 30, 31, 38, 56, 57, 62, 63, 85, 111, 162, 175, 176, 177, 180, 186, 192, 207
  see also competencies
slavery, 66, 79, 123
smoking, 107
sociability, 124, 125, 126, 127, 164, 165, 193, 194, 198
social, 120
  acceptability, 33
  access, 177
  actors, 10, 154, 202
  and state, 9, 12, 20, 23
  articulation, 46, 54, 64
  autonomy, 47, 137, 194
  backwardness, 130
  base, 20, 51, 58
  classes, 10, 47
  commitments, 132
  conditions, 3, 126
  consciousness, 84, 98
  councils, 54, 55
  critique, 107, 176
  democracy, 65, 70, 72, 75, 113
  dependency, 63
  destinies, 186
  development, 49, 133
  differends, 206
  economy, 119
  emancipation, 5, 15, 56, 63, 132, 158, 182, 183, 195
  epistemologies, 27
  ethics, 132
  exclusion, 2, 57, 64
  fabric, 147, 190
  formation, 11
  fragmentation, 3, 63
  function, 22
  goods, 3, 82, 154
  groups, 11, 63
  harmony, 175
  history, 44
  inclusion, 85
  inequalities, 48, 70, 177
  institutions, 10
  integration, 26, 98
  intimacy, 27
  justice, 33, 59, 71, 75, 84, 100, 107, 159, 189
  legitimacy, 150
  life, 1, 2, 15, 119, 157
  logics, 190
  management, 25
  media, 81, 191
  mobility, 41
  modernization, 26
  monological, 175
  needs, 70
  networking, 81
  order, 13, 120
  organization(s), 44, 45, 90, 119, 121, 133, 180, 203
  participation, 83, 100
  peace, 26
  policy, 25, 43, 51–2, 54, 55, 59, 63, 130, 139
  power, 7, 34, 78, 181
  practices, 14, 64, 84, 155
  precarity, 130
    as private, 166, 194
  problems/ills, 27, 28, 30, 40, 54, 57, 63, 84, 115, 150, 179, 181
  processes, 135, 182, 201
  production, 1, 62, 107, 120, 126, 182, 194
  programs, 70
  progress, 70
  projects, 64, 51, 55, 131, 139, 155, 169
  property, 78
  realm, 13, 120
  reconstruction, 85, 143, 197, 199
  reforms, 72, 74
  regulation, 28
  relation(ship)s, 5, 6, 8, 10, 12, 13, 15, 21, 26, 34, 40, 51, 63, 118, 119, 120, 122, 127, 133, 139, 143, 148, 153, 155, 160, 164, 165, 166, 167, 168, 169, 171, 175, 180, 181, 183, 188, 195, 198
  restructuring, 22
  revolution, 145
  rights, 69, 152
  risks, 49
  sciences, 31
  sectors, 46, 152, 153, 201
  security, 25
  sharing, 167
  situation/reality, 10, 102, 156
  sovereignty, 78
  spaces, 165
  strategy, 47
  structure, 3, 27, 30, 54
  struggle, 12, 169
  success, 3
  terrains, 3, 183

times, 178
transformation, 40, 74, 100, 107, 111, 112, 117, 131, 132, 160, 169, 171, 177, 184, 185, 186, 192, 196
understanding, 54
see also community
social movements, 4, 8, 33, 45, 46, 47, 50, 74, 117, 124, 126, 128, 132, 135, 143, 144, 152, 169, 182, 182, 187, 192, 194
see also activists
Social Reactivation Plan, 25
social reproduction, 9, 48, 120, 126, 134, 139, 192, 193
socialism, 5, 15, 16, 67, 78, 80, 81, 85, 92, 100, 169, 208
Socialist Outlook, 75
Socialist Plan, 108
socialization, 61, 77, 109, 114, 169, 188, 189
society
  and education, 112, 133, 149, 202
  as actor, 190, 203
  capitalist, 72, 78, 86, 100, 107, 113, 128
  civil, 9, 10, 12, 20, 54, 92, 122
  conceptions of, 153
  consumer, 27
  pluralistic, 82
  role of education in, 82
  socialist, 75, 82
  Western, 101
solidarity, 12, 20, 51, 63, 71, 93, 100, 101, 111, 114, 115, 117, 120, 122, 125, 127, 133, 135, 136, 137, 140, 147, 151, 160, 163, 170, 178, 184, 187, 191, 193, 194, 195
  cultures of, 155
  see also, affirmative concepts
solidarity economy, 47, 117–24, 130, 135, 137–40, 193, 195
Solzana, Gildifredo, 68
Sosa López, Carlos, 104, 105
South Africa, 205
South, global, 3, 29, 57, 177, 189
  see also Latin America, international division of labour, capitalist world system, particular countries
sovereignty, 48, 76, 78, 167
  see also forms of oppression
soya, 48
space, 7, 16, 21, 30, 40, 44, 61, 62, 64, 68, 72, 97, 98, 99, 100, 103, 109, 112, 119, 121, 122, 123, 125, 126, 127, 133, 134, 135, 136, 139, 140, 146, 147, 150, 151, 152, 153, 155, 157, 158, 159, 160, 162, 164, 165, 166, 169, 170, 175, 178, 181, 184, 186, 187, 188, 189, 190, 191, 192, 193, 194, 195, 196, 197, 198, 199, 201, 203, 204, 206, 207
  dialogical, 122, 184
  intimate, 194
  learning spaces, 135
  multiple scales of, 155
  occupations of, 127, 135, 136
  safe, 166, 193, 194
Spain, 111
Spanish language, 90, 162, 206
Spartacus League, 79
spatiality, 5, 6, 7, 124, 125, 152, 153, 155, 169, 178, 183
spectatorship, 159
speculative materialism, 205
spirituality, 5, 13, 14, 66, 67, 79, 80, 120, 121, 124, 128, 130, 135, 141, 156, 162, 168, 181, 185, 196, 198
  see also religion
sports, 103, 105, 150
Spronk and Webber, 75
stability, 23, 25, 29, 43, 51, 63
  democratic, 23, 33
  destabilization, 87, 190
  see also neoliberalism
standardization, 2, 3, 26, 29, 30, 31, 35, 53, 57, 63, 67, 80, 150, 176, 177, 178, 179, 180, 186
  see also quantification, neoliberalism
state
  as agent of change, 75
  and party, 46, 50, 69
  and society, 9, 20, 23, 25, 63, 74, 195
  anti-, 206
  antipopular, 2
  autonomy from, 144, 145, 169
  Bolivarian, 78
  bourgeois, 75, 91
  bureaucratic, 2, 76, 88, 119
  capitalist, 75, 78, 82, 188
  class politics of, 8, 48, 51, 63, 77
  communal, 75, 78
  controls on education, 2
  death of, 2, 59
  debate among Marxists, 78–9
  deinstitutionalization of, 22–3
  developmentalist, 139

state—*Continued*
  disciplinary, 2, 20, 25, 54, 63, 139, 187
  of emergency, 23
  enforcement of attendance, 22
  formal, 21
  forms of, 5, 187
  versus government, 88
  in Gramsci, 9–10
  internationalized, 19
  lack of capacity, 35
  versus market, 3, 24
  as market regulator, 26
  Marxist theories of, 75, 78–9
  militarized, 20, 38, 72, 188
  negotiations with, 126
  neoliberal, 38, 49, 187, 188
  neoliberal disciplinary, 25, 26, 28, 51, 56, 139
  not eradicated, 2
  oil companies, 71
  parastate, 3, 21, 22, 158
  power, 114, 132
  privatized, 22
  rational bureaucratic, 2
  responsibility for education, 59, 82
  restructuring of, 62
  salaries, 22
  as site of struggle, 12
  socialist, 75, 113, 188
  transformation in Colombia, 22–3
  unaccountable, 206
  violence, 21, 68, 114, 158, 187
  welfare, 45
  see also politics, bureaucracy
State University of Ceará, 132, 136
Stella Barreto, Alba, 160
stereotypes, 123, 162
  see also racism, discrimination, forms of oppression
Stokes, Doug, 20, 21
Stoler, 140
storytelling, 15, 122, 123, 134, 140, 151, 160, 161, 162, 163, 165, 168, 170, 185, 199
  see also affirmative concepts
stress, 58
struggle, 4, 5, 7, 8, 10, 11, 12, 16, 26, 33, 44, 45, 49, 64, 65, 66, 67, 72, 77, 79, 82, 84, 87, 89, 117, 119, 120, 123, 124, 125, 128, 129, 130, 131, 132, 133, 134, 135, 138, 139, 140, 144, 145, 146, 149, 153, 160, 163, 165, 169, 182, 183, 185, 186, 187, 188, 189, 190, 191, 192, 194, 195, 196, 198, 205, 206
students, 2, 3, 4, 8, 19, 26, 28, 29, 30, 31, 35, 36, 37, 38, 40, 57, 58, 59, 60, 62, 63, 64, 72, 84, 85, 89, 92, 97–108, 110–11, 115, 118, 134, 138, 143, 145, 148, 149–55, 155, 169, 179–82, 187, 189–92, 198, 201–4, 207
  see also universities, MANE
subalternity, 4, 6, 9, 10, 11, 12, 15, 40, 44, 45, 54, 55, 62, 63, 117, 119, 120, 122, 128, 133, 135, 137, 139, 140, 145, 146, 167, 170, 185, 188
subjectification, 3, 15, 40, 63, 121, 124, 125, 183, 186, 190
  gendered, 12
  neoliberal, 178
subjective
  conditions, 3
  epistemologies, 27
  listening, 196
  realm, 120
  transformation, 184, 193
subjectivity/subjects, 3, 6, 7, 9, 10, 12
  affective, 30
  alienated, 13, 14, 120, 176, 181
  alternative, 21, 180, 189, 190
  capitalist, 15
  competitive, 13
  counterhegemonic, 12, 14, 21, 26, 29, 32, 40, 58, 117, 152, 155, 180
  critical, 63
  decolonizing, 14, 183, 191
  democratic, 192, 194
  disciplined, 178
  dominant, 5, 7, 12, 15, 119, 128, 149, 181, 188, 192
  economic, 178
  educational, 64, 121, 140, 148, 188
  emancipatory, 167, 182, 192, 194
  embodied, 143, 193, 194
  emergence as, 190
  epistemological, 188
  European, 181
  everyday, 145
  gendered, 14
  hegemonic, 10, 12, 14, 22, 29, 30, 34, 155, 188
  historical, 10
  ideal, 28, 178
  imperial, 19, 130

individualized, 13, 175, 191
innovative, 7
inter-, 127, 166
interpellation of, 179
knowing/of knowledge, 6, 13, 14,
   15, 16, 26, 33, 36, 120, 130, 148,
   156, 183, 190, 197
liberated, 128–9
managerial, 30
marketized, 56, 57
modern, 188
monological, 14, 19, 180
multidimensional, 129
multiple, 169, 196, 199
neoliberal, 34, 57, 62
new, 127, 182
oppressed, 185
passive, 19, 144
political, 124, 125, 127, 129,
   139, 164, 165, 166, 190,
   191, 193, 194
popular, 8, 119, 139, 190, 193, 194
productive, 177
rational, 13
revolutionary, 139
self-disciplining, 2, 179
of social transformation, 107, 111
student, 4, 151, 180, 191
subaltern, 6, 120, 198
as subject of struggle, 12
survivor, 168–9
teacher, 3
transforming, 155
unlearning, 5, 121, 125, 158, 165,
   188, 192
violent, 159
see also self
subsistence, 126
suffering, 3, 59, 158, 159, 160, 162,
   184, 185, 194
Suggett, James, 67, 100, 101, 103
Sun, The (newspaper), 87
surveillance, 2, 30, 62, 63
   see also forms of oppression,
   invisibilization
sustainability, 2, 5, 21, 23, 54, 117, 119,
   123, 124, 128, 129, 156
synergy, 121
systematization, 8, 15, 130, 135,
   147, 148, 154, 156, 163, 164,
   165, 169, 182, 187, 192, 195,
   199, 202
Székely, Miguel, 54

Tamayo Valencia, 144, 145, 147
teacher training, 2, 7, 29, 31, 32, 40,
   55, 56, 63, 85, 108, 115, 127,
   130–4, 137, 148
teachers, 3, 11, 22, 27, 29–35, 40,
   55, 56, 57, 63, 83–5, 97, 99–113,
   115, 127, 130–2, 134, 136,
   140, 144–8, 150, 153, 154,
   176, 179, 186, 187, 188,
   207, 208
   see also educators
teaching. See education
technology, 1, 22, 29, 37, 38, 40, 48,
   64, 81, 92, 115, 152, 154, 155,
   180, 190
Teivanen, 23, 55
TeleSUR, 71
temporality, 48, 127, 134, 152, 166,
   178, 187, 191, 193, 201–3
tenderness, 166, 198
terrorism, 23
   as label for dissent, 23, 33, 99
   see also guerrillas, paramilitaries
Thatcher, Margaret, 114
theatre, 98, 124, 134, 135, 155–63,
   191, 206
   forum, 156, 206
   New, 156
   of the oppressed, 143, 155–6, 159,
   195, 206
   street, 157
theology, 122
   see also liberation theology,
   religion
theoretical structure, 67, 79
thinker, the (figure), 13
   versus doer, 14, 167, 184, 195
Thorning-Schmidt, Helle, 206
Tierra en Guerra (play), 162
Tiriba, Lia, 120, 122
Tolima Department, 24
torture, 21
touch, 135, 168, 196, 198
trades unions, 3, 21, 24, 32, 33, 34,
   44, 45, 46, 50, 77, 79, 118, 144,
   145, 146, 147, 149, 186
transformative tendency, 119
transgression, 7, 16, 44, 120, 121,
   127, 136, 140, 141, 143, 155,
   166, 168, 169, 185, 187, 191,
   195, 198
   see also resistance, boundaries
translation, 8, 82, 107, 167

transnational actors, 2, 20, 22, 23, 24, 27, 28, 35, 36, 37, 38, 39, 40, 49, 56, 64, 138, 176, 177, 180, 189. *See also* imperialism, international division of labour, capitalist world system
trauma, 159, 162, 163
trova, 111
trust, 43, 121, 135, 137, 147, 151, 165, 169, 179, 194, 196, 197, 207
Tygel and Souza de Alvear, 119

UBV, 70, 84, 85
UK (United Kingdom), 82, 113–14
UNASUR (Unión de Naciones Suramericanas), 71
underdevelopment, 13, 40, 130, 182, 183, 184
underside, 1, 2, 182
UNDP, 70
unemployment
 as threat, 2
UNESCO, 70
United Nations, 92
United Socialist Party of Venezuela (PSUV), 90, 110, 111
United States, 20, 66, 68, 71–2, 82, 87, 92
 Colombian FTA with, 38–9
 role in coup against Chavez, 86–7
Universidad del Valle, 146
Universidad Pedagogica Nacional, 148
Universidad Politecnica territorial del Estado Merida "Kleber Ramirez" (UPTM), 97, 108
Universidade para Todos, 59
University of Antioquia, 146
University of Cauca, 147
University of Ceará, 132, 136
unlearning, 5, 8, 11, 15, 107, 119, 121, 125, 141, 153, 155, 158, 165, 181, 183, 184, 188, 192, 194, 198
uprising, 1958, 65–7
urban land committees. See *Comites de Tierra Urbana*
URD. *See* Democratic Republican Union
Uribe, Alvarez, 1, 19, 22–3, 25, 26–9, 31, 33–6, 38, 40, 151, 190
Uruguay, water movement, 4
utopia, 128, 155, 163
 see also affirmative concepts
Uzcátegui, Rafael, 67, 79

vaccination, 53, 107
Valencia, 25, 32
valorization, 130, 132, 133, 137, 187
vanguardism, 66, 91, 120
Venezuela, 4, 5, 7, 8, 15, 54, 65–115, 169, 181, 182, 183, 185, 186, 187, 188, 205, 206, 207
venezuelanalysis.com, 97, 100, 101, 108, 207
verticalism, 185
Victor, Maria Paez, 68, 69, 71
Vidal, Jacqueline, 156
violence, 1, 8, 13, 20, 21, 24, 33, 34, 40, 78, 102, 103, 109, 123, 125, 143, 157, 158, 159, 160, 161, 163, 164, 165, 167, 169, 175, 179, 193, 198
 gendered, 157
 intimate partner, 123
 symbolic, 40
 see also forms of oppression
Vivas, Carolina, 157
vocationalization, 61
voice/speech, 74, 123, 141, 145, 156, 158, 161, 162, 165, 167, 170, 194, 196, 197
 against capitalism, 179
 children's/learners', 103–5, 111, 134, 207
 collective, 156, 166
 deep, 196
 dialogues of, 163, 165, 207
 dissenting, 22
 embodied, 6
 everyday speech, 111
 excluded, 32, 157, 165
 facilitation of, 158, 165
 of God, 67
 from the margins, 16, 199
 meaning of, 16, 141
 multiple, 5, 14, 16, 141, 199
 "other," 23
 for others, 170
 pedagogies of, 156
 public speaking, 81
 right to speak, 117, 193
 speaking over, 3, 195
 speaking the world, 184, 195
 speaking with, 5, 8, 184, 207
 versus violence, 103
 see also dialogue, listening, affirmative concepts
Vulliamy, Ed, 86–7

war, 20, 67, 80, 86, 162, 165
  see also guerrillas, terrorism, violence
Washington Consensus, 68
  see also neoliberalism
weaving, 6, 16, 24, 122, 127, 143, 145, 156, 157, 160, 166, 170, 193, 198, 199
Whalton, 32
White House, the, 86
Wilpert, Greg, 88
Wilson, Joshua, 106
Wirth, Fraga, and Novaes, 120
Woods, 88
word and world, 6, 12, 14, 166, 177, 183, 187, 191
worker management, 77
workers' control, 77
Workers' Party (Brazil). See *Partido Trabajadores*

working class, 45–7, 50–1, 54, 66, 72, 77, 99, 118, 126, 205, 206
working conditions, 3, 32, 34, 48, 56, 62, 81, 83, 136, 178, 179, 190
wounding, 163, 170, 196, 197
  see also forms of oppression
WTO, 205

ya basta, 127
yoga, 163
Yogev and Michaeli, 176
Young, Clifford, and Julio Franco, 70–1

Zambrano, Gerson, 105
Zapata, 39
Zembylas, Michalinos, 179
Žižek, Slavoj, 205–6
Zona Educativa, 110
Zuluaga, Olga Lucia, 146

GPSR Compliance
The European Union's (EU) General Product Safety Regulation (GPSR) is a set of rules that requires consumer products to be safe and our obligations to ensure this.

If you have any concerns about our products, you can contact us on

ProductSafety@springernature.com

In case Publisher is established outside the EU, the EU authorized representative is:

Springer Nature Customer Service Center GmbH
Europaplatz 3
69115 Heidelberg, Germany

www.ingramcontent.com/pod-product-compliance
Lightning Source LLC
LaVergne TN
LVHW011807060526
838200LV00053B/3692